SUSAN DALGETY has enjoyed a varied career in journ
on a range of governance projects in Malawi since
Scotsman and, pandemic permitting, travels widely
for six months in 2019 after a six-month road trip across the USA and a year-long journey across every country in the European Union. She was Editor of Scotland's leading community newspaper, the *Wester Hailes Sentinel*, Deputy Leader of Edinburgh City Council, Chief Writer for the *Edinburgh Evening News* and Chief Press Officer for Jack McConnell during his tenure as First Minister of Scotland. She is a trustee of the McConnell International Foundation, the Scotland Malawi Partnership and 500 miles, a Scottish charity that supports the development and delivery of prosthetic and orthotic services in Malawi and Zambia. She lives in Fisherrow, a former fishing village at Musselburgh with her husband, economic researcher Nigel Guy. She has two grown-up sons and four grandchildren.

The Spirit of Malawi

SUSAN DALGETY

Luath Press Limited
EDINBURGH
www.luath.co.uk

First published 2021

ISBN: 978-1-913025-46-5

The author's right to be identified as author of this book
under the Copyright, Designs and Patents Act 1988 has been asserted.

This book is made of materials from well-managed,
FSC®-certified forests and other controlled sources.

Printed and bound by
Ashford Colour Press, Gosport

Typeset in 11 point Sabon by
Main Point Books, Edinburgh

Photographs by Susan Dalgety unless otherwise indicated.

© Susan Dalgety 2021

To my mother Mary McShane, who tau[ght]
grandchildren Kyle, Iona, Arran and Sofia[...]
life; and Hombakazi Tanaach Reve Mbe[ki...]
princess and died a Malawi queen, age[d...]

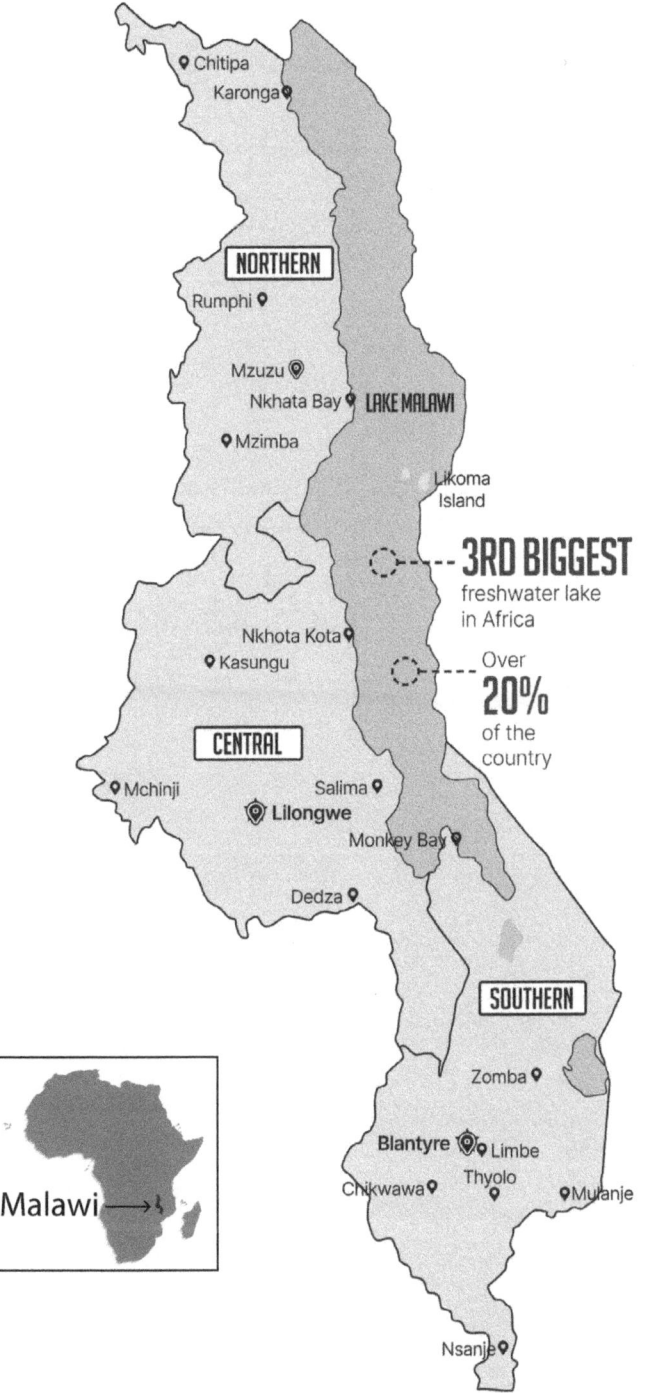

Contents

Acknowledgements		11
Foreword by Vera Kamtukule, Malawi Government Deputy Minister for Labour, Skills and Innovation		13
Foreword by Lord McConnell of Glenscorrodale		17
Preface		21
Map of Malawi		24

SECTION 1: The cycle of life

Chapter 1	The spirit of Malawi	27
Chapter 2	Birth of a nation	36
Chapter 3	The early years	44
Chapter 4	Four million children	51
Chapter 5	Typical teenagers	59
Chapter 6	Into adulthood	66
Chapter 7	Family life	74
Chapter 8	Growing old	82
Chapter 9	Health of a nation	90

SECTION 2: All in a day's work

Chapter 10	The economy	103
Chapter 11	Addicted to tobacco	114
Chapter 12	Business life	122

SECTION 3: The people's culture

Chapter 13	The lake of stars	133
Chapter 14	Tribal traditions	142
Chapter 15	In God we trust	150
Chapter 16	Creative forces	159

SECTION 4: A young democracy

Chapter 17	Colonialism to aid	171
Chapter 18	Governing Malawi	180
Chapter 19	Justice for all?	191
Chapter 20	Village to city life	199

SECTION 5: Whither Malawi?

Chapter 21	A hopeful future	209
Timeline		221
Notes and sources		225

Acknowledgements

THIS BOOK HAS taken 15 years to write. From the moment I first arrived in Malawi in April 2005 to help organise the forthcoming visit of Scotland's First Minister, I have loved this country and its people. I have visited many times since – for work, to spend time with friends and for the sheer joy of seeing familiar faces who are now part of our extended family. This book could not have been written without them, or the hundreds of Malawians I have worked with over the years, from senior government ministers to village leaders.

It is not my voice that is woven through the book, painting a vivid picture of real life in this small landlocked country, whose GDP per head was once bigger than China's and is now one of the world's poorest. Nor did I actively seek the views of any of the thousands of development professionals who work in Malawi. They do invaluable work, but this is not their country. The voices in this book are Malawians. All I have done over the years is listen.

I am especially grateful to everyone who agreed to be interviewed for the book; it would not exist without them. Sadly, I could not use every interview, not because they weren't interesting or illuminating, but because the book would have been twice the length, and I had a deadline to meet. But these conversations informed my writing as much as the ones I used.

And a once-in-a-century pandemic erupted just as the book was due to be published. So far Malawi has escaped the worst of the health effects of the virus, but the long-term impact on its society and economy will not be known for years.

Thanks to Ronex Nyamwera and his father Alum, Vitu Longwe, Rejoice Chimasula and the rest of her wonderful family; Charles Govati, Emmanuel Thuwala, former MP and now Education Minister, Agnes Nyalonje, James Lihoma, Agnes Mizere, John Bande MP, Susan Banda, Peter Massina and the indomitable Karen Gillon. Also the staff and board members of the Scotland Malawi Partnership and the Malawi Scotland Partnership and Dr Peter West, Honorary Consul for Malawi in Scotland. Your kindness and insight are on every page.

Warmest thanks also to Margaret Ngwira of Linga Wine, whose shortbread is a thing of beauty; Joseph Migeli, Blantyre's best taxi driver; all the staff of the Women's Legal Resources Centre (WOLREC) who teach me something new every time I visit; Olivia Giles of 500 miles for her encouragement and friendship; Danny Phillips for his companionship over the years. And thanks to everyone at Cakes Lodge – particularly Sille, Edson and baby Calvin – and to Maria and Frank Johnston for their wonderful hospitality during our 2019 research trip.

No one writes a book on their own, so I will be eternally grateful to my husband, researcher and copy-editor, Nigel Guy, whose love inspired me to get on with writing this book after years of talking about it; to Gavin MacDougall and his team at Luath Press for giving me the chance to finally, at the age of 64, publish my first book; and to Govati Nyirenda, whose photographs inspire me and whose friendship has sustained me since 2005.

And of course my warmest thanks to Jack McConnell, who as First Minister, decided that two small countries, Scotland and Malawi, should strengthen the bonds that had linked them since Dr David Livingstone's first visit in 1859. He took a courageous leap of faith in 2005, which has changed the lives of countless people for the better, including mine.

But most of all I want to thank all the Malawians I have met since that first visit, from the young boys on the northern lakeshore who, during our recent stay there, would regularly trade the same paw-paw for a few sweets, to the countless women I have danced with in villages over the years. This is your story.

Foreword by Vera Kamtukule
Deputy Minister for Labour, Skills and Innovation

The Spirit of Malawi is a book written from the front lines of the Malawian people by Susan Dalgety, an amazing woman with a proven love for my country. I could not have thought of a better person to tell this story than her.

It is a story told from the perspective of what others would call 'ordinary citizens'; but that would be inaccurate and a severe underestimation of remarkable people. A people who, in 2019 after a disputed presidential election, exuded unflinching and methodical resilience in the face of tyranny, and with righteous anger, mobilised and organised against all odds and, unarmed, marched relentlessly for months to demand justice over their stolen vote.

To cement it all, we had the impeccable and uncompromising five Constitutional Judges who deserve a place of distinction in the world's legal fraternity. In February 2020, they delivered a historical judgement that overturned the May 2019 presidential election and consequently ordered a fresh one.

And we salute the millions of people who braved the winter of June 2020 to queue for hours, to protect and cast their vote, ushering in a new administration built on the Tonse philosophy, which is all about collective responsibility. This is the spirit of Malawi.

Reading through the pages of this book, the brutalisation of the citizenry that has spanned decades and left the people in untold poverty cannot be hidden. This is largely due to corrupt practices perpetrated by those charged with the privileged responsibility to govern for over 26 years, thus bringing the country's economy to its knees and its people living as second class human beings, in abject squalor while a few elites lived in splendour.

This was a period in which decisions to do with people were made capriciously and without due process or respect for the rule of law; the nation was literally up for grabs for the politically connected.

The challenge for the new administration is to accelerate the nation's development agenda by 26 years; only we must do so in five years or less. However, if we are still standing after all we have been through as a nation, with the passion we have shown in the midst of disasters including the Covid-19 pandemic, then it goes without saying that there is nothing we cannot achieve, because that is the spirit of Malawi.

Malawians may sometimes appear cowed, fearful, lacking diligence when called upon to do so, but under no circumstances must such adjectives be mistaken for weakness, for we are well galvanised to conquer and defeat toxic systems.

To make Malawi the place we want for future generations will require practical, realistic, deliberate and methodical approaches. This will challenge people – because paradigms will be shifted and status quos changed, making people uneasy, and they will resist it.

And are things going to change in the short-term? Maybe, or maybe not! However the journey to a better Malawi will have started and that's the spirit with which we shall manifestly propel ourselves forward, as we look to the future with hope and absolute confidence in our own abilities.

We have been through situations as a nation that should have broken us entirely, but instead these unleashed our hidden potentials. We have always leaned on donor assistance in every sector, but of late we have learned to foot our own bills, stand on our own two feet and most of all, we have cultivated a communal way of living that was long eroded, because that is the spirit of Malawi.

Malawi is endowed with natural resources which until now have been either under-utilised or accessed only by corrupt individuals in the know. While we are in the process of changing things in that regard, we are strongly convinced that our greatest competitive edge remains the natural abilities of our people.

As can be seen in this book, our education system is unable to shape us to accurately respond to the ever-changing needs of our economy. But we can also not deny the fact that it is the very same system that produced the crop of earnest servant leaders like Dr Lazarus Chakwera and Vice President Dr Saulos Chilima.

Our health system is not universally accessible and we can do way better. However, flamboyant systems and strategies do not build a nation – the attitude and mindset of the people do.

Malawi is a land of survivors. It is blessed with people who possess unabashed passions and skills passed on from one generation to the other. This is what distinguishes us, it is what gives us our identity, a sense of belonging, for we know that to get to where we need to go, we must never lose track of what makes us who we really are.

Malawians have enough self-respect and drive to move their country forward, and the dignified men who are at the helm of government at the moment have their work cut out for them to leverage on the enthusiasm, willingness, keenness and dedication of the people to change things, and provide a framework that will promote patriotism, learning and hard work.

All of this will steer productivity that will move us out of the margins of society; for we have been here for far too long and we deserve better, because that is the spirit of Malawi.

As you read this book, you will be exposed to the other side of Malawi not yet discovered, the real stories of real people. While most of it provides interesting detail about different cultures and classes of people, the underlying intention is to arouse genuine interest of what else this country has to offer, both socially and economically. For it is an undeniable fact that for Malawi, things can only get better from here, because this is the spirit of Malawi.

Hon Vera Kamtukule
Deputy Minister for Labour, Skills and Innovation

Foreword by Lord McConnell of Glenscorrodale

Visiting a new country for the first time is always exciting, but for a politician leading a delegation with a large travelling media circus it is also fraught with danger. Protocol, language, stamina and the need to communicate a purpose – both on the visit and to the folks back home – were all in my thoughts as we touched down in Blantyre, Malawi. But I need not have worried, as I was about to fall in love.

It was May 2005. For the best part of a year I had been working with both Tony Blair and the Make Poverty History campaign to influence the Gleneagles G8 Summit due to take place in Scotland at the end of June. As First Minister I wanted to use the occasion to promote Scotland, but I knew that we should do more than just win investment from around the world to benefit Scots. We had responsibilities too.

Following re-election in 2003, we had established an international development policy for Scotland. The devolution settlement reserved international affairs to the UK government, but we had the power to support their development efforts and I was determined we would use it.

We had chosen to prioritise people-to-people connections, a mutually beneficial interaction that would share knowledge and skills. We had decided that our efforts would be especially, but not exclusively, focused on one country. Now it was time to talk to Malawi about a possible partnership.

Why Malawi? There were many reasons – not least because the Scotland Malawi Partnership, an embryonic civic organisation, had recently been formed by the cities of Glasgow and Edinburgh, and there was a strong connection that went back to Dr David Livingstone in the 19th century. I was wary of mentioning Livingstone. Would any reference to him feel like harking back to the days of Empire? But I need not have worried. On arrival, my Malawian hosts told me 'Dr Livingstone did not discover us, we discovered him'. The bond was set.

'I fell in love with the place at first sight' is an overused saying. And as I was whisked away by the Presidential motorcade through poverty-stricken people standing by the road, I wondered if I would feel uncomfortable for the whole trip. But over five days I did indeed fall in love. The Warm Heart of Africa had entered my soul.

Four Scottish midwives had been in touch. They were volunteering in Bottom Hospital, the world's worst-equipped maternity hospital, where 12,000 babies were born every year. Several died each day, babies and mothers. There was no fridge to keep medicines safe. Young terrified women and girls gave birth on the floor. One consultant, the inspirational Tarek Meguid, struggled to empower the women and save lives. Every visit made me more and more angry. This was the 21st century.

Young trainee nurses in a rural hospital working on the wards without vaccinations, endangering their own lives to help others and find a career. Teachers explaining that young girls missing school was not only a cultural or financial issue, but was linked to provision of toilets and safety.

And in villages with no clean water, electricity or sanitation, meeting children who now headed their households after the HIV/AIDS epidemic had taken their parents, but who really wanted to go back to school.

I stood in a 'classroom' with a straw roof and a mud floor where children learned algebra by memory as there were no writing materials. And a few metres away stood the sandstone block – the new school classroom – that had never opened because the £1,200 needed to add a corrugated iron roof had not been found.

Yet, everywhere, a warmth. And a warmth for Scotland. Stories passed from generation to generation of the Scots who came. Dr Livingstone who helped stop the slave trade. Those who built schools, hospitals, roads and churches. Those who stood side by side with Malawians when they were fighting for independence in the 1950s, and who challenged President Banda when his first post-independence government started to go rotten.

I knew then that the power here was in the people. Not governments and international NGOs, but people working with people, supporting each other, learning from each other, building capacity and skills.

Later that year, when President Bingu wa Mutharika came to Scotland, the Scotland Malawi Partnership was formally launched. He and I signed a document. But, as he said to a group of Malawians we met later that day, 'this is not the Jack and Bingu show'. We wanted to facilitate people-to-people partnerships, not be a substitute for them.

Today, the Scotland Malawi Partnership (SMP) has 1,200 members, with more than 109,000 Scots involved in a Malawi-related activity each year.

Scottish Government support has survived three First Ministers – unlike almost every other programme started back then.

And SMP now has the partner organisation we hoped for back in 2005. The Malawi Scotland Partnership is independent of government and has become a powerful civic voice in Malawi itself. And there are twice as many Malawians as Scots – 208,000 people – actively involved in the community partnerships between Scotland and Malawi.

This unique experiment is now a unique relationship between two countries. Despite all the political changes in both, and the occasional obstacles thrown in the way, the people of Malawi and Scotland have shown that our common humanity does indeed overcome our unequal development, our very different lives and the huge gap in our opportunities.

But that gap remains unacceptable. As ever, education is the key to unlocking progress. Of course the country cannot grow without more reliable electricity and other reforms. Of course it will not be safe and secure without action on climate change. But it is in education that empowerment leading to fundamental change is found.

The years since I first visited have been hard for Malawians. They have been let down by politicians and fallen off the radar of international organisations under the pressure of conflict, migration and extreme weather events elsewhere.

Ultimately, Malawians are going to have to fix this themselves. The international support will come and go, but development will only be sustainable with better governance and change led by local entrepreneurs, educators, medics and a free media.

Susan Dalgety was there in May 2005. She has been a driving force for the partnership ever since. Her love for Malawi and Malawians has driven her to write this book. Susan believes in the people, and her friends in Malawi believe in her. Enjoy the pictures she draws, the stories she tells and the lessons she draws. The Warm Heart of Africa is ready to welcome you too.

Lord McConnell of Glenscorrodale
First Minister of Scotland, 2001–07

Preface

When I emerged from Lilongwe airport for the first time, in April 2005, after an interminable 24-hour journey, I was greeted by a diffident young man, Peter Potani.

My companion, Rachel, and I were the advance party for a forthcoming official visit to Malawi by the First Minister of Scotland, Jack McConnell. Peter was to be our driver for our week-long recce, but he quickly became much more than that. He was our cultural guide, our translator, our fixer, and by the time he dropped us at the airport to start our journey home, he was my friend. He still is today.

Over the years since then, visiting Malawi as a governance adviser working with women MPs and councillors, I have made many more friends, becoming immersed in their lives as they have in mine.

We have celebrated family weddings together, mourned the loss of a much loved *agogo* (grandmother), laughed at the antics of Malawi politicians, cried at the devastation caused by floods, drought and corruption, shared more than a few *Kuche Kuche* (local beer) and cooked *chambo* (fish) together. And we have despaired at the general state of our world, from racism to Trump, misogyny to capitalism, and more recently, the terrible impact of Covid-19.

Of course, there are cultural differences, not least that most Malawians have faith, while the majority of Scots, who, more than 150 years ago, imported their Christianity to Malawi, no longer believe in a god of any denomination.

The biggest divide is economic. I may have been born into a poor family, but my homeland is one of the richest countries in the world. I benefit from a free health service, my sons don't need to spend half their income on school fees, and my mother enjoys a secure old age.

Life in Malawi, for all but a small elite, is a daily struggle. For many, the challenge from when they wake in the early morning is to find enough food to feed their family. For others, it is the constant stress of finding the money for their children's education. And as people age, they depend on the charity of others to survive.

Malawi is still striving to recover from the impact of colonialism, seven long decades when my country exploited Malawi's natural resources and its people for our own selfish ends. And climate change, global supply chains and digitalisation conspire to test the ability of even the most effective politicians and creative entrepreneurs to build an economy strong enough to support Malawi's ever-growing population.

Just as Scotland is much more than bearded men in kilts playing the bagpipes against the backdrop of a Highland loch, so Malawi is far more complex than the stereotypical images beloved of well-meaning charities.

The smiling but hungry child, staring into a white woman's camera, experiences the same emotions and has the same aspirations as her peers in richer countries, but her humanity is all too often portrayed as one-dimensional, nothing more than content for a fundraising campaign.

As my friendships in Malawi matured, and I began to understand better how the country worked, I nurtured an ambition to write a book that captured the essence of contemporary Malawi through the stories of its people.

It was important that the book was not my story. It should not be about my experience of 15 years working in Malawi, including the six months I lived there in 2019, though my visits have helped me better understand the context of people's lives.

Nor should it be a travelogue, charting Malawi's many beautiful natural resources, from Lake Malawi to Mount Mulanje; nor a treatise about development, informed by ex-pat 'experts' who are paid handsomely for their insights, honed in the universities of Europe, North America and increasingly Asia.

It is, as it must be, Clara's story, a 67-year-old woman who was given a death sentence 20 years ago when she was diagnosed as HIV positive, and who now, thanks to antiretroviral drugs (ARVs), is strong enough in her seventh decade to grow her own food.

It is Busisiwe's story, a single parent in her late 30s who runs her medical supplies business from home, juggling family duties with the demands of her business.

It is Chimwaza's story, who still lives in the northern lakeshore village he was born in more than 40 years ago, but whose family home now has electricity to power a fridge and a hot-plate, instead of a firewood stove.

It is Wezi's story, who dreams of hosting Africa's biggest fashion week.

It is Lazarus' story, who has partied with Madonna, but as an albino was almost killed for his body parts.

The single most important thing that I have learned is the essential truth of our shared humanity, despite all the things that appear to divide us. As Barack Obama writes in the preface of *A Promised Land*, humanity must now work together or perish; for us to co-operate, first we need to understand each other. And as the Black Lives Matter movement affirms, the colour of someone's skin must no longer bestow privilege or entrench disadvantage. We are one.

SECTION I

The cycle of life

CHAPTER 1

The spirit of Malawi

MALAWI IS A country of children. They tumble out of simple school blocks, their uniforms dusty with Africa's red soil, smiling broadly as they head home after a few hours of learning English and maths. Babies cling for dear life to the backs of girls barely older than the child they are carrying. Dark-eyed toddlers, wearing t-shirts discarded by rich European families and flown 5,000 miles to be sold in Malawi's roadside markets, sit quietly with their mothers, occasionally suckling on a casually offered breast. Footballs made of tightly bound plastic bags soar through the air, chased by scores of bare-footed little boys.

'*Azungu, azungu* (white people),' children cry delightedly when they spot white strangers in their township or village.

More than half of Malawi's 18 million population is under 18 years old. The statistics, gathered by the international agencies that hover over Malawi like a benevolent, if mildly censorious aunt, paint a depressing picture of a generation of children at risk from stunted growth, functional illiteracy and premature death. But the reality is so much more alive and hopeful than UNICEF's carefully researched infographics and strategic plans suggest. A girl born today can expect to live to 67 years – in 1960, she would have likely died before she was 40.

This small landlocked country does not have the natural riches found elsewhere in sub-Saharan Africa. There is very little gold, no copper or titanium. Oil may lurk deep in Lake Malawi, but no one, as yet, has exploited it. Malawi's children are its most precious resource.

Busisiwe (38) has just returned from a business trip to Johannesburg. She endured 48 hours on a crowded bus, travelling through Mozambique to South Africa so she could buy hospital blankets to sell on her return. Her modest medical supply business, which she runs from her late grandmother's rambling home on the edge of Blantyre, supports her and her six-year-old daughter. Her income also helps support her 15 nieces and nephews, many of whom live with Busisiwe, and two of her six siblings.

'Children are our life,' laughs Busisiwe as she picks up a stern-faced toddler. Brenda has just turned one and is the youngest of the Chimasula clan. 'They are expensive, school fees are our biggest headache, but we love all our children. They are very important in our culture.'

Malawi is a modest country. It is a narrow strip of land along the East African Rift Valley, squeezed between Mozambique, Tanzania and Zambia. It is around 560 miles long and 150 miles across at its widest part, similar in size to Bulgaria, and nearly 50 per cent bigger than Scotland. More than one-fifth of the country is taken up by Lake Malawi which, at over 360 miles long, is Africa's third-largest freshwater lake. Its beautiful beaches and gently lapping water are a magnet for rich, white gap year students, eager to experience the 'real' Africa. It is the heart of the country, providing fish to eat, water for irrigation and power and a home to one of the world's most important collections of freshwater fish. There are around 700 species of cichlids, the colourful fish that fill home aquariums, more than any other lake in the world. It is also, argue some, where human life began. Standing alone on a quiet beach anywhere along the lake's western shore, it is easy to imagine that this is where the story of our world started. That this tiny country, one of the poorest in the world, is our home village.

'Malawi is different,' says Govati Nyirenda, one of the country's first professional photographers and a well-travelled man. He pauses, then his rich, brown voice picks up his theme. 'To my mind, a Malawian is someone who loves people, who welcomes them. Having visited some other countries in Africa, I feel that we are different to most of the nationalities around this part of Africa. We are kinder, open-hearted people, we welcome foreigners. I know the slogan "Warm Heart of Africa" is for tourists, but I think it is true,' he laughs, slightly embarrassed at the cliché.

Malawi's history is not chronicled in the same way as the stories of European civilisations. There are no soaring cathedrals. No ancient texts or printed volumes of plays and poems from 400 years ago. Stories are carefully passed down from generation to generation, woven into the fabric of daily life over centuries. *Agogos* (grandparents) tell tales of great chiefs and bloody battles, of wizards and lions, deadly snakes and magic dancers.

There is some hard evidence of very early life in Malawi. The rock paintings at Chongoni, a UNESCO World Heritage site, were drawn by hunter-gatherers, some dating as far back as the 6th century BCE. Malawi's first known tribe was the legendary Akafula people. They are described as people of short stature with copper skin. They lived a peaceful existence along the shores of Lake Malawi, happily mingling with sporadic waves of Bantu-speaking people who travelled to the area from the 1st century.

It was not until the 13th century that another, more determined, influx of Bantu-speaking people from the north and west, including the Congo area, settled permanently in the region. This new population were farmers, bringing with them yams and bananas, as well as iron tools. They also introduced a system of formal government, and in 1480 the Bantu tribes united several settlements under one political state, the Maravi Confederacy, which at its height included large parts of present-day Zambia and Mozambique, as well as Malawi.

Govati recalls stories from these peaceful times, before the arrival of Arab slave traders and white colonialists. 'Our old parents [ancestors] lived a peaceful life, where people looked after each other. For example, in my father's village in the north, the women would prepare food together, and eat together. They would also send it to the lakeshore, where most of the men lived and worked, so they could eat. It is that ancient community that makes me feel Malawian.'

That community, which had started to develop more productive farming methods and to grow a wider range of crops, including cassava and rice, was largely made up of three tribes: the Anyanja, the lake people, the Atumbuka in the northern region and the Achewa who lived in the central plateau. Today, the Chewa are Malawi's biggest tribe. Their increasingly prosperous, agrarian idyll was shattered forever by a series of invaders. Portuguese traders arrived in the 16th century, first to trade in ivory and gold, and later in people. The height of Malawi's exposure to the slave trade was in the 19th century, when Swahili-speaking Arabs, and the Yao people from what is now Mozambique, stole thousands of healthy young men and women to sell in the slave markets of Zanzibar and Mombasa.

The Yao settled along the lakeshore and in the Shire Highlands in the south, bringing with them their Islamic faith. Today, around one in seven of Malawi's population are Muslim. From the south came the Ngoni people, armed refugees fleeing from the Zulu states. They settled in the north and the central regions after making peace with the Tumbuka and Chewa tribes. Then came the white missionaries. The first, and most famous, was Dr David Livingstone, a Scottish missionary, explorer and humanitarian, who first visited in 1859. His influence, and that of the Scottish missionaries who followed in his wake, remains visible in Malawi today. The country's oldest city, and its commercial heart, is named after Livingstone's birthplace – Blantyre, a small former mill town in central Scotland. Its most influential denomination, the Church of Central Africa Presbyterian (CCAP), is a sister church of the Church of Scotland and, since 2005, there has been a formal co-operation agreement between the governments of Scotland and Malawi.

The SMP and its sister organisation, the Malawi Scotland Partnership, support hundreds of civil society links. This relationship, built on a high-minded but practical principle of mutual solidarity, is rooted firmly in a common vision of humanity. 'Somehow, I feel that many of the donors just pull us backwards,' muses Govati. 'I like what Scotland does with Malawi. She is not a donor, Scotland is a partner. We exchange experiences, we exchange skills and friendship.' He stops for a moment, then reworks an old saying in his own words, 'You should teach someone to fish by giving him fish nets, so he can catch the food himself. Don't give him fish.'

The Scottish missionaries, who were quickly followed by the Dutch Reformed Church of South Africa and Roman Catholics from France, gave Malawi a new God to worship, as well as basic formal education and rudimentary health care in some areas. They also opened the door to colonialism, white farmers and businessmen eager to exploit the fertile lands of Malawi.

In 1891, the British established the Nyasaland Districts Protectorate, shortened in 1907 to Nyasaland. Malawi was now under the 'protection' of the British state, their new 'chief' was King Edward VII, and their new village elders the civil servants of the colonial administration. This new tribe of white settlers built roads and railways, some grew rich on cash crops such as tea and tobacco, and generally enjoyed a comfortable colonial life, while doing very little to improve the lot of ordinary Malawians. Colonial rule came to an end on 6 July 1964, when Malawi became an independent member of the British Commonwealth and Hastings Banda was confirmed as Prime Minister.

Banda, a medical doctor, freedom fighter and Anglophile, was educated in the USA and the UK. He practised as a GP in North Shields and London before returning to his native land in 1958 as its saviour. But within weeks of becoming Prime Minister, his dictatorial tendencies emerged. He fell out with his most of his cabinet ministers after they tried to limit his powers. He sacked some, others resigned and many fled the country into decades of exile. On Independence Day in 1966, Malawi became a republic and Banda its President. In 1971, he was made President-for-life.

Under his leadership, Malawi became a conservative, pro-Western one-party state. He supported apartheid South Africa, isolating the small country from the rest of the region. Political enemies were imprisoned or murdered. The country's few trains ran on time, but the people were not free.

Govati remembers the Banda years with a wry smile. 'The old life was oppressive,' he says, then stops for a moment, struggling to find the right words to convey what followed in 1994, when, after a peaceful referendum, the first free elections in more than 30 years took place. Banda, by then 96 years old, lost to Bakili Muluzi, leader of the new United Democratic Front party (UDF).

'My thinking is that we did not have a proper transition from one-party to multi-party democracy,' he says. 'We kind of jumped into multi-party, people thought it meant doing what you want, it was like a free-for-all, until maybe after ten years or so, people's minds started thinking about how to run the country, but by then bad habits had set in.'

By 'bad habits' Govati means the low-level corruption that is a depressingly regular feature of daily life. Many civil servants will not attend a meeting with external partners unless they receive an allowance. Police officers ask, politely, for a 'Fanta' – common slang for a bribe – when they stop drivers at the roadblocks dotted at regular intervals along the country's main roads. But that is nothing compared to the corruption scandal that erupted in 2013. Cashgate saw a gang of government ministers and civil servants loot the nation's coffers of around £25 million in just six months. Angry country donors such as the UK and Germany withdrew direct budget support to the Malawi government, diverting aid instead to large international organisations to deliver health care and other essential services.

The elections held in May 2019 saw the incumbent, Peter Mutharika, returned for a second term, but the ballot was riddled with irregularities. The main opposition parties, the Malawi Congress Party (MCP) and the new United Transformation Movement (UTM), sought justice in the courts, and on 3 February 2020, a panel of five High Court judges declared the election null and void and ruled that there should be fresh presidential elections, with a 50 per cent plus one majority required.

The rule of law had prevailed, and on 23 June 2020, Dr Lazarus Chakwera, leader of the MCP, was elected sixth President of the Republic of Malawi, with 58.6 per cent of the vote.

Chakwera, a former pastor, born in 1955, wakes every morning to what must seem like insurmountable challenges. Malawi is bursting with people. The population was four million in 1966, when Hastings Banda became President, a million fewer people than currently live in Scotland or Yorkshire. Only a decade ago, the population was 13 million. Today it is over 18 million, growing at just under three per cent a year. In ten years' time, it could be 23 million or more.

The majority of Malawians – around 15 million people – live in *mudzi* (rural villages) where their life has a similar rhythm to that of their ancestors. The settlements are organised around extended families who grow their own food and fetch water from a borehole if they are lucky, or a nearby stream or well if they are not. Slowly, the traditional round mud houses with grass roofs are being replaced by square ones built of fired bricks and topped with iron sheets. Electricity remains a distant dream for most villagers, and so the main dish of the day, *nsima* (maize porridge), is cooked as it always has been, on charcoal or firewood. Ancient traditions and beliefs, from puberty rites of passage to witch doctors, play as big a part in most villagers' lives as the churches and mosques imported only 150 years ago. And most villagers are poor. In 2016, 70 per cent of Malawians lived in extreme poverty – surviving on less than £1.50 a day.

'Poverty is rampant, we cannot deny that,' says Govati. 'It makes most of us sad, but when I visit the villages for work, or to see family, you notice people are happy. They are not happy because they are poor, but because he or she has a free mind, they live their life as free people.'

Villagers may be cash-poor, but most have land. Customary land, where land in a village belongs to the community, accounts for 70 to 80 per cent of the country's total area. Individual families have the right to use the land for growing crops and can dispose of it, but only within the limit of their tribal laws. Malawi's network of Traditional Authorities (chiefs) and village headmen acts as guardians of these laws.

In recent years, there has been an exodus to the four cities: Mzuzu in the north, Blantyre in the south, Zomba in the south-east, and the capital, Lilongwe, which sits in the middle of the country. Life in the cities for the 2.8 million people who live there can be very comfortable, if they have money to spare. South African-owned superstores sell everything from the latest laptops to locally grown tomatoes and avocados. An efficient, if expensive, 4G mobile network, provided by private companies such as Airtel Malawi, and a buoyant market in Chinese smartphones, means that even some of the poorest city dwellers are on Facebook. Everyone, it seems, communicates by WhatsApp. The country's best public and private hospitals and clinics are found in the cities, and medical evacuations to Johannesburg are common for those patients with good medical insurance, or deep pockets.

But poverty stalks the overcrowded, badly planned townships and suburbs, just as it does the villages. In 2013, the majority of people in work earned less than 10,000 Malawian *kwacha* (MK) a month (£10.50). Only 11 per cent of jobs are in formal employment, where employers are subject to labour laws such as the minimum wage.

Most people work, but their employment is precarious. 'That is why we have to create our own jobs, you cannot depend on other people,' explains Busisiwe. She buys and sells basic medical equipment, from batteries for respirators to bed sheets. 'We all have to earn money whatever way we can,' she adds.

Her sister Debra is a dressmaker, working at night when her children are in bed. Her brother, Leonard, makes cane furniture, while another sister, Rejoice, a primary school teacher, supplements the extended family income by selling second-hand goods.

Blantyre, where Busisiwe lives, is the oldest city, with a population of around 800,000. It is the country's commercial heart, with a relatively small manufacturing base. Malawi's beer is brewed here. Until it sold its majority stake to French company Castel in 2016, Carlsberg owned the brewery, its first outside Denmark. It can produce 38 million litres of Carlsberg beers under licence every year, as well as millions of bottles of Coca-Cola and the iconic Malawi gin, distilled since 1961 and now a favourite of middle-class Malawians, ex-pats and tourists.

'We Malawians like our beer, gin is for the *azungu*,' laughs Debra's husband, mechanic Peter Potani (38), brandishing a bottle of Carlsberg Chill. 'I am Ngoni and we really like our beer. It is the tradition here that men drink. In the villages, the old women make *kachasu* (moonshine) from maize or sugar cane.'

Zomba, only an hour's drive from Blantyre, is a university town, and the former capital. Its wide main street, tree-lined avenues and red-brick campus are reminders of Malawi's colonial period. Mzuzu, in the north, is the gateway to Malawi's highland region. Coffee is grown here, and a relatively new public university, focusing on science, has attracted thousands of students since it opened in 1997.

The climate is colder and wetter than the rest of the country. 'Some say it is our Scotland, because of the pine trees and mountains,' says Peter.

In the middle of the country sits Lilongwe, the capital since 1975. This is where the national parliament sits, and where international embassies and aid agencies ply their trade. International aid is big business in Malawi. Around a fifth of the country's economy – one billion pounds a year – comes from developed countries such as the UK, Japan and America, and the main international donors like the UN or the World Bank, though India and China are increasingly playing a role in Malawi's development.

Lilongwe is the first destination for most visitors to Malawi, as Kamuzu International Airport is on its outskirts. Split in two, the Old Town is where Malawi life explodes early every morning. Here are the local markets, the Chinese shops and the curio stalls for open-mouthed tourists, spellbound by fast-talking Rasta boys selling over-priced *chitenje* (cloth) and wooden trinkets.

Capital City is where the country's power lies. Designed in the 1960s and '70s with help from South African urban planners, this soulless sector is busy throughout the working day with politicians, civil servants and aid workers driving from meeting to meeting in their pristine 4x4s. At night, its offices and public buildings lie dark and empty.

This is where the decisions are made about how much aid should be spent on HIV/AIDS as compared to maternal health or malaria. Nearly one million people are HIV positive but, thanks to the Ministry of Health, working with international agencies, Malawi has one of the best antiretroviral (ARV) drug programmes in sub-Saharan Africa. HIV is no longer the death sentence it once was. It is here that development experts from across the world gather every day to plan Malawi's future. Decisions made in Oslo or Washington about whether to focus on economic development or humanitarian aid will directly affect the life chances of Malawians across the country, from Karonga in the north to the arid plains of Nsanje in the south. It is also home to Malawi's National Assembly, its parliament, which is housed in a rather austere building, paid for by the Chinese government. Its 193 MPs enjoy raucous debates, cheerfully covered in full every day by the two national newspapers, *The Nation* and *The Daily Times*, the state broadcaster, the Malawi Broadcasting Company (MBC), and vibrant private radio stations such as Zodiak FM. And this is where government ministers make solemn speeches about (slow) progress in rural development, electrification and job creation.

But with an annual government budget of MK 1.7 trillion (£1.8 billion), Malawi's democratically elected politicians have only slightly more resources to spend each year on their country's development than the international aid community.

Govati, who, at 53, was born the year Hastings Banda become President, ponders this hard fact for a moment. Like most Malawians, he acknowledges the important contribution international aid plays in Malawi life.

'The NGOs and donors are helping us, they do a good job, but I feel we need to move away from dependency on those things. We need to build up our people so that they can do things on their own. We should look to our traditions. If you are able to share what you have, you become happier. That is what our old grandparents taught us.

'The hope for Malawi, for the world, is that the only way we will survive is if we bind ourselves together. In our tradition that means if you are hurt or needing help, your community will be there for you, when you are happy, they will be there for you. We are one of the friendliest people in the world, that is our wealth. It is my wish that our children, our grandchildren, behave Malawian. If we lose that, we lose the spirit of Malawi.'

CHAPTER 2

Birth of a nation

THERE ARE AROUND 1,700 babies born every day in Malawi. Over 600,000 a year. Some will die only hours after drawing their first breath. Many more will die before their first birthday. Around 70 of those babies born each day will not reach their fifth birthday. The tiny, malaria-infected mosquito will kill some, fever and diarrhoea others. Measles is a common killer, as are respiratory diseases. And sepsis is on the increase, a humanitarian disaster in a country where antibiotics are scarce.

Nine-month-old Lizeveta is even more at risk. Sitting contentedly on her mother's knee, she looks the picture of health in her hand-knitted cardigan and bootees. But her mother Rose (29) was diagnosed HIV positive 13 years ago, at the time of her first pregnancy. ARVs keep Rose alive, but her baby girl was still at risk of being born positive. Sixty-five thousand children currently under 15 live with HIV.

'When she was born, they gave her a drug for a few weeks to stop the disease,' explains Rose. She picks up her daughter's ankle. 'And she was tested at six weeks, then again recently.' She grins, her smile lighting up her gaunt face. 'She is free of the disease,' she says. 'She will grow strong.'

Rose gave birth in the local clinic, a few kilometres from her village home, Mtwiche, in the Zomba district. It is a simple red-brick building, with a large post-natal room with six beds, and a much smaller labour ward, with only two beds. The clinic is clean, if basic. There is no bedding. Women wrap themselves in their colourful cotton *chitenjes*, the lengths of fabric that serve as everything from a towel to a dress. They bring their own plastic sheet – a mackintosh – to lay on the bed before giving birth, as well as string to tie the umbilical cord. A female relative – their guardian – will stay with them, supplying food and comfort.

Fathers are rarely welcome in the labour ward. In the villages of Malawi, where the majority of the population live, childbirth remains the private domain of women. That doesn't bother Rose. She looks perplexed when asked if her husband was at Lizeveta's birth. She shakes her head, laughing at the very idea.

'I only stayed one night,' she says. 'The birth was easy, the channel opened at 4.00pm and I gave birth soon after. There was no pain. So the next day, I got a bicycle taxi home.'

The bicycle taxi – a *njinga* – is a common sight in Malawi. A narrow, lightly padded seat is added to a bike's luggage rack, transforming it into an affordable mode of public transport. It is powered by the strong legs and lungs of young men, providing them with an income in a country where there are few formal jobs outside the cities. But they are hardly comfortable, and 24 hours after giving birth, the four-kilometre ride home must have been excruciating.

'It was fine,' says Rose. 'We are used,' she adds, smiling.

It is not just newborn babies who are at risk of dying. Malawi is one of the most dangerous places in the world for a woman to give birth, despite significant progress made in maternity care in recent years. Twenty years ago, one woman in 90 died giving birth. The latest figures from 2016 show a fall of more than a half, but still one in 200 are dying. This revolution came about because women are now encouraged to give birth in their nearest clinic, rather than at home with a traditional birth attendant. The government banned the use of these village midwives in 2007 but, somewhat surprisingly, the decision was reversed three years later.

However, women are now actively discouraged from using their services. Many local chiefs impose a fine of a chicken or a goat on women who use them rather than go to a clinic. But in a country where there are only 3,400 registered midwives against a required 23,600, village midwives still have a role to play, provided they are properly trained. International charities, such as Christian Aid, work with Malawi's Ministry of Health to help the women change their role from midwife to 'mother adviser'.

Now, instead of delivering a baby on a straw mat on the dirt floor of a village house, armed with nothing more than a plastic bag, a reel of cotton and some water, the women encourage pregnant women to get HIV testing, refer them to the local clinic for proper ante-natal care, and even accompany them while they give birth in the hospital. Some, however, have reluctantly retired.

Emeles Kachala doesn't know when she was born, but the tendrils of grey hair peeking out from her woollen hat suggest she is in her 60s. Sitting outside her village home in Zomba district, with one of her 15 'or maybe 20' grandchildren, she talks shyly of her 20-year career as a village midwife.

'It was an inheritance from my mother,' she says. 'She taught me how to birth babies. But I can't do it anymore, because of orders from the chief. A woman must go to the hospital, or she can be fined 5,000 *kwacha* [just over £5].

'No babies ever died with me, or mothers,' she insists, which is hard to believe when she goes on to explain how she dealt with a difficult birth. 'If the baby was stuck, then I took some pumpkin seeds and some ash from the fire and mixed them up for the woman to eat. Then I pushed down on the mother's stomach.'

A sudden, very loud, clap of thunder startles Emeles. Black clouds threaten a deluge of rain. She pulls her *chitenje* tighter round her waist. 'I miss helping mothers,' she says. 'Even now, people ask me to help deliver their baby, but because of the rules, I am not allowed. But I would do it again.'

Today, babies in Malawi are delivered by trained midwives, like 41-year-old Richard Ndala. He works at Machinjiri Clinic, several kilometres from Emeles' home. The clinic is typical of the hundreds of government units scattered across Malawi and looks identical to the one where Rose gave birth to Lizeveta. Outside sits a shiny new white pre-fabricated building, emblazoned with government logos from the USA and Britain. It is enclosed by an intimidating metal fence, topped off with vicious barbed wire. It looks like a nuclear weapons storage unit.

'It is for storing our drugs,' laughs Richard. 'We don't have that many, but we keep them in this new store we got from the donors.'

The clinic is powered by two small solar panels, hooked up to a bright yellow inverter in the labour ward. 'It is not always reliable,' says Richard, 'which can cause us problems at night. But the water is worse.' He points to the sink, where a bright green plastic urn sits on the draining board with a neatly written sign exclaiming its important purpose: 'BACKUP HANDWASHING WATER.'

'Our water supply is gravity fed, but because of our position, sometimes the water pressure is too low to make it through the taps, so we always have to have a back-up supply.'

Richard's typical day at the clinic begins at 7.30am. 'When I arrive, I get a handover from my colleague about the status of the women in labour. We then make sure the ward is clean and assess the foetal and maternal condition regularly. If we detect any complications, we call an ambulance instantly, and the patient is referred to the central hospital in Zomba, which is just under an hour's drive away.'

Richard says that, like most clinics in the rural areas, there are only two beds in the labour ward. 'We average around two births a day, but sometimes we can have three, even four women in labour. We put a mattress on the floor, spread their mackintosh on it, then a cloth on top and we lie them there. Some days we can have more than three patients, we lie those in the corridor and she delivers there.'

Women deliver their babies without painkillers. Whatever medication is securely locked in the shiny new storage unit, there are none of the effective drugs often given to women in rich countries. No gas and air, no pethidine and certainly no epidurals.

'We will give them paracetamol after they deliver,' says Richard, kindly.

He says that most births are straightforward. 'If a woman has a complication like pre-eclampsia, she will go to the big hospital. But sometime their family doesn't want them to travel, they want them to stay here, close to home. That can be difficult.'

But his biggest professional challenge is the number of teenage mothers. Around 30 per cent of women aged between 15 and 19 years old will give birth. 'The girls lie about their age,' says Richard. 'Some are younger than even 15. Their bones are not strong enough for labour.'

He leans against the empty labour bed. It is a Saturday afternoon, and the ward is, unusually, empty.

'The most fulfilling part of my job is when I deliver a baby and it cries right away. I know it is going to be all right. If it doesn't cry immediately, I try everything I can to make it happen. If a baby dies, I am haunted.'

Three hundred kilometres to the north of Richard's clinic lies the capital, Lilongwe. An ever-expanding city of one million people, it is home to some of the country's richest families, as well as thousands of urban poor, living in crowded townships with little or no sanitation or safe drinking water. Here, too, is the country's biggest maternity hospital, Bwaila, where 50 babies are born each day.

'Sometimes it can hit 85,' Lilongwe district health officer Alinafe Mbewe told *The Nation* newspaper during a visit by humanitarian Graca Machel, the widow of Nelson Mandela.

At the time of Machel's visit, the hospital only had one functioning incubator and one theatre that was in use. She couldn't hold back her anger. 'It is not proper for such a busy hospital to have only one functional incubator... being a woman, I feel bad.' She called on the private sector to get involved, but it will take more than the donation of a few incubators, welcome though they would be, to bring Malawi's maternity services into the 21st century.

There was a brief period several years ago when maternal health was the government's top priority. Joyce Banda, only Africa's second woman head of state, put her campaign, Maternal Health and Safe Motherhood, centre stage when she became President in 2012, promising to reduce maternal deaths significantly. Her presidential tenure ended after only two years when she was defeated in the 2014 elections. Many would argue, perhaps unfairly, that the campaign lost momentum under her successor Peter Mutharika.

Charity Salima (60), or Mama Salima as she is known in her community, certainly thinks much more needs to be done. A force of nature, she gave up a secure job as a senior research nurse ten years ago to open her own community clinic in Area 23, one of Lilongwe's most crowded and poverty-stricken townships.

'My family were confused,' she laughs, remembering their reaction. '"How will you eat?" they asked. I told them, "The Lord is my shepherd," and look, he has provided.'

Charity and her team of staff and volunteers have delivered 8,000 babies in a decade. All survived, a remarkable record in a country with one of the highest maternal mortality rates in the world. What is Charity's secret?

'Experience,' she says. 'I know how long a labour should last. And if there are any signs of distress, in the mother or the baby, then we send her to Bwaila.'

Charity's immaculate clinic has none of the high-tech, eye-wateringly expensive equipment found in labour wards in the UK. There are no birthing pools, and no anxious fathers.

'We encourage men to come,' says Charity. 'In our culture, childbirth is only for women, but it is changing. And I expect the man to come when we have family planning sessions. A woman does not get pregnant alone,' she guffaws.

Charity has won many accolades. She is dubbed Malawi's Florence Nightingale, her work has been featured on CNN, and in 2019, she was presented with a Commonwealth Point of Light Award for her work by the British High Commission. But even the indomitable Charity cannot work miracles on her own. 'We need support all the time. Money is always a worry. We always need new equipment.'

Top of Charity's wish list is a £1,000 machine that will help deliver oxygen to newborn babies in distress. Even a few minutes of oxygen deprivation at birth can cause life-changing conditions such as cerebral palsy, or even death. But very few labour wards in Malawi have one.

In the waiting room of Charity's clinic sits a young woman with a tiny baby. She looks scared. Charity bends down and firmly pulls out the young woman's breast from under her *chitenje*. Speaking softly but firmly, she explained to her how the tiny baby in her arms needed to latch on to her engorged nipple.

'Like this,' smiles Charity, pushing the mother's breast closer. And just like that, mother and baby are bonded. The young woman visibly relaxed as her first-born began to feed, and Charity steps back, satisfied.

'She gave birth in the hospital, not here in my clinic,' explains Charity. 'They don't have time to properly explain how breastfeeding works, so often women will come to me when their baby is crying, because they are not feeding well.'

A few kilometres from Charity's clinic, accountants Vitumbiko and Clever are sitting in the sunshine at Coco's Café in Lilongwe's newest shopping mall. They could be a young professional couple from anywhere in the world. He looks on tenderly as his wife of two years toys with her avocado on toast.

'Basically, in Malawi, once you get married, society expects you to have a baby,' she giggles. 'And you know, people may ask you directly, depending on how close you are to them… some will be straightforward and say, "Ah, any news?"'

Vitumbiko (25), whose baby daughter, Viwemi, was born a few weeks earlier, says her experience of childbirth was completely different to that endured by the majority of women in Malawi. She works for an international accountancy firm, and her medical insurance covered the costs of her antenatal visits and the birth, as she explains.

'We are lucky, my work paid for it. Private hospitals are very expensive here, so if you have private insurance, you are sure of getting better services than the ones you get at the government hospitals like Bwaila. This is now a big thing here in Malawi for the middle-class and the high class. Almost everyone wants to be on a scheme. The clinic we found was new and it is really modern, and fancy. And our doctor was a good guy, understanding and the like.'

Vitumbiko may have enjoyed the best modern care her private insurance scheme can buy but she is a young Malawian mother in a society where pregnancy is still considered private business. She hesitates for a moment, 'Basically, people are still quite closed. If you know the gender of the child, you don't share it. You don't talk in an open place about the pregnancy. But for us, we were having a hard time because we were excited, and we wanted to share the excitement.'

Recalling her recent pregnancy, she says, 'Whenever you touch your stomach, people look at you. They are not comfortable, but it is natural you want to hold your bump and the like.'

Clever, who is a year older than his wife, looks up from his burger and chips. 'I think here it is because of these superstitions that people like to keep the pregnancy very private,' he chimes in. 'You know witchcraft in Africa is still a big thing. And it is real. Not everyone will be pleased to see you have a baby, so because of the old beliefs some will choose to be private about it and won't share the news until the baby is born. They won't even put pictures on social media, they will try and keep it private. People are scared to tell people in case they do something and the baby miscarries. And it is not just in the rural villages. Even here in the city, people believe such things. If your mother lives in the village, she may tell you, "don't tell anyone," because she does believe such things.'

Clever is as relaxed talking about witchcraft as he is discussing Manchester United's recent game. This is not unusual. Malawians will happily mix ancient beliefs with Christianity or Islam, and many will visit their local witch doctor when they are ill, instead of going to a clinic. Vitumbiko agrees with her husband that it is not just people living in the rural areas who hold fast to the old traditions.

'I took a picture of myself and had it on WhatsApp and some friends were like, "Why are you putting your picture there, you are not supposed to show your pictures," and the like. For me it doesn't make sense. And my mum thinks the same. But there are still people in town that are educated but believe that people will come and harm their baby while they are expecting.'

Vitumbiko looks slightly puzzled when asked if she is breastfeeding her baby. 'Of course I am,' she says, then adds, as if only just remembering that her time at home with Viwemi will be limited to her three months' maternity leave, 'but of course, when I go back to work I will start with a bottle. Bottle milk is so expensive. Everyone wants to save, so you have to breastfeed, unless there is the other problem.'

The 'other problem' is HIV. Breastfeeding used to risk mother-to-child transmission of the disease, a huge challenge in a country where formula milk costs twice what it is in Britain. Since the introduction of Option B+, where every pregnant woman with HIV is given ARVs, regardless of the stage of their disease, the transmission is comparable to that in many developed countries.

Back in Mtwiche village, Rose casually pulls out her right breast for Lizeveta to suckle on. She does not care that there is a stranger watching her, or that there are men from the village wandering past. There is no stigma to breastfeeding here. In the villages, babies stay close to their mothers for the first two years of life, strapped to their back with a *chitenje*, quietly feeding on demand, sleeping in the same bed or mat on the floor. You rarely hear a baby cry, unless it is in acute distress. Breastfeeding is an ancient tradition that women, whether urban professionals or villagers, are happy to follow.

Vitumbiko laughs, 'Even if you make the choice not to [breastfeed], when your mother comes, and your mother's sisters, I don't think they would tolerate that.'

The contrast between Rose and Vitumbiko could not be starker. Rose had her first child when she was 16 and was infected with the HIV virus at the same time. Now a mother of three, her very life depends on the antiretroviral drugs she takes every day. Her home is a small house, made of unburnt bricks, with a roof of tin sheets and a dirt floor. She has no electricity and no running water. She charges her cheap Chinese mobile phone at the local trading centre and carries water from a borehole for washing and drinking. She and her husband, Menard, survive by growing maize to eat. Their three children will go to the local government primary school, and maybe, if there is enough spare money, they will get a secondary education.

Vitumbiko was 25 years old when she became pregnant with her first child. She gave birth in a modern clinic, and her husband drove her home the next day in their pale blue Toyota. They live in a small, modern home in a suburb of Lilongwe with running water, electricity and a kitchen full of gadgets. Their smartphones connect them to the rest of the world. Their first-born will go to a private school, and then university.

Both children, Rose's nine-month-old Lizeveta and Vitumbiko's six-month-old daughter, will decide Malawi's future. But first, they have to survive their first five years.

CHAPTER 3

The early years

JESSIE EVERSON MAPAYANI is a lively four-year-old girl. She enjoys playing with her friends and her favourite game is *chiterera*, where the children gather in circle to sing traditional songs, with each girl taking turn to be in the centre.

'She loves it,' says her father Everson (29), a former councillor who lives in Mooza village, near the shores of Lake Malawi.

When her parents can afford it, she attends a local nursery class, where she learns to recite the alphabet, the days of the week and some common prayers in English, rather than her native tongue, Chichewa. In the villages of Malawi, girls are taught their primary role in life, that of mother and homemaker, from as soon as they can walk so, even though Jessie is barely three-feet-tall, she helps her mother look after her newborn baby brother, John Everson, tending to the child while her mother, Mercy, prepares *nsima* or washes clothes.

There are 2.6 million children aged under five in Malawi. Deaths among this vulnerable age-group have reduced dramatically in recent years, thanks in part to the government's community health strategy, supported by UNICEF and other donors. Yet more than 25,000 babies and toddlers still die each year from largely preventable diseases such as diarrhoea, pneumonia and malaria. Malawi's death rate is ten times higher than that of the UK. Jessie has already suffered two bouts of malaria which required hospital treatment, and she is at constant risk of the disease.

'Losing one child is a loss to the nation, as well as the family,' says Jessie's father. 'They are the future of our country, and we cannot afford for them to die. But it is difficult here in the village. When a child gets sick you have to take them to the clinic, which is usually miles away. And both times Jessie was sick with malaria, we had to use a private clinic and that cost us money, around MK 4,000 [£4.20] each time.'

Less than half of the population live within a five-kilometre radius of a formal health facility – public or private – while only 20 per cent are within 25 kilometres of a hospital. And very few families have easy access to transport. When a child falls ill, parents often have to borrow money from family or friends to take their sick child for diagnosis or treatment.

'It is always a worry,' says Everson. 'And at our home, which only has two small rooms, the whole family sleeps together in one bed. And we don't have a mosquito net,' he adds, 'That means the mosquitos find it easier to bite us, as we are all in one bed.'

Recent figures show that one-third of under-fives (32 per cent) sleep without nets, and that progress in reducing this figure even further may have stalled in the last few years. Anecdotal evidence suggests that many families, particularly those living near the lakeshore, use their nets for fishing; others sell the insecticide-treated nets, donated by international agencies, for extra cash.

While Jessie and her friends play happily outside in the sunshine, hidden inside thousands of village homes across the country are babies and children with disabilities, from albinism to cerebral palsy. It is almost impossible to get an accurate figure for the number of under-fives with a disability because Malawi's traditional culture means that many children are hidden from view.

The 2018 Census, which defines disability as 'difficulty with seeing, hearing, walking, speaking, intellectual, self-care or other' found that 1.6 million people (10 per cent of the population over five) had at least one of these difficulties. The most common is with sight – 760,000 people – and nearly 250,000 suffer from epilepsy.

'In the rural areas, disability was traditionally associated with witchcraft,' explains Frank Maliko, a disability expert from Lilongwe. 'So, when a woman gave birth to a child with any type of disability she was deemed to have been cursed, or that she had been practising witchcraft, and that caused a lot of discrimination.

'So many parents neglected their disabled child, not taking very good care of them, for instance, hiding them in their homes, that happened quite a lot. Some even discarded their child. That still continues today, which is why the government, through the Malawi Council for the Handicapped (MACHOA), mainly does community orientation programmes, to help parents and the community understand disability.'

Bertha Magomobo struggles to care for her disabled child against almost insurmountable odds. Her seven-year-old son, Skeffa, has cerebral palsy and cannot walk or feed himself, and his speech is impaired.

According to Frank, cerebral palsy is all too common in Malawi. 'It is an accident of childbirth or comes from malaria seizures when they are around three or four,' he explains.

Several years ago, one local organisation, the Parents of Disabled Children Association, estimated that 80 per cent of disabled children had cerebral palsy, and a 2017 study by the London School of Hygiene and Tropical Medicine and Malawi's College of Medicine, concluded that cerebral palsy was the most commonly seen disability, but no one really understands the true extent of the condition.

Bertha lives in a village several kilometres from a main road, in Zomba district, and has no easy access to transport.

'She was told if she had been able to take him to Blantyre – which is two hours' drive from her village – when Skeffa was a baby, he might have been able to walk, with the help of braces, but it was impossible,' explains Imedi Jafali, a local community worker who has been helping the family.

Imedi was able to raise enough money from well-wishers to buy Skeffa a basic tricycle wheelchair, which means that, for now, his life, and that of his mother, has improved significantly.

'Now he can go to school,' explains Imedi, 'and Bertha doesn't have to carry him everywhere. But what will happen to him when he is a grown man?' he asks sadly. He knows the answer only too well.

Early Childhood Development (ECD) is one of the Malawi government's many priorities, supported by donors, big and small, from UNICEF and World Vision to celebrities like Roger Federer and Madonna. Federer's foundation has a ten-year plan to improve the lives of 150,000 children in Malawi by 2021, by investing in pre-school education. 'Early education is the foundation of learning,' says the father of four. And Madonna's charity, Raising Malawi, recently built the Mercy James Institute for Paediatric Surgery and Intensive Care in Blantyre's Queen Elizabeth II hospital, the first facility of its kind in the country. The children's wing, named after one of the four children Madonna adopted from Malawi, includes three operating rooms dedicated to children's surgery, a day clinic and a 45-bed ward. During a recent tour of the facility, which boasts colourful murals of Nelson Mandela as well as the latest equipment, Madonna told *The Nation* newspaper, 'There was a time in Malawi when there was no intensive care unit for children. So it means a lot to me that we have been functioning well... the centre makes all the difference,' she said.

Evidence shows that the first few years make a significant difference to a child's life chances. A toddler needs the right nutrition, good health and enough learning and love to flourish. But as UNICEF Malawi points out, the majority of under-fives face challenges from the day they are born.

Their parents – or guardians – don't have the opportunity to develop positive parenting skills, the children suffer poor health and nutrition, they don't benefit from early learning and they are at high risk of natural disasters such as floods, or major epidemics like HIV/AIDS. And a recent report by the Ministry of Education, Science and Technology showed that 87 per cent of children in primary school could not read, write or do basic arithmetic by the time they were halfway through their eight years of primary education.

World Vision is just one of the organisations that has transformed its education programme to spend more on early years, as their communications director, Charles Gwengwe, explained recently in a newspaper interview.

'Until recently, most of our education funding went to help communities build schools, as well as to provide uniforms, fees and other school supplies. However, analyses have shown that children were not necessarily learning while they attended these schools. Against this background, we have strengthened our work on ECD centres... to unlock and boost literacy.'

World Vision has now trained nearly 2,000 caregivers to work in community-based childcare centres, with more planned.

The government, too, has turned its attention to nursery education, borrowing £38 million from the World Bank in 2019 to extend community classes across 13 districts, almost half the country. But, according to the Association of Early Childhood Development in Malawi, much more needs to be done if Malawi's children are to fulfil their potential.

'More than half of our children under five do not go to an early development centre. And there is a problem with the capacity of the caregivers, less than half have had any proper training,' said their spokesperson recently.

Jessie Mapayani's experience of early years education is typical. According to her father, her nursery school is very basic.

'She learns some simple things, such as how to introduce herself, songs and the days of the week. And they do some physical exercise, such as running. But the class is four kilometres from our home, and it is hard to take her every day. It costs MK 1,000 (£1) by motorbike taxi, so she failed to attend all the classes last year.'

Everson is not alone in his struggle to afford nursery education for his eldest child, as he explains, 'Most of the children in our community stay at home because their parents don't have the money to pay the monthly fee (MK 1,500) and the transportation. My assessment is that only five per cent in our community attend nursery school.'

And he is doubtful about the quality of the teaching at community-based nurseries. 'My observations suggest that the facilitators have not undergone nursery training, and because they are unpaid volunteers, they don't take their duties as seriously as they would if they were paid.'

His fatherly concern about the quality of nursery classes is confirmed by community development worker, Amos Mlotha (30), who works in villages across Salima district.

'Early years development is very important, which is why the government and some donors are right to prioritise it. But the challenge is that the caregivers are not always trained and some of them have not even been to school themselves.'

Drive through any suburb of Malawi's two main cities, Lilongwe and Blantyre, and you will see many brightly coloured signs offering nursery classes. Some even offer Montessori education, but according to Vitumbiko, who works for an international accountancy firm, those are only for white people or very rich Malawians.

'Nurseries in Malawi go as much as a million *kwacha* [£1,050] per term, you're talking of the Montessori schools. Others are MK 70,000 [£74] a term, which is fair. Some cost around MK 200,000. But when you compromise on the price, you compromise on the care that is given.'

Her baby daughter, Viwemi, will go to nursery when she is two and a half years old, 'or maybe three, but it will have to be affordable,' laughs Vitumbiko.

But Viwemi does have a nanny. 'Every working mother has someone to help her with the children,' explains Vitumbiko. 'Otherwise we could not work. It is perfectly normal for ordinary people to have a maid. Our nanny is called Yanjanani, which means "brings us together" in Chichewa. She lives with us and works five and a half days a week.'

Like most female domestic workers in Malawi's towns and cities, Yanjanani is from a village. Her home, and where her sons live, is in Thyolo, a six-hour bus ride from Lilongwe.

As Vitumbiko explains, 'She came to the town to find work, and she has been here for some time, seven years or so. Her sister looks after her boys. I have still to make an agreement with her for time to see them, but basically, I will give her two weeks off in December and at Easter as well, five days.

Since her children are older, she will be more flexible. If they were younger, she would have to go there more often.'

Like nursery fees, a nanny's wages vary according to the status of their employer. Vitumbiko, who lives in Area 25, a township on the edge of Lilongwe, pays Yanjanani a modest monthly salary.

'I have started her with MK 25,000 [£26] a month, plus board and lodging. We give her bedding, soap, whatever she needs. The rates for the nannies can go as high as MK 50,000 a month, it depends on the location and the like. For example, one of my bosses pays MK 40,000 a month for her nanny.'

And while it has taken Vitumbiko and her husband, Clever, some time to adjust to sharing their small home with a stranger, they are slowly getting used to it.

'If you think about it, it is much better than day care. Day care has several babies, but here you are talking about only one person taking care of your baby.'

Viwemi and Jessie are lucky. Their parents may sometimes struggle to afford quality childcare, or even to pay the rent, but their future is much brighter than the millions of children classed as 'vulnerable.'

The government's 'National Plan for Action for Vulnerable Children', published in 2015, suggests that there are upwards of two million vulnerable children under 18 in Malawi. This group includes orphans who have lost one or both parents, usually to HIV/AIDS; children who are not living with either parent, or with parents who have no education and almost no household income; and children living on the streets, or in institutions.

Amos explains that in the villages, grandparents will often try to take on the role of mother or father for vulnerable children.

'If a child becomes an orphan, and their *agogo* [grandparent] has the financial muscle, they will take care of that child,' he explains. 'Or an auntie or uncle, sometimes even well-wishers who are not related to the child, will take on the responsibility. But most of the times, it is the grandparent. But if the child does not have relatives with the good heart to take care of her, then she will end up in an orphanage, or even the street.'

It was from one of these orphanages that Madonna plucked her four children, transforming their lives overnight. But for the two million vulnerable children remaining, they face the prospect of a future filled with violence, child labour, teenage pregnancy, conflict with the law and poor health.

Malawi's most vulnerable children do not have access to even the most basic commodities, such as regular food, clothes, or proper shelter. In every village, there are toddlers dressed in rags, their faces dirty, their skin showing signs of infection, their bellies distended from hunger. They gather round strangers, staring silently at them, their lives stunted before they reach primary school age.

'These children don't have enough to eat, and they are at constant risk of infection,' says Amos. 'And they suffer from emotional deprivation, from the love and care of parents. It is very sad, and very frustrating that we cannot do more to help them.'

There is a plethora of interventions designed to support vulnerable children, from direct cash payments to the adults who care for them (social cash transfers) to school feeding programmes and community-based childcare centres. There is a country-wide network of social welfare officers, child protection officers and community development assistants, each with a role to play in protecting vulnerable children. There are hundreds of local and international charities, big and small, all focused on supporting these silent, hungry, lonely children.

The Malawi government has adopted most international treaties and conventions on child rights, and Chapter 4, Section 23 of the country's constitution provides the basis for the protection of all children. Yet not all children can be protected.

'There are just so many,' says Amos.

As little Jessie Mapayani and her friends play *phada* – or hopscotch – on the sandy earth outside her two-room home, her mother Mercy watching on, there is a little boy, around three years old, standing close by. He is dressed only in a filthy, torn white t-shirt, three sizes too big for him. He is barefoot, mucus dripping from his nose, his black hair almost red with dust. Jessie is looking forward to starting primary school in two years' time.

'I am going to learn to write,' she tells her father. 'And I want to be a teacher when I grow up.'

The little boy looks on in silence.

CHAPTER 4

Four million children

EIGHT-YEAR-OLD Faisa looks glum, a rudimentary cast weighing down his lower right arm, and his spirits.

'His friends were pushing him around, and this happens. The arm broke,' explains his father Imedi Jafali, 'The clinic said it will take six weeks to mend. Boys are boys.'

The offer of a bottle of Coke brings a smile to Faisa's face, and he cheerfully climbs into the back of the car as it sets off to Napalo Primary School, deep in the heart of Zomba district, 90 minutes' drive from Blantyre, Malawi's commercial city.

Imedi, who gave up his job as a boarding school manager to become a councillor in 2014, is now struggling to find work after losing his seat in the 2019 elections. He does community work, but that does not pay well, and with four children at school, he regularly has sleepless nights worrying how he is going to pay for their education.

'My wife and I have discussed it, and I may have to go to South Africa to look for work,' he says, with deep resignation.

His two eldest boys, Brandina and Halima, are at a government secondary school, and his 12-year-old daughter Veronica is finishing her primary education at a faith-based school, an hour's minibus ride from her home. 'It costs MK 1,000 (£1) a day for her to travel there,' he says.

Faisa, his youngest, attends a private primary school, and these annual fees of around MK 50,000 (£53) are the main source of Imedi's anxiety. 'I just don't know how I can continue to pay them without a proper job.'

There are 4.1 million children in Malawi in the official primary school age-group between six and 13 years – nearly a quarter of the population. It will be Faisa and his generation that will take on the task of transforming Malawi from one of the poorest countries in the world into a middle-income nation. And the quality of their education will be key to whether they succeed or not.

Since 1994, every child in Malawi has been entitled to attend primary school, free of charge. The commitment to free, universal primary education was made by President Bakili Muluzi during the country's first multi-party democratic election campaign, and he fulfilled his election campaign promise, 'Education for All,' almost immediately he took office on 24 May 1994.

One thousand new classrooms were built. Thousands of new teachers were trained quickly – perhaps too quickly. A new curriculum was rolled out to 5,500 primary schools and feeding programmes were introduced as the number of pupils grew by 50 per cent, or almost a million, within the first year.

And in Muluzi's inaugural speech at the start of his second term in 1999, he promised the government would continue with its primary education programme, and 'where necessary new primary and secondary schools will be built, technical institutions will grow during the next five years.

'Our teachers everywhere will receive special attention under a new programme that will ensure that they are well and properly accommodated within their teaching environment,' he said.

Muluzi's campaign promise of education for all has proved to be much harder to fulfil than to make. Primary education is only nominally free, as most government schools now charge parents a 'development' fee of at least MK 2,000 per year, and children have to pay to sit their end-of-year exams. The strain on family budgets, already over-stretched, means that many children have to drop out as their parents simply cannot afford to send them to school. Twenty-five years after universal primary education was introduced, only half of pupils complete their schooling, and perhaps four in ten of those will go on to secondary education.

University lecturer and education expert, Dr Yonah Matemba, who lives in Scotland, says there are many reasons why children leave school. 'The first is the abject poverty which most people in the rural areas suffer from, so they cannot afford the cost of school uniforms and the development fee. Sometimes the home environment is not supportive, or family illness, such as HIV/AIDS, forces children to stay at home to help out, and of course our traditional cultural practices that force children to work in the family gardens [small plots where food is grown] mean many do not attend classes. And for older girls, pregnancy and marriage contribute.'

He is clear about what needs to be done to support all Malawi's children to finish at least their primary education. 'The school development fees should be abolished, and schools need to be less stringent about uniforms. It should be an offence if a child does not attend school. I know implementation might be problematic, but fear of sanction could be a first step. And there should be a unit that follows up on non-attendance.'

Reflecting on 25 years of free schooling, Yonah is ambivalent about whether Muluzi's bold policy has paid off.

'My views are mixed,' he says, 'On one hand, free primary education has opened doors previously closed to millions of children from poor families. After all, those kids with parents who can afford it have always accessed education. But the quality of education has been compromised due to, among other things, lack of investment for new school buildings, teachers' housing, training of teachers, their salaries and, of course, learning materials.'

Wandering round the sandy grounds of Napalo Primary School in the bright lunchtime sunshine, it is easy to see that the development of Malawi's primary education is an ongoing battle between quality and quantity. The school is typical of the red-bricked campuses dotted across Malawi. There are four blocks, with two classrooms in each. Two toilet blocks, one for boys and one for girls, and each housing four pit latrines, provide basic sanitation. And there is a rudimentary kitchen where parents volunteer to prepare a basic meal for the children – usually porridge.

'But we struggle to raise the money to buy the flour and sugar,' says head teacher Geofrey Chipala.

'We have 720 pupils enrolled,' he whispers. A mysterious virus three years ago has left him permanently hoarse. 'Not good for a headmaster,' he laughs, softly. 'That means an average of 90 children per classroom, which is why some have to be taught outside.' He points to a few trees and a haphazard pile of handmade red bricks. 'The community has started to mobilise bricks, see over there, but these are inadequate, and the parents don't have the money to build a new classroom block…' he tails off, perhaps mindful that his story is repeated across the country.

Every public primary school needs more classrooms, more books, more equipment, more teachers. 'I have 15 teachers on staff,' says Mr Chipala, 'with another seven student teachers from Machinga Teachers Training College. The teacher-pupil ratio is just too high.'

Children start primary school officially at six years old, but some private schools will enrol children a year earlier, and many village children do not start until they are eight or nine. Primary education lasts for eight years. In the first four, children are taught in Chichewa, the national language.

From Standard 5, classes are taught in English. At the end of their eight years, those fortunate enough still to be at school will sit exams for their Primary School Leaving Certificate of Education (PSLCE). These exams will decide whether a child is eligible to progress to secondary school. Failure means an end to a child's education at 13.

Teaching is traditional. If they are lucky, children sit quietly in rows of wooden desks while their teacher uses a blackboard to explain the finer points of arithmetic and agriculture. If their school is over-subscribed, as many are, they will sit outside to learn, under trees or in makeshift shelters.

There are now more than 80,000 primary school teachers in the country, with 7,000 graduating each year from a network of government teacher training colleges, supported by a number of private colleges, all accredited by the Ministry of Education.

The latest figures show that there are more than 6,000 primary schools, and of those almost 600 are private, four times the number nine years ago. As government schools struggle to keep pace with the country's population explosion – it has jumped from under ten million to 18 million since 1994 – even parents with a modest income send their children to private school, particularly those living in urban areas, where there is more choice.

Mabvuto Salirana (42), a taxi driver based in the capital Lilongwe, works 12 hours a day, seven days a week, so he can afford fees to send his ten-year-old daughter Sarah to her local Catholic primary school. 'The fees are around MK 70,000 (£74) a year, but it is worth it because the classes are better there, especially English lessons.'

Mabvuto is unusual in that he sends his daughter to a private school, while her twin brother, Sam, goes to the local government one. 'The girl always grows faster than the boy, and she enjoys the high competition,' he explains, diplomatically. 'She wants to be a doctor.'

Mabvuto, an astute businessman, has earned enough to build two large houses with running water and electricity, one for his family, another to rent. But despite his success, Mabvuto is embarrassed he did not finish his secondary education, which is why he is determined his children – his daughter as well as his son – will get the best education he can afford.

Not all parents believe education is as much a right for their daughters as their sons. The 2017 Household Survey shows that more girls than boys go to school up to the age of 13, but after that, girls drop out faster. Puberty is a challenging time for a girl, as traditionally it marked the transition into adult life. Many parents in the rural areas cling to their ancient tribal customs, forcing their daughters to abandon schooling for motherhood.

UNICEF says that nine per cent of girls are married before they are 15, with nearly half wed by the time they are 18. One-in-five are victims of sexual violence, with most abusers being people that the girls trust, such as an uncle, step-father or even their primary school teacher.

Malawi's two national newspapers, *The Nation* and *The Daily Times*, regularly carry headlines such as 'Herd boy jailed for defilement.' The 'boy' in question was a 28-year-old man, and his victim, who he violently raped, was an eight-year-old girl. And there are thousands of similar cases that go unreported every year.

Life for boys can be harsh too. The official working age is 14, but extreme poverty makes many parents break the law, particularly in the rural areas. There are estimated to be two million child labourers in Malawi, with boys aged ten to 13 years old most likely to be working. Children are employed, for a pittance, in fishing, forestry, domestic work and shop work, with the overwhelming majority of older children working in agriculture. Over one million work in conditions that are considered hazardous.

'Our culture is different from that of white people,' one smallholder farmer tells *Africa News*. 'We believe in training our young people to become independent as adults. We do not consider this as child labour.'

His view is becoming increasingly outdated, however. The government is committed to ending child labour, and the Malawi Congress of Trade Unions, supported by local and international organisations, campaigns vigorously against the practice.

The loudest and probably the most effective voice against child labour is the International Labour Organisation (ILO), which has been working for 25 years to end the practice across sub-Saharan Africa. Their latest focus in Malawi is on the tea and coffee sector, but the most gruelling and dangerous work children are forced to endure is in the tobacco fields.

Tobacco is Malawi's most important crop, providing around half of the country's precious foreign exchange earnings, and worth up to one tenth of its GDP. Most of the tobacco is produced by small-scale tenant farmers, who spend ten months of the year sowing, weeding and harvesting their deadly crop, for very little reward, which is why many feel they have no option but to use their children as free labour.

Felix Thole, Chief Executive of the biggest and oldest tobacco growers' association, the TAMA Farmers Trust is, perhaps understandably, slightly defensive when asked about child labour.

'We have made progress reducing it,' he insists. 'It is true that in the past, working in the tobacco fields was a family activity, but we need to make sure that the children get an education. So we work with the ILO, the tobacco companies, our farmers and leaders in the community – the chiefs and headteachers – to come up with solutions. Our children must go to school.'

But as well as missing school, child labourers are often exposed to acute nicotine poisoning – the equivalent of 50 cigarettes a day, according to one study – as well as toxic pesticides, and they can work in searing temperatures, with no protection, for up to 12 hours a day.

Fifteen-year-old Joel, from Kasungu in the central region, says, 'It is difficult work, harvesting, then sewing the leaves. Sometimes I don't feel so good, my stomach and head hurt. I don't like this work, but my brothers and I have to help our mother.'

In a surprise move in October 2019, British law firm Leigh Day announced it was taking a class action case against British American Tobacco on behalf of 2,000 Malawian farmers, including hundreds of children, for forced labour. And the USA immediately suspended imports of tobacco from Malawi, saying it had information that showed it was being produced using child labour. The ban has since been lifted, but it exposed Malawi's reliance on tobacco exports as its main source of foreign income.

Mr Thole said his association was taken aback by America's decision. He said, 'More money has been spent by the industry stakeholders, including tobacco buying companies. Malawi has done a lot in fighting child labour and it was surprising to ourselves.'

Almost every child in Malawi is expected to help their mother and father at home, from fetching water from the borehole to tending the garden. Accountant Vitumbiko recalls how she learned to cook and run a home at an early age. 'I started getting chores to do around eight, learning to clean and how to cook. By the time I was 13, I could do a family meal, and I didn't think anything about it. It is normal.'

She laughs when she remembers her first attempt at cooking *nsima*, Malawi's national dish. It may be a simple porridge, made from maize flour and water, but it requires practise to perfect the technique. 'I remember I got burned that first time,' she laughs. 'When I got to the time when you have to harden it, when it starts to bubble, it burned my hand.

'Girls do all the chores inside the house, and no one complains,' she goes on. 'No, we would not do that, we wouldn't complain to our parents.' She laughs. 'Even if you do complain, nothing changes, you still have to do it.'

Vitumbiko may have a nanny, a university degree and an Instagram account, but when it comes to child-rearing, she is as traditional in her attitudes as her grandmother, Dorothy, who lives in a village. 'Family life in the city is the same as the village,' she says. 'When my daughter, Viwemi, is old enough she will have to learn how to cook, and clean as well. She needs to be able to manage a home. But she will also go to university,' she adds quickly. 'Boys do learn household chores, but for them it is lighter, they do less, and the focus is much more on the outside, such as gardening and the like.'

While life for the majority of Malawi's children is much tougher than it is for the average nine year old in Europe, most still enjoy their childhood years. Their footballs may be made of tightly bound plastic bags, and sweets only a very occasional treat, usually handed out by passing *azungu* (white people), but they still have fun.

For one group of children, though, every waking moment is a living hell – Malawi's street children. Visitors to the country are visibly shocked the first time they are assailed by filthy children, dressed quite literally in rags, their hand outstretched, pleading plaintively, '*Bwana, bwana*, give me money. Hungry *bwana* [boss], hungry.'

Some children are abandoned by their parents, or extended family, because they simply cannot afford to feed and clothe them. Others are orphans, or have run away from abuse, only to find that they are at much bigger risk of sexual and physical assault on the streets.

Michael, now 19 and at secondary school, recalled his six years as a street child in Zomba in a 2019 newspaper interview to mark International Day for Street Children.

'Life became unbearable at home because my mother could hardly afford to take care of me and my two siblings,' he explained. 'Each time dusk approached, it was a difficult moment for me because I used to sleep on the veranda of a shop and sometimes under benches at Zomba market.'

And he could not forget the terrible abuse he suffered at the hands of older boys. 'They usually force younger ones into sex, as well as giving them money targets to be surrendered to them on a particular day,' he said.

Michael was rescued by a local charity, Mlambe Health and Social Trust, who are helping him rebuild his shattered life, but there are an estimated 6,000 children still surviving on the streets.

Godknows Maseko, who spent several years on the streets as a young teenager, is now step-father to 73 of them. The youngest is four-year-old Benjamin, who was abandoned on the streets soon after he was born. The eldest is Charles (26), who was Godknows' and Helen's first child when they opened the Steka care home in 2007.

'Steka stands for "step kids aware",' insists Godknows, 'not "street kids aware". The children are our family, we are their step-parents. People think that children begging on the street are looking for food, for a bed. They are looking for love. For the love of a parent.'

A recent report by Malawi's Ombudsman, Martha Chizuma, criticised Malawi's government for abandoning street children. 'No matter how we ignore them, they are still Malawians and it is a matter of national issue, these children have the same human rights as others,' she said.

Godknows is philosophical about his government's apparent lack of interest in the fate of Malawi's most vulnerable children. 'That's the way it is,' he shrugs.

He and Helen raise money to feed and clothe their impossibly large family through a number of small enterprises, from raising chickens to running a nursery school for local children.

Their main focus, however, is on raising funds to build a vocational centre where his children can learn skills for life. 'All my children go to school, and some will go on to university, but not all of them. That is why I am building the new centre,' explains Godknows. 'Where will the money come?'

He smiles. 'That is a tricky question. We work hard 24 hours a day to raise the money. And God always provides.'

CHAPTER 5

Typical teenagers

BILL DROPS HIS bulging backpack on the concrete floor and stands clutching his Chipiku plastic bag, packed full of cheap noodles, crisps and biscuits.

'We have the worst hostel,' he says, looking round the room at the battered iron bunk beds with stained, flea-bitten foam mattresses, the bare wires where light switches once were and the graffiti-scarred, poorly plastered walls.

'It is because we are year one,' he says cheerfully. 'It will be better next year, we may even have showers.'

Fourteen-year-old Bill Potani is one of the few thousand teenagers who spend their four years of secondary education at a boarding school. But these institutions should not be confused with boarding schools in rich countries. The conditions are spartan, to say the least. Bill doesn't mind sharing a room with 13 other boys, or even the lack of running water in the mouldy shower block. 'We use a bucket to wash,' he explains.

It's the food he hates. 'Beans and *nsima*, every meal,' he grimaces. 'And they are not cooked properly, they taste horrible. I hate them,' he says with all the feeling a teenager can muster. So why was he so keen to come to boarding school, instead of a day school in his home city of Lilongwe?

'The teachers here are very, very good,' he pronounces seriously, blinking through his newly acquired glasses. 'That is all that matters. The teachers are good.'

And that is all that matters to the lucky few who manage to get a place at a secondary school. Adolescence is when the deep inequality that characterises Malawi society becomes entrenched. Every child is entitled to free primary education, from age six to 13, but secondary education – whether at a public or private school – is only for a privileged few. The government announced an end to formal fees for public secondary schools in the run up to the 2019 elections, but these have been replaced by 'development' fees, which can be as high as MK 5,000 (around £5.25) a term. And students who board have to pay for the privilege of sharing a dingy hostel with up to 20 in a room.

Where you live matters. One-third of teenagers living in the cities go to secondary school, but only a little over ten per cent of children in rural Malawi. It is no surprise, then, that the latest government figures suggest that less than one-fifth of 14 to 17 year olds – 297,000 teenagers – currently benefit from secondary education. There are another 90,000 or so older students still in class, doggedly trying to finish their secondary education. It is not unusual for someone to still be in school when they reach their 20s, having repeated several years.

Winning a coveted place at one of the country's 1,100 public secondary schools is the aim of every child who sits the PSLCE at the end of Standard 8. But even those who pass will be very lucky to get a place. In 2019, nearly 220,000 pupils passed the exam, but only 82,000 were selected for a national secondary school. The remaining students may, if their parents can afford the fees, opt for one of the growing number of private secondary schools scattered across the country. Bill's school is run by the Seventh Day Adventist Church, and charges MK 200,000 a term (MK 600,000 a year, or £630), money his parents, Peter and Debra, simply could not afford to pay without help from their extended family.

Rich parents will happily shell out thousands of pounds a year to secure their child a coveted place in one of the international secondary schools, such as Bishop Mackenzie's in Lilongwe, which offer international examinations. But for most teenagers, their formal education will stop just as they reach adolescence. Even those lucky enough to be selected for secondary school can face financial pressure so intense that it sometimes puts an end to their dreams.

Everson Mapayani (29), who lives in Mooza village in Salima district, was one of those fortunate – and bright enough – to win a place at a highly regarded public secondary school, as he recalls.

'My parents are poor villagers,' says Everson, now a father of two, and an energetic community activist. 'I was selected to go to Chipoka Secondary School. It is a boarding school, a good one. I was so happy. My mother and father gave me MK 3,000 (£3), half of my fees for the term, but when the school distributed the card for school meals, I did not get one as I had not paid the full amount. I survived two days without eating, then I decided to go home, as my parents could not find the remaining MK 3,000.' He stops for a moment, then says, quietly, 'I did not learn anything in the first term.'

His parents were determined that their eldest child should continue his education, as Everson explains. 'They cultivated cotton in readiness for the fees for the second term, so I went back to school. But the cotton price that year dropped to MK ten per kg, and they could not even sell because the market was at Balaka, which was too far.

'So once again, I stayed for a few days without eating, but then I decided to go home. I had to sell my belt to a fellow student to afford the bus fare home.'

Sitting at home, his dreams of university fading, Everson and his father decided that he should try to get a place in the local Community Day Secondary School (CDSS), within walking distance of their village home.

The overwhelming majority of Malawi's secondary schools are CDSSs. There is a network of around 1,000 across the country, many built by donors such as USAID, America's international development agency. Most of the students walk to school, sometimes up to ten kilometres each way. Some schools provide very basic hostels for those who live too far to make the daily journey.

The quality of the teaching and resources varies from school to school and is often dependent on the school leadership. Everson's future depended on whether he could persuade the head teacher of Kaphirintiwa CDSS to admit him halfway through year one.

'The headmaster, one Mark Kalilombe, told me to write an application letter, telling him why I wanted to go to school, and I was lucky, he admitted me.'

Everson's school career quickly took off. He won a scholarship and towards the end of his first year, he was selected as a member of Malawi's Youth Parliament, a post he held for three years. His family poverty meant that, even though he passed his final secondary school exams – the Malawi School Certificate of Education (MSCE) – with good grades, he could not afford to go to university or college.

'I was top in my class from year one to year four in humanities and languages,' he says, his pride at his teenage achievements still obvious, 'So I am very sad that I was not able to undertake higher education because of poverty,' he says, 'I dreamt of doing social work or community development...' he tails off, before rallying.

Everson was the local councillor for his area for five years, until he lost his seat in the 2019 elections. 'I would love to find the funds to continue with my education,' he says, 'but I am searching for a job. I have children to raise, and I am determined they will go to secondary school. No one can take your education from you once you have it. It will make them self-reliant, as

I have become, and it means they can help develop their community, and the country at large.'

Malawi is full of bright, ambitious teenagers like Everson. Sixteen-year-old Gift Wyson, who attends the Holy Family CDSS in Phalombe, in southern Malawi, is an electronics wizard. His inventions so far include a machine that works as an auto-teller to count *kwacha* notes, a photocopier, a wind vane and a chemical tester, and he is planning more inventions, including Malawi's first home-grown motor engine, and an electric generator.

He told *The Sunday Times* newspaper that he puts his success down to the science lessons he gets in his school. 'When I learn things in class, I do not simply understand them for the sake of obtaining good grades during examinations,' he explained. 'I usually try to apply the basic principles to my everyday life activities, thus translating the lessons from class into the operation of these machines.'

His father, Richard, is a self-taught motor mechanic whose parents could not afford to send him to secondary school.

'My family needed support for its daily survival, and as our parents grew older, they could not provide for us,' he said, adding that he is now trying to increase his income so that he can support his son's ambitions.

The future life chances of Malawi teenagers are not only deeply divided by household income – virtually no child goes to secondary school unless their parents are in the richest 20 per cent of the population. Sex plays a significant factor too.

Malawi's traditional cultures, developed over centuries and still celebrated today in the rural areas, dictate that once a girl reaches puberty – when she starts to menstruate – she is ready for marriage and childbirth. While more girls than boys go to primary school from age six to 13, the number of girls in education starts to drop off after 13. And even those girls who have made it as far as secondary school can find their education cut short by marriage.

Masozi was married just before her 16th birthday, when she was halfway through her second year at Mhlafuta CDSS, in the Mzimba district. Now pregnant, she is trapped in a marriage forced on her by her parents, in return for a *lobola* (dowry).

'I grew up harbouring an ambition to be a nurse, so that I could save and serve my area, which is grappling with the problem of compromised health services. That is why I worked hard at secondary school, because I knew pretty well that I could not achieve my dream without education,' she told campaigners against early marriage.

A determined alliance of Malawi's chiefs – its traditional leaders – the government and civil society, supported by the UN, the EU and other major donors, is working hard to end child marriages. In 2017, the government increased the legal age of marriage to 18 years, for both boys and girls, but despite the change in the law, traditional culture still determines many girls' futures. Nearly half of girls (42 per cent) are married by the time they are 18, and almost one in ten before their 15th birthday.

Maggie Banda, founder and executive director of WOLREC, bemoans her country's stubborn adherence to 'tradition'. 'Some of our social and cultural practices, such as early marriage, are very harmful to girls. And we find people hide behind culture and tradition to violate girls' rights. There have been attempts to address the issues of social and cultural practices through national and local laws, but up to now they are still rampant. These practices destroy the life chances of far too many of our young women.'

While Masozi, and thousands of teenage girls like her, are coping with breastfeeding and coming to terms with marriage to a man they barely know, Lizziness (17) and her 16-year-old sister, Clever, are busy planning their lives.

The Banda sisters are lucky. Their father, Frank, has a steady job as a driver for the World Bank and their mother, Gloria, has a diploma in procurement. She finds work regularly on short-term contracts, including the 2019 voter registration drive. Both girls won places to a prestigious Catholic girls' boarding school, from where Lizziness has just graduated, and while Frank and Gloria occasionally struggle to meet the girls' school fees, they always manage.

'Education is our family priority,' says Frank.

Watching Lizziness collect the school prize for social studies at her recent graduation, it is hard not to feel some optimism for Malawi's future. She and her group of Year 4 friends are strong, healthy young women, poised and confident in their abilities, ready, it seems, for whatever the future holds.

Lizziness, who is hoping to win a place at university to study economics, already has a clear plan. 'I want to be self-employed,' she asserts. 'I am going to be an entrepreneur and open my own coffee-processing business.'

In the meantime, she spends her time watching movies – Bollywood is a family favourite – and shopping at the 'bend-down boutiques' – the Malawi nickname for second-hand clothes markets – with her mother and sister.

Clever still has a year at secondary school to complete and will sit her MSCE exams at the end of her final term. It is these exams, which test all eight secondary school subjects, that will determine whether she, and her sister, progress to university.

'The lower the points you get, the better you have done,' explains Frank. 'Last year someone had six points, which is the very best you can get. I don't think my girls will do that,' he laughs, 'but they will try very hard.'

Clever, whose favourite subjects are English, biology and chemistry, wants to study engineering if she gets good enough grades. 'I realise a lot of girls don't go for engineering or science courses because they think they are too tough for them, but that is not true. We can do the same as boys,' she says determinedly.

She also enjoys her compulsory life skills lessons, because, she says, they tackle the gender divide that holds back so many Malawi girls and women. 'It helps us question many of the traditional practices and cultures in our country. And to understand why girls have issues, such as wanting to lose weight. It also shows us how social media can negatively affect our behaviour,' she laughs, holding on to her Chinese phone, which is banned at school.

While Clever and Lizziness are preparing for an adult life that they hope will offer all sorts of possibilities, from a professional career to a happy marriage and a home of their own in the city, teenage girls like Memory have only traditional village life to look forward to.

Memory is typical of the one million or more 14 to 17 year olds who cannot afford secondary education, or who dropped out of school to help at home. She starts her day at 5.00am, before the sun rises, by preparing food for her younger brothers and sisters to take to school. 'They like Irish potatoes,' she says.

Next on her list of chores is fetching water from the borehole and heating it over firewood so the family can wash. Only then can she consider her own needs, when she dons her bright blue school uniform and heads off to primary school. She may be 17, but Memory is only in Standard 5, where the average age of her classmates is 11.

She missed years of primary education because she had to stay at home to help her mother grow crops and look after her siblings, after her father died. But she is determined to finish her primary education. 'I want to be a driver, or a nurse, so that I can help my mother feed the family, and to help pay school fees for my brothers and sisters,' she says cheerfully.

While Lizziness and Clever spend their afternoons catching up with friends on social media, or watching movies, Memory hoes the rich red earth outside her family compound, in preparation to plant cassava and maize.

'We don't eat much meat or eggs,' she says, while stirring the pot of *nsima* ready for the family's evening meal. 'They are too expensive, so we eat beans and relish [greens cooked with groundnut flour, tomatoes and onions] with our *nsima*.'

Her day ends by the light of a crudely made paraffin lamp, as she does her English homework. She smiles as she closes her dog-eared book, which she shares with a friend, 'It is my favourite subject, I enjoy learning it.'

Bill, sisters Lizziness and Clever and Memory are each, in their own way, typical Malawi teenagers. What lies ahead for them as they prepare for adulthood?

CHAPTER 6

Into adulthood

SITTING IN A burger bar in central Lilongwe, Alexander plays with his 'all-day breakfast' as he recalls the start of his university career.

'It was 6 February 2010, a Saturday,' he says. 'I won't forget that day because it was one of the happiest moments of my life. I had arrived at Chancellor College, in Zomba, the mother university. The first and one of the biggest of our public colleges.'

It was one of Clara Galimoto's happiest moments too. Alexander, the youngest of her seven children, was the first in her family ever to go to university. A widow since 2000, she has struggled financially after her husband, Stexie, died from AIDS. In the week before his death, she too had tested positive.

After his funeral, she was forced to leave their city home in Mzuzu and head back to her home village on the outskirts of Lilongwe, where her brother gave her and her children a house – but she had no income. Her oldest son, Gifted, was forced to abandon his dreams of a university career and find work, while Clara learned how to be a village woman again, growing maize to eat and selling the surplus to buy soap and salt. But she was determined that her baby, Alexander, would go to university. 'He is the cleverest, he is our future,' she reminded everyone on a regular basis.

Like Clara, the government believes that its graduates are the country's future. The government invests around a third of its education budget in higher education, compared to just over ten per cent in secondary schools. Malawi has the most expensive university system in Africa, according to the World Bank, with one year of study for one student costing the same as 250 primary school pupils. And yet the return on its investment has still to bear fruit. In 2018, fewer than 100,000 Malawians had a degree – little more than one per cent of the over-21 population.

Malawi has four public universities, with plans for a fifth. The University of Malawi, established in 1964, has four colleges: Chancellor (often known as 'Chanco'), the Polytechnic, the Kamuzu College of Nursing and the highly rated College of Medicine. The nursing and medical colleges are hoping to merge to establish a medical university. There is Mzuzu University in the north and the Malawi University of Science and Technology (MUST) in Thyolo, in the southern region, which offers largely science and technology courses. And Lilongwe University of Agriculture and Natural Resources (LUANAR) focuses on Malawi's most important industry, farming, and its most important natural resources, its land and lake.

There are a number of other public higher education institutions, from the Marine College to the Malawi Institute of Management, which offer professional qualifications in a range of disciplines. And there is a growing number of private colleges and universities, but as Alexander points out, 'Many of them are not accredited, so everyone wants to get into a public university.'

Entry into one of the public institutions depends on two things: a student's performance at the MSCE and their ability to afford the tuition fees and living expenses.

'We get points for our MSCE exams,' explains Alexander. 'You need to get between six (the best score) and 36. I got 15, so I made it.

'You have three choices when you apply, so economics was my first choice, with accountancy my second and business management my third. But these are popular courses, and it happened I wasn't even given one of them. I was enrolled to study biological science. My understanding was that many people wanted to get into the courses I chose, and the competition was too hard, so I wasn't picked, but I had to be offered something. Unfortunately, they didn't give me a choice, they made it for me, that's how it operated then. I hear now people have to make seven choices.'

Despite being forced into a course he didn't have any interest in, or particular aptitude for, Alexander was happy. 'Very happy,' he recalls, 'Not because I was doing biological science, but because I was going to university. In my first year, I didn't care what I was studying, all I cared about was that I was in college.'

His happiness ended almost as soon his second year started. 'The fees in first year were MK 50,000 (£53) a year, and I got a scholarship which helped with my fees and living expenses. But there was a fees hike in 2011, to MK 250,000, and I didn't get help. My family had to find the money. It was tough for them and for me. It is even worse now for students, the fees are around MK 500,000 a year, with living expenses on top of that.'

Hundreds of Malawi undergraduates now struggle to afford their studies, with reports of some forced to sleep in lecture theatres because they cannot afford to rent a room, while others go hungry for several days at a time. 'Others lack even pens and notebooks. It is just too much,' bemoaned Luciano Ndalama, Dean of Students at the Polytechnic, in a newspaper interview recently.

The Higher Education Students and Loan Board offers help, but the demand outstrips its meagre resources. 'It is very clear the Board seems to be overwhelmed…' thundered a leader in *The Daily Times* in 2019. 'In the past, the government took it upon itself to educate its citizens and it did so by taking full responsibility for those who showed potential… Things have completely changed as priorities have been skewed. Education is no longer given priority, except on paper. That is why being selected to university has become a curse to parents and students…'

Realising his dream of a place at university proved to be a curse for Alexander. He dropped out at the end of his second year. 'I got diverted,' he remembers, 'it never ended well… I failed my exams and only sat one of the resits.'

He was advised to take a year out on the promise that he could return. 'I went home, I studied, but when I went back to register the following year my name wasn't there. I had to accept it, there was no choice.'

Alexander struggles to describe the years that followed, as he entered his 20s, a university drop-out and unemployed. 'I wasn't myself,' he says. 'It took me nearly four years to recover. In 2016, I decided I won't be like this forever, I have to move past it.'

He tried to find a job, desperately, as he recalls. 'I keep records. Since leaving university, I have applied for more than 400 jobs. From the 400, I have been called for interview not more than ten times. I have had two jobs.'

In desperation, he managed to raise enough money to study for a diploma in accounting at the Malawi College of Accountancy. 'I got it in one year, it is accredited by the UK's Institute of Chartered Accountants.'

He now has a job as a loan officer with a subsidiary of the large international charity, World Vision. After deductions for tax and medical insurance, he is left with MK 84,000 (£88) a month to live on.

'You need to find a friend to live with, as a decent place to stay starts around MK 50,000 a month. I like my job, but there is no real chance of getting promoted. You can only go as far as a supervisor, that's your bar. Then I would have to go somewhere else.

'I would like to get a job where we reach out to people, to see people smiling, not just office work, but in the field. And I want a better salary, to save, to have a better home. And one day get married. I used to dream about it at university, imagining my home, my wife, my kids. And then when my life turned upside down, those dreams passed.'

Alexander has not ruled out finishing his education. 'I like economics, I would love to complete my studies, do an economics degree, to understand how the economy operates, what are the problems and failings in Malawi.'

And Clara, how does she feel when her youngest son has not yet fulfilled the family dream of being the first Galimoto to get a degree? 'I am happy now,' she says quietly. 'Alexander was so sad for a long time. Now he is working, he is much happier. He will be fine.'

The transition from adolescent to adult has been tough for Alexander, but at 27 he says he is getting stronger. 'Sometimes when I am alone, I get so emotional. But I realise I can't dictate how my life will turn out, but I can dictate how I should take it. I am learning from things that happen to me.'

The majority of young Malawians have no choice over the direction life will take once they leave school. Their adult lives will be like those of their great-grandparents, and for many, not very different to how their ancestors lived before colonial times. Adulthood for most Malawians comes with puberty, then marriage, not a degree or a job. Young teenagers in Malawi's villages, where 84 per cent of the population live, will go through an ancient rite of passage to mark their new status.

The practices differ from one tribe to another, and from one area to the next, but the main purpose is the same: to teach the child what is expected of him or her as an adult. The most elaborate practices are reserved for girls, because, according to an old Chewa saying, *'mwamuna sauzidwa'* – a man doesn't need to be told what to do.

The initiation ceremonies range from the straightforward *chinamwali*, in the north, where a girl is counselled by an aunt or her grandmother about menstruation, how to show respect for her elders and told to avoid sex before marriage, for fear of pregnancy. She is also instructed to stop playing with those of her friends who have not yet reached puberty, as she is now a grown-up and must associate with adults. In the southern region, girls are still taught *thedzo* (dances) that show them how to please their future partners sexually. After a month of tuition from older women, they gather at the chief's house to show what they have learned. At the end of this ceremony, they are invited to choose a boy to lose their virginity to, or *kusasa fumbi* (removing dust). And across all three regions of Malawi, girls are taught how to pull each other's labia so that over time, they grow long, like fingers (*makuna*). Men, it is said, prefer to marry a woman with *makuna*. Even the brightest of village girls find it hard to escape their destiny as wives and mothers, with most village women having four or five children, compared to three for urban women.

Most boys enjoy an informal introduction to adulthood, with advice on how to take care of the sick and elderly as they mature, how they should not fear dead bodies, as they are required to attend all funerals in their community, and how to enjoy sex. According to research by Malawi's Human Rights Commission, nearly a fifth of boys will undergo *jando* (circumcision) when they reach puberty, or even younger. The age it happens, and methods used – whether cutting off the foreskin with a knife or fingernails – vary from district to district, but all boys are considered adults once it has been done and are advised to have sex as soon as possible.

Perhaps the most visible of traditional rites of passage for boys is *kumeta nyau*, joining the *nyau* cult, which is most common among the Chewa people in Dowa and Mchinji. *Kulowa Gule* is a central part of the Chewa culture, and boys are introduced to the secret society as teenagers, from about ten years old up to 20, depending on where they live. As well as advice on how to conduct themselves as members of the cult, they are taught practical skills such as building a house, mat-weaving and making hoes for cultivating the crops that will be essential to their adult life.

Most Malawian men will never find a full-time job with a regular salary, subject to tax and employment law. The formal labour market in Malawi is tiny, with little more than ten per cent of the adult population enjoying that kind of job security. But almost all possess a range of practical skills, from being able to fire bricks to building a two-roomed family home, to growing the food their family depends on for survival. And every village has at least one highly skilled, self-taught engineer who can mend an ancient TV set or fix a car engine.

The government and its skills agency, TEVETA, preside over a country-wide network of vocational training. There are nine technical colleges which offer a range of apprenticeships, from administrative studies to plumbing. But the entry requirement is an MSCE, putting these opportunities out of reach of most young Malawians.

In 2015, the first of 25 community technical colleges to be built across

Malawi opened its doors, offering vocational training to young people who can read and write basic English.

John Lanjesi (25) left school in Standard 7 of primary school to look after his brothers and sisters after their parents died. He had given up hope of ever getting a job that would allow him to have his own family, depending instead on piece work, digging pit latrines for his survival. He was one of the first to enrol at Chilombwe Community Technical College on the outskirts of Blantyre, where he trained as a bricklayer, and now he says his future is assured. 'I can get married.'

Lifa Kamwendo (29) walked 20 kilometres every day so he could attend Ngodzi Community Skills Development Centre, where he trained to be a carpenter. His business in thriving. 'After one person gave me a deposit to make a dining set, that was the start,' he says. 'And now I make a profit of MK 200,000 (£211) a month. As a father, nothing brings a better feeling than being able to provide for all your family's needs.'

Nthanda Manduwi (24) is the very epitome of a confident young creative at the start of a glittering career. She graduated from Chancellor College with a degree in economics and demographic studies. She now blogs, makes short films, writes self-help books and is one of Malawi's few travel writers. She is also a tax collector. 'I work for the Malawi Revenue Authority,' she smiles. 'The salary means I can do my creative work.'

Her experience of university was in complete contrast to Alexander's. While she says her family is not rich, her mother was Malawi's first female ship's captain, and now owns a private primary and secondary school. Her father is an engineer.

'We are not poor,' she says, 'but my mum struggled at university, she was studying at Chanco, but her dad passed away in her third year and she couldn't afford to go back, so she dropped out. Someone sent her an application for the Marine College in Monkey Bay, and she thought, "Why not? They are going to educate me while they are paying me." She was the only woman in a class of 12. My dad was there and that is how they met.

'So, we are middle-class, but I grew up in Mangochi, not in the city. So even though I was driven to primary school, I grew up with the kids from the villages, who live in huts. Unlike my rich friends, I know what it means for people not to have food for a day.'

Nthanda loved her university experience. 'I guess I was finally myself, I didn't have rules, I didn't have people telling me what to do, so for the first time I was free to be me and figure out what I wanted to do with my life.'

She quickly figured out that she wanted to be a writer. 'University is where I stumbled upon blogging, and I invested time in that, and it has grown from there.'

She also discovered a talent for business, when she found she could not survive on the government scholarship programme of MK 50,000 (£53) a term. 'It was not enough to live on, so most of us had small businesses to raise more money. I used to love doing hair to earn some extra money. There were a few businesses on campus, so in my third year, when the university put the lease of a salon out to tender, I pitched for that, and got it. So, for two years I ran a hairdressing salon, with two employees. I needed the money, but I also wanted to explore entrepreneurship.'

Most students find it difficult to combine their studies with their social life, let alone build a successful small business, but Nthanda combined all three with ease, as she recalls. 'It wasn't difficult. I did my business in my free time. I was also really active in student entertainment, so I was always organising events, like pageants and shows, and no, it wasn't hard to balance.'

She stops for a moment. 'Okay, maybe if I had dropped the business and my social life, I would have got better grades, but it wasn't something I regret.'

She is very happy to have had the opportunity to go to a public university. 'You're not valued without a degree,' she states. 'You're just not taken seriously. I wouldn't be able to do what I am doing now – my job and my creative life – without a degree, or definitely not at the level I am at now.'

The statistics bear her out. Graduates are far more likely to be in employment by the time they hit 35 than any other Malawian and will earn five times more than someone whose education ended at secondary school.

The contrast between the life chances of a girl born in a village and one born into Malawi's small, but very visible, middle-class are so stark as to be almost grotesque.

'It is huge,' acknowledges Nthanda. 'Life in the villages is very much as it was hundreds of years ago. It is a pretty tricky situation. I got a rude awakening a few months ago. I was doing a talk for girls on menstruation, teenagers, in a township outside Lilongwe. These were girls from very poor families… only three out of a couple of hundred engaged with me, the rest were completely passive. They will leave school and get married. I have no idea how to change that, how are we going to make the poor people included?

'I think there can be improvements made. Students need better guidance on what courses to choose. And obviously, there are lot of young Malawians who are very intelligent but fail to get into scholarship programmes.' She adds, 'The fees are very high, so I think maybe there should be more scholarships for very smart people, no matter where they come from.'

CHAPTER 7

Family life

AMOS MLOTHA CELEBRATED his 30th birthday recently. The community development worker earns an above average salary, working for one of the country's most successful NGOs.

He is a handsome man, with a gentle sense of humour and a keen intellect. He is also unmarried. By Malawian standards, he is too old to be single. The average age for a man to get married is 23 and has been for nearly three decades. Before that, it was even younger. But there is a good reason for his reluctance to tie the knot with his girlfriend and mother of their young son.

'I can't afford to make that commitment just yet,' he says, with more than a hint of regret. 'Not until my sisters finish college. I have to pay their school fees. One is at Chancellor College, the other two are at private institutions. Their fees are around MK 2.5 million (£2,600) a year.' He stops, as if the magnitude of his family responsibility had suddenly become clear to him.

'I earn MK 400,000 (£420) a month,' he continues after a moment. 'My net pay is MK 275,000 a month, or MK 3.3 million (£3,500) a year. So, you can see I am not even left with close to half. My life is on hold. It is very difficult. What it simply means if I am to progress in my life, I have to wait until these guys are finished school.'

Amos' dilemma is not unusual in Malawi, where there is no welfare state. Family obligations are paramount, particularly it seems for the first-born, as Amos explains.

'When you are the first-born son, or the first-born daughter, the whole family expects you to support the rest of the brothers and sisters. You are more or less like a breadwinner, you take over from the parents.'

Amos' father, an accountant for a secondary school, supported him through university, but as soon as Amos started earning, the responsibility shifted to him.

'My father's financial capacity means he cannot afford to pay school fees for all of us,' explains Amos. 'When I started work, I took over responsibility, paying school fees for my two younger brothers. One is finished college now and working with Mary's Meals, the charity. I am remaining with the other brother, who is almost finished. Now since the responsibility of paying school fees for these two is almost done, I have taken over the fees for my three sisters.'

He is at pains to explain that his father contributes. 'Whenever I am totally stuck, my father comes in. He can cover minor issues, like clothes, shoes and transport. What I am targeting are the school fees, because with his financial muscle he cannot afford the fees.'

But Amos' family obligations mean he cannot start investing in his own family's future.

'So, this responsibility means I cannot start my life until these people finish school. It is a challenge. It is a block. Even though my girlfriend has accepted it, her life is disturbed, so we cannot invest, we cannot set up home together.'

Surprisingly, he is not resentful of this burden. 'No, I am not,' he smiles, but he is aware that the situation is not particularly fair.

'The sad thing is you support your brothers and cousins, you help them excel. Maybe they will get better qualifications and a better job than you, because you were supporting them, but they will never think of helping you. We don't benefit. It is not a good thing to be the first-born,' he laughs, a little ruefully.

Family is the defining feature of Malawi society. In a country with no state support for people with a disability, the unemployed or the destitute, no state pension and where only rudimentary healthcare is free, families are the welfare state.

Several generations of one family will live happily together, with cousins and step-brothers, aunties and in-laws included. And this traditional family life is as common in city homes as it is in village compounds, where families will group their one-roomed homes together. Living alone is a strange concept to most Malawians. There are only around 275,000 single person households (7 per cent), compared to 29 per cent (8 million people) in the UK. Solitude is not yet an aspiration, even among those seeking a better life.

Busisiwe Chimasula tracks down products from across the world for her medical supply business, while perched precariously with her laptop in the middle of a room full of laughing children. She jostles for space amid the jumble of family life: towering stacks of clothes, school books and mismatched shoes, cartoons blaring on the ancient television in the corner as she negotiates online with a supplier in India.

Since the death of her grandmother, Homba Mbekeani, in 2019, Busisiwe has taken on the role of the family matriarch. She shares her family's large, if dilapidated, house with two of her six siblings and their six children. Another sister lives in a smaller house on the edge of their large garden. And during long school holidays, the house can be home for up to 15 children and teenagers as well as half a dozen adults, as cousins gather at the family home.

'I have learned so much about life in recent years, and I pass that on to my daughter Chipo and my sisters and their children. I teach them about the importance of church, and to work hard at school. And the importance of family,' she says.

Busisiwe and her five sisters are not unusual in that they are all single parents, apart from Debra, who lives 300 kilometres away in Lilongwe with her husband, Peter Potani.

'Marriage, for this current generation, is not as important as it used to be,' explains Busisiwe. 'This generation wants an easy ride, an easy way to get everything. I think that is why we have a higher divorce rate, or women do not get married.

'Most people prefer being on their own, and independent, like I am. And nowadays, with more freedom and more rights, then we don't care as much about marriage.'

Research suggests that one-third of marriages will end in divorce within 20 years, and unlike the UK, where divorce rates are now at 42 per cent, this is not a new reality. Marriage breakdowns have been a feature of Malawi life for the last 100 years, since studies began. The HIV epidemic, which saw upwards of 1.5 million people die, created a sharp increase in single parent households, not only through death, but also from divorces, with research suggesting people get divorced to protect themselves from possible infection.

But everyone loves a wedding, and they are an especially joyous occasion in Malawi, whether an expensive religious ceremony in a city church followed by a reception at a top hotel, or a customary event in a village, barely unchanged in centuries. Even rich young Malawians, with their expensive German cars and clothes imported from the UK or America, will follow age-old courtship and marriage traditions.

The National Assembly (Malawi's parliament) passed the Marriage, Divorce and Family Relations Act in 2015. It recognises four different forms of marriage: civil marriage, where the ceremony is conducted by a public official; religious marriage, customary marriage and marriage by reputation or permanent cohabitation. The minimum marriage age is 18 years, including for customary and religious rites, which previously had set the onset of puberty as the age for marriage. And polygamy, which is still widely practised in some districts, remains an offence, punishable by up to five years in prison and a fine of MK 100,000 (£105), but only if the second marriage is a civil (statutory) one. Polygamous marriages are allowed if confirmed by religious or customary rite.

The simplest form of polygamy, or *mitala* as it is commonly known, is for a man to have two or three wives, although there are examples of men with up to eight wives in the northern region. The wives may stay in the same compound as each other and their husband, but they will each have their own small mud-brick house. Some will earn their own money, but most will help grow the family's cash crop. The husband will control the family's income.

Malawians give many reasons for *mitala*. Some men, particularly chiefs, regard several wives as an outward sign they are wealthy. Others marry if they want to 'punish' their first wife when she loses her looks, or nags too much. And some men consider their wives – and children – as nothing more than a source of cheap labour.

Women, too, have their own reasons for agreeing to be a second wife, or for their husband to marry a younger woman. A young woman earns respect when she is married, so many prefer a polygamous marriage to the stigma of being single. Some are pressured into marriage because they are 'old', and many are encouraged by their parents to marry a man who has wealth. It doesn't matter if he has several wives.

Vitumbiko is in the third year of her married life, and she laughs at the thought of her husband, Clever, bringing another wife into their two-bedroom home in Area 25, a township on the edge of Lilongwe.

'Noooo, it cannot happen,' she says. 'Not here, not in the city. Yes, in the rural areas, particularly among Muslims, but not here.'

While Vitumbiko dismisses polygamy as an out-of-date tradition, only practised by villagers, she holds dear to other family traditions, particularly counselling, as she explains.

'When you agree to get engaged, you seek guidance from your parents about who should be your marriage counsellor. We call them *ankhoswe* [uncle]. In fact, a marriage is as much about the families as it is about you. You can even have the engagement – *chinkhoswe* – in your absence. It is possible. In the old days that would happen a lot, it still happens in the rural areas.

'The *ankhoswe* is usually a relative. Our culture is matrilineal, so it has to be someone from your mother's side, a brother or cousin. And someone from your partner's mother's family. It is only in the north that it is from your father's side.'

As Vitumbiko feeds her baby girl, Viwemi, she sets out the role her *ankhoswe* will play in her family.

'If I have a problem with my marriage, for example if Clever was not giving me support, I would have to report that to his uncle, or aunt. These days your *ankhoswe* can be a woman too. They will then come to our home and discuss the matter with us. They offer advice, then will check progress.'

Vitumbiko is happy enough to go along with the tradition, but only up to a point. Her *ankhoswe* helped organise both her engagement party and wedding. She is less comfortable about the prospect of sharing intimate secrets with them.

'For me it would make me feel uncomfortable, telling someone else my problems,' she says. 'I think it is easier to sort them out ourselves, but it is part of our culture and most people are still comfortable with it. And your *ankhoswe* is supposed to keep your confidence, they shouldn't say to others, maybe only your parents.'

And she acknowledges the *ankhoswe* could have an important role to play if a young couple were experiencing problems.

'I think it would be easier for me to tell my parents if I had a problem, but if Clever had wronged me, my parents would be harsher on him. The *ankhoswe* is much calmer and more objective. But it is changing.'

Another ancient tradition that is evolving is that of *lobola*, or dowry. A major study by the Malawi Human Rights Commission into cultural practices suggests that two-thirds of marriages across the country are still formalised by some sort of payment.

'Clever did not pay a *lobola* for me,' laughs Vitumbiko. 'But I did have a wedding shower.'

City brides may prefer food mixers to heads of cattle, but in the rural areas where ancient customs are still held dear, the 'bride price' will vary according to the behaviour of the bride-to-be. The better behaved she is, the higher her dowry. A woman who is a virgin, or has not given birth, attracts a premium. And the wealth of her parents is taken into consideration – the more affluent a family, the higher the *lobola*.

Village families will use the *ankhoswe* to negotiate the dowry at the time of the engagement. There is usually a preliminary payment such as a *mamotcho* – a pack of soft drinks, soap, salt and other essential items – followed by a more substantial dowry of cattle or cash. After the dowry is paid, the couple can either live together immediately or arrange a religious ceremony or a customary wedding. However they choose to celebrate their newly married state, their *ankhoswe* will counsel them on sex, money and how to handle their relatives immediately after the wedding.

Even Vitumbiko and Clever enjoyed a *chilangizo* (counselling session) before their reception began. 'It is the way,' she laughs, remembering how she was told that the way to a man's heart is through his stomach.

Food is central to Malawi family life. Village women, helped by their daughters and granddaughters, will spend much of their day gathering and preparing food.

A typical day will start at around 4.00am, before the sun rises. A woman will get up to collect water from the nearest borehole, then heat it over firewood for the breakfast porridge or Irish potatoes. After the children leave for school, she will go to the family's garden, or small field, to help tend the crops, and while there she will collect relish – usually rape leaves – to cook with tomatoes and onion for the midday meal. And in the early evening she will collect more relish, before starting the ritual of cooking *nsima*, Malawi's national dish.

Most Malawians, rich and poor, young and old, will say they have not eaten if they have not had *nsima* as part of their meal. Many villagers will eat it three times a day, if they have sufficient flour.

Maize was introduced to East Africa in the 16th century by the Portuguese, and changed forever how Malawians eat, and how they farm. Families, even rich ones, will grow maize wherever they can. And for the majority of the population, it is not only their staple diet, but their main source of income, since most Malawians, especially outside the cities, don't have regular paid employment.

Vitumbiko was taught how to prepare *nsima* by her mother, Thoko, when she was eight or nine. 'The cooking technique may be straightforward, but it takes practise to get it just right,' she says.

'First thing you have to heat your water, and before it gets to a boiling point you have to put in your flour, maybe a handful, it depends how many people you are feeding. After that, you stir it and let it boil up maybe five or ten or minutes, then you start adding in the rest of flour, the *ufa*, to make it thick. You add it slowly, stirring and adding, with a porridge stick.

'Experience tells you when you have enough *ufa*,' she laughs. 'And it depends how you like it. Some people like it soft, some people like it very hard. The type of *ufa* will make a difference. There is the white *ufa*. *Ufa oyera*. Then we have the *mgayiwa*, the third one is the ground meal, this one is very dark, the *mgayiwa* is in-between. The process is the same, but the amount of flour varies. The white *ufa* is soft, while if you put in a lot of ground meal flour, the *nsima* will be hard, so you have to be careful.

'From adding the *ufa*, we are beating it all the time, so it becomes smooth. It has no time, you just know. It is fine, it is hard work. At a funeral, there are very big pots, which need two women to cook the *nsima*.'

Vitumbiko says she had no lessons on how to prepare relish. 'As for the vegetables, you observe when your mother is doing it, then you try it.'

Even in urban households, the majority of household chores fall to the women and girls, and while Vitumbiko is a professional woman, with a promising career as an accountant, she holds fast to Malawi's traditional division of household labour.

She acknowledges that girls have a tougher childhood than their brothers but seems content with the status quo. 'Yes, sometimes it seems not fair. But sometimes we think it is fair, because it is easy for a woman to stop working and be a housewife. Our culture gives our men the responsibility to earn money for housing and clothing, the husband has to be the provider.'

As Vitumbiko prepares to go back to work after three months' paid maternity leave, she has just employed Yanjanani, a 33-year-old woman, as her live-in help. But she would prefer not to have to rely on Yanjanani for her childcare needs.

'If mum was not working, I would not have even got a nanny. I would have dropped Viwemi in the morning at her place. That is very, very normal in our culture. *Agogo* – the grandmother – is the one who brings up the children. And in the village, the older women, the grandmothers, are often the main caretaker. It is very normal for grandmothers to raise the children while the mothers work in their gardens, or if the parents have died.'

Best estimates suggest that around one million children in Malawi have lost one or both parents, with 670,000 designated as orphans due to HIV/AIDS. And one in eight children do not live with their biological parents, even if they are alive. The communal nature of Malawi village life, where family homes are built close together and household chores like cooking, gathering firewood and water are shared, means that children grow up in extended families, where grandparents, aunts and uncles play as big a role in child-rearing as mothers and fathers.

Everson Mapayani and his wife, Mercy, have two children, four-year-old Jessie and baby John. 'My mother, their *agogo*, is the one who takes care of John and Jessie on a daily basis, while Mercy is busy doing laundry and tending the garden. *Agogo* is the one who baths them and carries John on her back.

'In our culture, grandparents are very significant, as they teach us our traditions, and how to live. My own *agogo*, Lenia Thom, my mother's mother, is still alive, and took very good care of me from when I was born. And even though she is very old, she was born in 1940, she still cares for my children too, as her house is just behind mine in our compound.'

As Everson's grandmother and his parents enters their elder years, Everson starts to assume the role of their guardian, just as they cared for him as a child.

'I have great responsibility to my parents and *agogo*,' he says. 'I help them with soap, with cloth and with food. And I built them a house. They are now under my care, for the tremendous deeds they did bringing me up.'

But not every older person in Malawi has a son or daughter to care for them, and in a country where there is no state pension provision, life after 60 can be very tough. Almost unbearable.

CHAPTER 8

Growing old

THE TWO OLD women, one bent almost double with arthritis, walked slowly down the red road, pausing outside the chief's house, then picked up their pace a little as they headed towards their homes.

'If they are lucky, their family will look after them,' says community worker Amos Mlotha, who spends most of his working week among villagers. 'If they are not, if they have no children or grandchildren close by, they will go hungry some days. Some elderly do work, the women can make local beer and sell it. If they are still strong, they can grow vegetables, but if they cannot, they depend on others to feed them.

'Some days they can live without eating *nsima*, they will go to bed hungry,' he states, matter-of-factly. 'And it is hard for them to fetch water and firewood, they need help, and if they don't get it, they suffer.'

It is an accepted fact of Malawi life that most of its elderly population (650,000, or four per cent of the population) depend on their family for their very survival. And the majority – over 600,000 people – live in the rural areas. In a society that ostensibly reveres its elders and where grandparents play an important role in child-rearing, the plight of many old people is harrowing. Even so, they are considered the lucky ones in society to have survived, as Malawi's current life expectancy is still low compared to rich countries, at 61 years for men and 67 years for women.

In the first ever national policy paper on the elderly, published in 2016, the government admitted that Malawi's elderly population suffered a range of challenges, from poor nutrition to physical abuse. Nearly one-fifth have a chronic disease, while over half of men (60 per cent) and 42 per cent of women aged over 85 years old say they still work, mostly growing food.

Most Malawians, particularly those in the rural areas, still hold fast to their traditional beliefs, while also devoutly practising Christianity or Islam. Sudden deaths are attributed to witchcraft, people will turn to traditional medicine first before going to their local health clinic, and wealth and power is regarded as having been won by magic.

Older village women, in particular, are often verbally or physically attacked on suspicion of practising *ufiti* – witchcraft – as 67-year-old Clara Galimoto recalls.

'It was a Friday night,' she remembers, 'local youths started throwing stones at my home. They broke the glass in the windows, and I was frightened they would kill me. It was because someone said I was a witch, that I was putting bad spells on people. My son came and stopped them, but I was very worried.'

Clara, who is barely four feet ten inches tall, is philosophical about the attack. 'It is what happens,' she shrugs.

But shocking incidents, like the 2016 slaughter of the four grandparents of a 17-year-old girl by an angry mob, have forced the government to act. The four villagers, ranging in age from 69 to 86 years old, were murdered after their neighbours decided their granddaughter's death from a lightning strike had been caused by witchcraft, and her grandparents were responsible.

A commission was set up to review the 1911 Witchcraft Act, which bans the practice, and a new law is promised. It cannot come soon enough say campaigners, but like most of Malawi's legislation, enactment will be the real challenge.

'We have good laws,' says Maggie Banda, head of a leading NGO, WOLREC. 'But delivery on the ground is slow.'

By far the biggest challenge facing older people in Malawi is poverty, and by extension, poor health. There is no state pension, so the overwhelming majority of over-60s have to depend on their extended family to eat. A motion passed by the National Assembly in December 2018 called on the government to introduce a monthly pension of MK 20,000 (£21) for everyone over the age of 60, but it is unlikely to become law any time soon.

And while public hospitals are free, the treatment is often very basic, particularly for diseases such as cancer, heart disease and stroke. Malawi is like most sub-Saharan countries, where non-communicable diseases such as cancer are on track to be the leading cause of death by 2030.

Jack Juma, a former welder, is one of the lucky ones. His eight children make sure his old age is comfortable. Sitting in his village home in Thyolo, with his wife Dorothy preparing *nsima* outside, Jack recalls his working life.

'Dorothy and I married here in this village in 1959, when I was 21 years. In 1961, I went to Zimbabwe for work, like a lot of Malawians, where I stayed for 16 years. That is where I learned my work as a welder, at technical college there. I came back in 1975, and worked for Escom, the electricity company. Then I joined Mandala Body Shop, where I was producing bodies for lorries.'

He stops to cough, then continues, 'After that, I joined Air Malawi as an aircraft welder. I stayed there for 15 years, then I left and started my own business, which I was calling 'Jack's Metal Work'. And in 2006, when I was 68 years, I came back here, I came home. My wife was already here for six years.'

Jack may have been reluctant to leave city life in Blantyre after 45 years but he admits now that it was the right decision.

He laughs, 'I decided to come home because I wanted to rest. I had been working for a long time, and since I came back to the village, I am staying comfortable.' He stops, coughs again, 'Except I developed a problem in my spine, but that is because of old age.'

Jack and Dorothy's village home is more substantial than most. It has several rooms, and a secure tin-sheet roof. The outside kitchen is in a solid outhouse and the pit latrine toilet boasts a comfortable cast-concrete seat, so there is no need to squat. 'For old bones,' laughs Jack.

'I have no pension,' says Jack explaining how he and Dorothy survive. 'I did not get a pension even from Air Malawi, it is not a government, it is a company. They gave me some lump sum at the end, but that was all. But anyway, we praise God, we are now depending on our children. That is where we are getting our living. We praise God because he gave us children, we have eight, seven daughters.'

Jack's grown-up children live across the country and each one contributes to their parent's household income.

Their daughter, Thoko, who lives in Lilongwe, 350 kilometres from Jack and Dorothy's home, explains, 'We pay what we can afford. My husband and I pay my parents' medical insurance, and we help out with other things when we can.'

And, with help, Jack and Dorothy still grow their own food. He says, 'We grow maize, pigeon peas, cassava, sweet potatoes and other crops. Some people help me work in the garden, they are being paid by our children, who also get some of the maize flour.'

Jack acknowledges that he and his wife are luckier than most elderly people. 'If someone here in Malawi doesn't have any children, they have a very difficult life, a very difficult life, because they have no one to support them. They suffer terribly. And it is not just food. When we need medical attention, our children send us an ambulance and it takes us to the hospital. This thing is not happening to other people here. They might have children, but because those children didn't go to school, they have no money to help.'

Jack is adamant that the reason for his good fortune was his decision, an unusual one for a working man in 1970s Malawi, to educate his seven daughters. He explains, 'Those people whose children have no money, they had no money to send them to school. When I was working, I wanted my children to go to school. I knew if they went to school, even the girls, they would not suffer.

'And now I am happy that my children are not depending on anyone. We are now depending on them. We look after each other. We looked after them when they were young, now they look after us. It is the cycle of life. If I didn't send them to school, when I retired, I would have suffered. But it is not the case, I am not suffering.'

Homba Mbekeani suffered terribly during the last two years of her life. Struck down by a series of strokes after her 90th birthday, she was confined to a wheelchair. Her left arm and leg were paralysed, and while her mind was still sharp, her speech grew increasingly frail. Cataracts in both eyes meant she was virtually blind. Over one-quarter of all older Malawians have difficulty with their sight.

'I'm alive,' she would rasp, when visitors asked how she was, but her deteriorating health meant her quality of life was poor. It would have been much worse if she did not have three of her six granddaughters and their children living with her, providing 24-hour care.

There is no specialised stroke unit in Malawi, meaning that those struck down either have to be flown to South Africa for treatment – if they are fit enough and can afford it – or hope for the best.

After her first major stroke, Homba was sent home after a few days to recover, or not. Her family, led by Busisiwe, who moved her daughter and her medical supplies business from the capital to her grandmother's home in Blantyre, took over her treatment. They massaged her limbs several times a day, bathed and fed her, carried her to the bathroom during the day, and at night pulled on the adult 'nappies' that Homba so despised. But only when they could afford them.

As Busisiwe remembers, 'The disposable pants are very expensive, so we had to go without other things to buy them and depend on well-wishers to help out. And *agogo* hated them. "They are for babies," she used to say.'

Busisiwe and her sisters never complained about the demands of caring for their grandmother. 'What else should we do?' she asks. 'She raised us, more or less. It was our turn to care for her. And we loved her.'

A few weeks before she died, Busisiwe tracked down Homba's closest remaining blood relative, her cousin, Felicia, in South Africa. Homba had moved to Malawi in 1954 when she married Jarvis, a young Malawian lab technician she had met while training as a nurse in Durban.

Her mother later moved from the Eastern Cape to live with her, and Homba never returned home. 'I want to visit before I die,' she used to say but she never quite managed the trip.

Busisiwe found Felicia, the daughter of Homba's mother's brother, through Facebook, and desperately tried to raise the money for her flight to Malawi to see Homba.

'It is important that *agogo* meets with her own family before she dies,' explained Busisiwe. 'She should be buried in her home village back in South Africa, but that can't happen. This is the next best thing.'

Malawians, even the most sophisticated urbanite, believe that they must be buried in their family's home village, no matter where their home was during their lifetime. Traditional Authority Chikumbu of Mulanje told *The Nation* newspaper recently that, despite spiralling funeral costs, chiefs were right to respect traditional customs.

He said, 'It is not asking too much if we insist that villagers whose relatives die away from the village should bring their dead for a decent burial in the village. It is the way things should be. In fact, if it was not for the financial difficulties that people face on a daily basis, we would have wished all to be buried in the village.'

Sadly, financial difficulties prevented Homba from being reunited with her cousin, and therefore her culture, before her death.

'Felicia had no passport,' Busisiwe said later. 'And even if she had, we struggled to find the money for her airfare as she needed to come with her granddaughter.'

Homba died in her sleep in the early morning of 24 July 2019, nearly three weeks after her 92nd birthday. Surrounded by most of her 28 grandchildren and great-grandchildren, and a few neighbours, she had marked her birthday with her favourite chocolate cake.

'Never thought it would come to this,' she whispered as she sat, lopsided in her wheelchair, a six-year-old great-granddaughter holding her cake.

'Never wanted to end up here.' She struggled, but kept on, 'Worked too much, was too obedient, you suffer for that... you will be okay doing what you like.'

Homba's funeral combined Christian traditions with the ancient burial rites of the Ngoni tribe, of which her husband Jarvis was a member. In the hours after her death, senior members of the family gathered to discuss burial arrangements and, crucially, to agree who would pay for each item, from her coffin to the hire of chairs for the CCAP service that would precede her burial.

As news of her death became known, friends and neighbours arrived with gifts of food. 'There was even a cow given,' smiles Busisiwe. The grieving family, whether in a village or a city setting, are expected to feed the constant stream of mourners who attend the vigil and burial.

Homba's large living room, once her pride and joy, but now a rather dilapidated space with a pocked concrete floor, was transformed with reed mats into a *nsiwa*, a vigil room where her body would lie for 24 hours before burial. Those women closest to her slept here, guarding her body while the men gathered outside, listening to the women sing, in soaring, poignant voices, a constant stream of hymns.

Women play a central role in Malawi funerals, whatever the religion or tribe. '*Amayi amafungatira bwino maliro*' – women know how best to take care of the dead body, said one respondent to the Malawi Human Rights Commission study into cultural practices. They are also believed to be more compassionate than men, and according to folklore, men used to stay outside the *nsiwa* to scare away any wild animals. Nowadays, they chat quietly.

The members of Homba's prayer group and women's choir at Chirimba CCAP Church, dressed in their trademark white blouses and headscarves, accompanied her body to the cemetery at the Henry Henderson Institute, followed by a procession of family, friends and neighbours. Shopkeepers came out onto their verandas to pay their respects as the cortege passed by. Strangers stood silently, seemingly in prayer. Even the children were quiet. Drivers are expected to get out of their car if they meet a funeral procession and face a local fine if they do not. Death is taken very seriously in Malawi.

As her body was lowered into the deep grave, dug that morning by half a dozen bare-footed gravediggers, the minister from St Michael and All Angels Church, the oldest in the country, built in 1891, said a prayer in Chichewa. Reed mats, the traditional burial covering, were placed carefully on top of her coffin, then concrete was quickly shovelled over them. 'To stop thieves,' whispered someone.

Mourners watched silently in the hot afternoon sun as the grave was filled in and a three-foot-high mound carefully constructed to mark her resting place. A tombstone will be placed there in a special 'unveiling' ceremony about 12 months after her death.

A final farewell from her 16-year-old great-granddaughter, on behalf of her family, marked the end of the ceremony, and as Busisiwe walked away, she said, 'We did our best, we gave *agogo* the funeral she deserved. She is happy.'

The cemetery at the Henry Henderson campus is unusual in that it looks like any graveyard in Britain, with granite headstones, some almost 100 years old, marking the lives – and deaths – of many prominent Malawians, and many who were not. Village cemeteries are often mistaken for small woods, close to a settlement, but hidden among the trees and shrubs are grave markers, some elaborate, many in simple stone or wood.

And in Malawi's tens of thousands of villages, people still adhere to ancient burial rites. The Ngoni and Chewa people brew *mowa* – beer – which is sprinkled around the graveyard after a burial, followed by a village feast. If this ritual is not carried out, people fear the dead person's spirit will haunt the village. In some districts, people prepare *mowa* and its non-alcoholic equivalent, *thobwa*, to be drunk by everyone at a ceremony one month after a burial, to mark the end of the mourning period, and beer is poured on the deceased's clothes to cleanse them before others can wear them.

And, to the dismay of human rights and health campaigners, sex is still an important part of death. *Kugoneka mizimu* (pacifying the dead) is the ritual where a bereaved woman is forced to have sex with one of her husband's relatives, usually his brother, in his attempt to secure the dead man's inheritance. *Kulowa kufa* is the practice where a man – the cleanser – has sex with a woman whose son or husband has just died, to put the dead person's spirit to rest.

And across the country, the formal dissolution of a marriage is carried out after the death of a spouse to allow the surviving partner to remarry or move. In Chewa communities, a widow is free to return to her home village one year after her husband's death, and when a *chiliza* (tombstone) has been built in his memory. In some areas in the south, the relatives of the deceased will give the surviving spouse a token to mark the dissolution of the marriage. Women will get new clothes and some money, while men get a razor blade and cash.

But whatever ancient ritual marks the death of a Malawian, the health of the nation is getting better, slowly. People are living longer. In 1964, at the time of independence, life expectancy at birth was only 38 years, compared to 71 in the UK. Maternal deaths have more than halved over the last two decades, from over 1,100 deaths in every 100,000 births in 2000 to just under 500 in 2016, but it is still one of the most dangerous countries in the world to give birth. And Malawi, considered by some as a fragile state, has enjoyed remarkable success in tackling the HIV/AIDS epidemic that only a few years ago threatened to wipe out a generation.

It is one of the few countries in sub-Saharan Africa that is on track to achieve the UN's '90-90-90' target: 90 per cent of people with HIV knowing their status; 90 per cent of these accessing ARVs, and 90 per cent of those on treatment being virally suppressed. But it still only has a few hundred doctors for a population of 18 million.

CHAPTER 9

Health of a nation

MARIA SPREADS OUT the reed mat in the shade of an acacia tree a few yards from her village home, and, gathering her *chitenje* more tightly round her waist, sits down.

'I am a *sing'anga* – a spiritual healer,' she says. 'I was born around 1950, many, many years ago. During my childhood, colonial rule was still here, and we were fighting for this land.'

She stops, and points to the three simple mud-brick houses behind her, where a small group of women and children were preparing food.

'I have two children, a boy and a girl, and several grandchildren. Some live close by, some further away. My husband Paul, he has passed,' she adds.

'I learned about traditional medicine from my dreams. It was about 15 years ago, because of Alinafe, my last born, she is disabled. She was fine when she was born and was walking, but from the age of four, she stopped walking. At first her neck changed, and she was unable to turn it. We went to the healers to find medicine. Her body was very weak. Then her body became strong again, but her legs didn't work. One leg is now able to work but the other cannot. She needs a wheelchair to move around.'

Maria recalls how she tried to find a cure for her daughter's paralysis, most likely caused by malaria. 'I tried many clinics, Malosa, Zomba, Domasi, none were able to help,' she says.

It was around that time that her dreams began. 'There was a young girl sick in our village. One night, I dreamt that I had to go to the bush and get trees, make ashes from them, then cut the body of the girl and apply the ash. So, I did that and gave her some other medicine to drink. The following day the child passed diarrhoea, blood and other things came out, and the girl was better.'

Maria is one of thousands of traditional healers in Malawi. They provide the most basic primary care for upwards of 80 per cent of the population, offering to cure everything from headaches to HIV/AIDS with their herbal medicines. This dependence on centuries-old medicines may seem strange to people living in rich countries, but research shows that more than half of adult cancer patients in the USA use complementary therapies alongside bio-medical treatments such as chemotherapy and surgery, while an estimated nine million people use complementary and alternative medicine in the UK.

A point not lost on Maria. 'Traditional medicine and the white man medicine work together. Sometimes when people come to me, I advise them to go straight to the clinic. Other times I treat them first.

'A lot of people come to me with headaches, diarrhoea, skin infections, difficulty passing water. Also, women with problems, women who are not fertile, some women who complain that their husband cannot do anything, they want me to give him power,' she laughs. 'Really, it depends on the sickness, but most people prefer to come here before going to the clinic.'

Malawi's traditional healers have been healing the nation for centuries, but until 1953, no single African doctor or registered nurse was employed by the colonial government, and at the time of independence, 1964, there were only five doctors, of any ethnicity, working in the country. Today, the most recent figures suggest there are only around 600 doctors in Malawi, serving a population of 18 million, or four doctors for every 100,000 people, compared to 280 doctors per 100,000 in the UK.

UK health expenditure per person is about 120 times higher than in Malawi, which only spends about £25 a head, with more than half of that money coming from the donor community.

The clinical challenges facing the health service are overwhelming. One million people are HIV positive, malaria kills between 4,000 and 8,000 people a year, and one in every 50 babies die at birth. Non-communicable diseases such as cancer, hypertension and diabetes are on the increase. More than one-fifth of adult Malawians have high blood pressure, and it has one of the highest rates of cervical cancer in the world. And there are more than 1.5 million people living with a disability, from toddlers with cerebral palsy caused by a bout of malaria to construction workers paralysed by a fall on a building site with no health and safety rules.

Healthcare is delivered by a range of providers, and surprisingly for a country whose government has so few resources, its public health services are free. It was a policy instituted in 1964 by President Hastings Banda – the second Malawian to qualify as a doctor – and no leader since has considered changing it.

The government is the biggest provider. It runs the country's four central hospitals, which focus on advanced, specialised care. There are 26 district hospitals offering interventions such as caesarean sections and life-saving emergency surgery. Each district hospital has between ten and 40 health centres in its catchment area, and these provide basic primary health care, including HIV/AIDS treatment as well as maternity services. And in the community, a national network of 11,000 community health assistants provide preventative health care advice, including immunisation campaigns.

The Christian Health Association of Malawi (CHAM) provides almost 30 per cent of all health services and is contracted by the government to operate around 160 health centres and rural clinics. The growing private sector has 250 facilities, mostly urban clinics, but the small number of Malawians who can afford it travel to South Africa, or increasingly India, for medical treatment.

The man responsible for training the key medical staff for his country is Dr Mwapatsa Mipando, principal of the College of Medicine, and keen Liverpool FC supporter.

'I love football,' he laughs. 'I remember when I was in hospital as a child,' he recalls, 'I had injured myself in a game. You could hear the intercom, "Calling doctor so and so". My father said, "I want my oldest son to do that."'

Dr Mipando didn't quite realise his father's ambition. He studied biology and education at Chancellor College, and, after two years teaching in a secondary school, he joined the staff of the recently opened College of Medicine as a physiology lecturer.

And then his dream came true, 'I got a place at Liverpool University to do my Masters,' he says, 'No scholarship, but they waived my fees, so I survived. And it was the city of my favourite football team.'

He returned from England in 2000 as Malawi's first fully trained physiologist. And after securing his PhD thanks to a Norwegian scholarship, he found himself head of the department. 'When I came back from Durban, where I did my doctorate, the two white staff members, said "Okay here is a Malawian, we are off, bye-bye." So I was the only member of staff, the head of the department and the junior.'

Four years ago, he became college principal. 'It was a big moment for my father,' he says. 'He is very proud.'

But Dr Mipando faced two major problems when he moved into the principal's office. 'It hasn't been easy,' he admits. 'The issue of Cashgate – the government corruption scandal – had an impact on funding. The donors stopped budget support to the ministries, so we suffered. And the college was not very close to the donors.' Malawi's health services, including the College of Medicine, depend on the international aid community for their survival. External donors spent over £13 per person in 2017 – two-thirds more than the government of Malawi.

'I have had to rebuild trust after Cashgate,' he explains. 'It means putting systems in place that can gain the trust of the donors. We put our audits on our website. We market what we are doing. When I am invited to embassies, I make myself available. It has taken time, but we are rebuilding that trust.'

But even the persuasive Dr Mipando cannot convince a donor to support his plans if they do not fit with their own strategy for development.

'I really like working with the Norwegians,' he says. 'They listen to what we need, while the others, the Americans, the Germans, even the British, say "We have this priority," and you have to squeeze yourself into that. It is frustrating.

'Take dentistry for example. When I looked at our strategic plan, a dental school was supposed to have started a long time ago. The Irish government wanted to support it, but then the financial crash happened. I went to see the Irish ambassador when I became principal, and I had a very good tea with her. But they were no longer interested. So I went to the Japanese, but oral health was of no interest to them.'

Dr Mipando then approached the Chinese. 'But they only listen to politicians,' he laughs. 'But they gave me a gift of a fryer.

'Finally, I spent two hours with the Indian ambassador, but the only thing I came back with was this clock,' he smiles, pointing to an ornate timepiece.

It was the head of Glasgow University's dental school, Professor Jeremy Bagg, who came to his rescue. With a grant from the Scottish Government, he helped Dr Mipando establish Malawi's first dental school in 2019.

'So now we have 14 undergraduate programmes, including dentistry,' declares Dr Mipando. 'And an intake of around 1,600 students a year. We started with 12 students in 1991.'

Two years after the college opened, the 1993 official statistics showed that, of the 120 doctors working in Malawi, only 30 were Malawian. And in 2002, donors, led by the British government, started supporting the training of clinical officers rather than doctors, in part to try and stem the number of Malawian medics emigrating to the USA or the UK.

'But now we have an intake of around 120 medical students each year,' reveals Dr Mipando. 'We are making progress.'

Malawi is also making remarkable progress in tackling three killer diseases: HIV/AIDS, malaria and TB.

Since the first HIV diagnosis was made in 1985, at least 1.5 million Malawians, probably closer to two million, have died of the disease. At its peak, in the early-to-mid-2000s, 100,000 people were dying every year, and it seemed as if the disease would wipe out an entire generation, leaving behind only the elderly and children.

Then three Presidents, one in the White House, and two in Lilongwe, took decisions that would save millions of lives.

In January 2003, George W Bush unveiled the President's Emergency Plan for AIDS Relief (PEPFAR), which today still supports 50 countries in their fight against the disease, including Malawi. A year later, while South Africa's President, Thabo Mbeki, was still describing ARVs as 'poison' and dismissing the link between HIV and AIDS, Malawi's President Muluzi agreed a comprehensive HIV strategy. And in 2005, his successor, Bingu wa Mutharika, launched a nationwide plan to deliver free ARVs for all, so saving countless lives.

One of the first Malawians to benefit from the new treatment was Clara Galimoto, who found out she was HIV positive a few days before her husband died in 2000. She recalls the terrifying moment she learned of her possible death sentence. 'Stexie was very ill in hospital and I did not know what the cause was. Then the doctor told me he was positive, and that I should get tested. So I did. And yes, he passed the disease to me.'

Clara, who lives in a village on the outskirts of Lilongwe, was one of the first to benefit from the free ARV treatment. 'I didn't know if they would save me, but what else could I do?

'Now, 15 years later, I am strong. I am still working in the garden, growing maize, even though I am an *agogo*,' she smiles. At 67 years old, she is a living testament to the success of the global effort to tackle this major health pandemic.

Malawi still has one of the highest occurrences of HIV in the world – the one million people affected represent nearly ten per cent of the adult population. Approximately 670,000 children have been orphaned by the disease, and women are disproportionately affected, with girls and women under 25 most at risk of infection.

But the country has made remarkable progress in recent years. More than 800,000 people take ARVs every day. Self-testing is now common, giving people the privacy they crave, and Malawi was the first country in the world to adopt

Option B+, a measure to stop mother-to-baby transmission.

'Most people know someone who is HIV positive,' says Thoko Nyirenda (51), a nurse who now runs her own private health clinic in Area 25, a Lilongwe township. 'It's part of life now. But it didn't use to be like that. When I worked on the Johns Hopkins' HIV project with women who were diagnosed positive, their reaction was terrible. They were angry, or depressed, or both. Some would scream and cry, some would stay very quiet. They all thought they would die.'

Thoko's clinic, and her small pharmacy next door, offer basic primary health care, as she explains. 'We are the first stop for people who are sick. We do testing for malaria, for blood sugar, pregnancy and HIV. There are not enough government clinics, and most people don't have private health insurance, so clinics like mine are a big part of the health service.

'When someone comes and asks for an HIV test, I have to counsel them first. I tell them that if they are positive, they have to go to a hospital for treatment. I tell them they have to abstain from unprotected sex.' She pauses, then laughs, 'No one can abstain from sex. And I tell them it is not the end of the world. There is far less stigma now, and if they take their medication, and eat well, then they will live as long as me.'

The whole population is at risk of malaria. There are around six million confirmed cases of the disease a year, it is responsible for a third of out-patient visits, and kills almost 3,000 under-fives a year.

But another global effort, led by George W Bush's 2006 President's Malaria Initiative, has seen the death rates among under-fives slashed by half between 2006 and 2015, from 122 deaths per 1,000 to 64. The disease is not yet under control. One-third of under-fives have the malaria parasite, and thousands of people still die each year. But, thanks to the widespread use of treated bed-nets and insecticides, there is progress in tackling the disease. And in April 2019, Malawi became one of first countries in the world to immunise young children against malaria. It joined, along with Ghana and Kenya, a World Health Organisation (WHO) pilot of the first vaccine that gives partial protection against the disease.

'Nobody is suggesting that this is a magic bullet,' said Dr David Schellenberg, scientific adviser to the WHO's Global Malaria Programme, in an interview with the BBC at the time.

'It may not sound like much, but we're talking about 40 per cent reduction in severe malaria, which unfortunately still has high mortality, even when you have good access to good treatment.'

Malawi's battle against HIV/AIDS and malaria may make global headlines, but according to orthopaedic surgeon, Dr Leonard Banza, the focus on these two killer diseases means other health challenges are largely ignored by both the government and the international community.

Fifty-year-old Dr Banza arrived in Malawi 18 years ago, when he and his wife walked out of war-torn Democratic Republic of Congo with nothing but the clothes on their back. He is now one of the country's leading orthopaedic surgeons, one of only 12 in the country.

'The donors focus on HIV, malaria, TB, that is it. Orthopaedics, road traffic accidents, not a big deal. But this is what I deal with all the time.'

As in every sphere of life in Malawi, statistics vary according to which organisation compiles them, but even the most conservative estimate of road deaths in Malawi is chilling. The WHO's most recent report said that nearly 6,000 people a year are killed on Malawi's roads, making it the third most dangerous place in the world, after Venezuela and Thailand. Kamuzu Central Hospital, where Dr Banza is the head of the orthopaedic department, treats about 4,000 road traffic accident victims a year.

'I am the only member, so I am the junior as well,' he laughs, half-heartedly.

The number is projected to double in the next ten years, according to a research paper co-written by Dr Banza in 2016.

'The motorbikes from China, the minibus drivers, you know how they drive. They hit people then just continue, no one cares. We have to pick up the pieces, to fix people. But there are only two theatres available to us, and we don't have enough equipment to use both. Sometimes we don't have drips, or gowns. Often there isn't an anaesthetist on duty, or when there is, there are not enough nurses. Or blood in the blood bank. And hardware, we never have enough bone screws.'

Dr Banza is supported in his work by Norwegian surgeon, Dr Sven Young, who spends much of his year in Malawi. 'Thanks to his friends, we get money to buy hardware from India,' says Dr Banza. 'We don't get anything from the hospital. If we tell them we can't operate because we don't have screws, they just look at you.'

Femoral – thigh bone – fractures account for nearly a third of Dr Banza's workload, and many are among women over 50.

'Let me give you an example,' he offers. 'If I am in a high-income country, most patients above 50 with a proximal femur fracture will go for a hip replacement. Here, we treat them with traction. We just put them on a bed.

This is very, very abnormal.'

He continues, 'After two weeks, you say now you can go home on crutches. But she will be on crutches for the rest of her life. I can take you now to ward 3A and you will see how many women have these fractures, and none of them will be operated on because we don't have the capacity. All of them on traction until the pain subsides, then they will be on crutches. This means they are not going to walk normally. Their lifestyle is going to be compromised.'

The burden of being unable to treat patients as he knows he should weighs heavily on him. 'There are many patients I cannot help. They will become disabled. Yet my whole purpose as a doctor is to make people's lives better. It is very draining.

'The women ask, "How long will I have to use crutches, up to when?" And I have to say, "Probably for the rest of your life." Imagine in a village on crutches. These women have to go to their farm, to grow food. They have to get the firewood on their head, to carry the water, use a pit latrine, while on crutches. People with HIV, now they get ARVs, they can work, their life expectancy is good. But someone with a proximal femur fracture, her life is changed forever.'

The 2018 Census found that 14,000 people say they cannot walk at all, a further 56,000 have a lot of difficulty in getting around, and another 350,000 have some form of mobility problem. For those Malawians with serious spinal injuries, life is almost unimaginable, as Dr Banza describes.

'This morning I had a patient, a man in his 40s who fell from a mango tree. He has no sensation up to his nipple. This is the end, the rest of his life gone, all for a mango. There is nothing for a quadriplegic in Malawi, nothing. In Europe, I would operate immediately, so the patient can be in a wheelchair as soon as possible. All we do here is wait for the pressure sores. Once they come, that is the end. All for going up a tree.'

Dr Banza was clearly affected by his patient's plight. 'This guy is married. He has five children. He is never going to be able to do anything again. He will just lie in bed. The first day, he won't realise he will never walk again. The second day, he will know he cannot move anything. That is when he will start thinking. "What is going to happen to my wife, someone is going to take her… what will happen to my children, who will feed them?" And the poor guy, he will stop eating. We will try counselling, but he will get smaller and smaller, until one day, he is no longer there…'

He pauses. 'I cry, because I am not treating patients the way they should be treated. The hospital managers say we don't have the money, but somehow there is money to do other things. Our field is neglected.

'But it is not just the money,' he insists. 'Most of our patients come from the districts, we serve the whole of the central region, six million people. First, they go to their district hospital, where their condition is badly managed by the clinical officers. So, when they come here, you have to start all over again.

'A case that could have taken 30 to 45 minutes takes three hours, because you have to dismantle everything. Their body is trying to repair, but in a very awkward way. So, then you see instead of operating for 30 minutes, you need three hours. You get physically and emotionally exhausted. The patient may need blood, but there is no blood in the blood bank. Then you start thinking, "Is it worth operating this case, or will I just leave them?"'

But the former refugee is at heart an optimist. 'Yes, there are lot of challenges, too many, but I get a lot of satisfaction when I see a patient get better, someone who was struggling to walk, who was getting bullied at school. It is a joy.

'Later this week we are going to operate on a patient who fractured his femur in 2016. I saw him during an outreach clinic in Dowa a few months ago. He had stopped going to farm, he had stopped living. Imagine his joy when he is able to put on weight on his leg and start walking normally. Of course, I could go and start working in a hospital that has everything, but it is not a calling.'

Dr Banza and his surgeon colleagues will soon have a clinic that has almost everything. The Lilongwe Institute of Orthopaedics and Neurosurgery (Lions) is under construction at Kamuzu Central Hospital, and will provide an out-patient department, purpose-built theatres and wards and staff houses so that doctors can be on-call.

The money for the building, as well as a CAT scanner, vital for orthopaedics and brain surgery, has come from a consortium of international donors, including Norwegian philanthropist Trond Mohn, the Alliance Foundation, Auckland University Hospital and the Norwegian Government.

'It will change how we work,' says Dr Banza. 'It means we can take the service out of the main hospital system and change the culture.'

Dr Banza does not know if he will spend the rest of his career in Malawi. 'Everyone asks me that,' he says. 'I always think twice before answering. The future is always difficult to tell. For now, I am in Malawi. I am happy to spend the rest of my life in Malawi… for now, at least that is how I am.'

He finds it easier to predict the future for Malawi's over-burdened health service. 'When I came here, I was a bit shocked, coming from the Congo where people paid for health treatment, but here everything was free. The government must have money, I thought, then I realised they don't have money, but they are trying to do it with the money from outside. Honestly, it is not sustainable. So, if this situation of everything for free continues, I don't think healthcare standards will improve. The hospital will just be providing paracetamol.'

He pauses again. 'I did some of my training in Aberdeen, but we don't have national insurance here, like the UK. Everything is free, including the food. I don't know how the government will cope, they don't have enough money. And the quality of care suffers. If the economy of the country does not improve, it will be very tricky. Impossible, I think.'

SECTION 2

All in a day's work

CHAPTER 10

The economy

THE GOVERNOR OF the Reserve Bank had clearly lost his patience. Taking the microphone from the Finance Minister by his side, he declared, 'A hundred dollars per capita. One hundred dollars. Free education. Free health service. [Farming] subsidies. The police.'

He paused for effect then continued, his exasperation almost under control. 'Everything has to be provided from those $100. In some countries, the health budget alone is equal to $5,000 per person. In Malawi, the minister has only $100 to allocate to everything. Can you imagine a household with $100 only?

'We are sitting on huge domestic and international debt. In the current budget as much as MK 224 billion (£235 million) is allocated towards debt repayments, it is statutory expenditure. So the minister has to deal with it. We need to reduce our debt repayments to make fiscal space for future spending.'

Dr Dalitso Kabambe, who took over as head of the Reserve Bank in 2017, was speaking at a public consultation meeting hosted by Malawi's newly appointed Finance Minister, Joseph Mwanamvekha, only a few weeks after the 2019 elections.

The event, held in the cavernous Bingu International Convention Centre – built in 2012 with a loan from the Chinese government – was billed as an opportunity for the Finance Minister to 'solicit views, contributions and inputs from all stakeholders on the government's 2019/20 budget.' Presentations by the minister, agricultural economists and economic justice campaigners had all acknowledged that agriculture was the country's biggest driver of wealth, but no one, it seemed, had an answer to the question, 'Why is Malawi so poor?' Instead, every vested interest in the room had made a bid for more government cash, hence Dr Kabambe's frustration.

He continued, 'Now, listening to all the presentations… we need more in health, we need more in education, we need more in energy. The best advice [for the minister] should be let's cut from here and put here, cut from there, put there. As you reduce domestic debt, you put the savings where? As you raise additional revenues from taxes, it can be used for what? The minister needs focused advice, he needs ideas.

'He is facing a huge challenge, because with that $100 he must service debts, he needs around $20 for that, with more for civil servant salaries. That means he may only have $50 per head to move forward the country.'

He paused and finished with the simplest summation possible. 'We need to generate more revenue for future resource mobilisation. We all know where we are as a country.'

Where Malawi is as a country is near the bottom of every poverty league table since gaining its independence in 1964. According to World Bank data on national GDP (Gross Domestic Product, a measure of total income), only two countries have remained consistently in the bottom ten in the world since then: Burundi and Malawi. Yet in 1964, Malawi was richer than China, the country it now depends on for much of its imports and infrastructure. Malawi's GDP per head then was £182 (in 2010 prices), compared to £126 in China.

Today, China has an annual income per head of over £8,000 while Malawi languishes on £323. The average growth rate of GDP per person in Malawi since 1964 is 1.4 per cent per year. Even the UK, generally seen as an underperforming economy for many decades, managed 2.1 per cent each year on average from 1964 to 2018. The total size of Malawi's economy is less than a quarter of that of the city of Edinburgh.

Agriculture is the mainstay of the economy, just as it has been for over a century, while tobacco still accounts for around half of all exports. Malawi is, according to Antwerp University, the most tobacco-reliant economy in the world. The overwhelming majority of the population – 84 per cent, or 15 million people – live in rural villages, eking out a living by growing maize and beans.

The country is hugely dependent on international donations for essential services such as health and education. Annual aid in 2018 was around one billion pounds, only slightly less than the government's entire annual budget.

To appreciate the state of Malawi's contemporary economy, you have to understand its colonial past and the post-independence regime of Dr Hastings Banda. Malawi has two significant natural resources: the magnificent Lake Malawi, which covers one-fifth of its land mass, and its arable land which, if well-managed, can grow a wide selection of cash crops, from tea and sugar to tobacco and cotton.

Early European settlers recognised the value of Malawi's land, particularly the rich soils in the south around the Shire River, and, according to Bridglal Pachai writing in the *Journal of African History* (1973), they 'took advantage of the friendliness and gullibility of the people... to lay claims to vast extents of land.'

As Chief Kadwere of Chiradzulu explained in 1915, the white settlers tricked chiefs with bales of cloth. 'When a planter came to the village, he asked the chief to sell him a place where he could build his house, and this is the only plot the chief signed for,' he told a commission of enquiry, held by the new colonial government.

The planters then laid claim to large tracts of the surrounding tribal land, leaving the Malawians dependent on the largesse of the new owners to remain in their homes. The concept of private land ownership was alien to the Malawi people. In traditional sub-Saharan African societies, land belongs to everyone, to the living and the dead. It is the role of the chiefs to protect this customary land for its current occupants, and for future generations. Land is not the basis of personal wealth, but a community resource.

After Malawi became a British Protectorate in 1891, Bridglal Pachai describes how the colonial administration 'carved up the country into virtual principalities, presided over by large European-owned companies'. These plantation owners had rights over 15 per cent of the total land area, including 867,000 acres in the Shire Highlands, home to the country's finest arable land. By 1945, nearly one-third of the total population lived and worked on private estates in the Shire.

Malawians were forced to work on the plantations in exchange for the right to live on the land, and this exploitation led directly to the Chilembwe Rising of 1915, where a group of Malawians, led by a Baptist preacher, John Chilembwe, killed three Europeans in a failed rebellion against colonial rule. Today, Chilembwe is a national hero, a freedom fighter whose portrait adorns Malawi banknotes.

In the decades before the Second World War, the British Colonial Office made various attempts to protect Malawians' security of tenure on the big estates, eventually deciding that the best option was to buy back land from the plantation owners. By 1954, in recognition that 'the African and European enterprise in Nyasaland are complementary and interdependent,' the freehold land owned by Europeans had shrunk from 15 to just under four per cent, and by the time of independence in 1964 it was only two per cent. Malawi's land was back where it belonged, with its people, but that did not herald a new era of prosperity.

When Malawi became an independent state on 6 July 1964 and Prime Minister, Dr Hastings Kamuzu Banda, assumed complete control over his country's economic and social development, it was ranked as one of the poorest countries in the world. Over 90 per cent of its four million people lived in rural villages on customary land, and they survived by subsistence farming. Malawi's manufacturing sector was in its infancy, contributing less than ten per cent of total economic activity, and the country was spending more on public services than it earned.

There was no central banking system, no statistical service necessary for planning and managing an economy and very few experts in monetary or fiscal policy. The transport infrastructure was inadequate, with only 3,000 miles of all-weather roads. There were only 6,000 pupils starting secondary education each year, and primary school enrolment had been dropping since 1956, despite a big increase in the population. And it was clear that the new country would have to rely on external funders, in particular the British government, for much of its development. Indeed, many analysts predicted Malawi's economy would collapse soon after independence.

Even Dr Banda described the economy as 'frail', but he had a plan. Unlike many of his African contemporaries, he rejected communism. '[It] does not and cannot succeed, does not or cannot work,' he said, preferring instead a mixed economy approach, similar to that of Malawi's former colonial master, the UK. He prioritised economic development over social protection, encouraged British civil servants to stay in post after independence and promoted foreign investment. And, crucially, he decided that Malawi's prosperity lay in agriculture. He offered his fellow politicians and senior civil servants 'soft' loans to buy large estates to grow cash crops for export. He instituted a national rural development programme in an attempt to modernise farming methods, and he exploited a global market opportunity in tobacco, as Professor Ben Kaluwa points out.

Professor Kaluwa is one of Malawi's pre-eminent economists, and his academic career stretches back into the Banda era. 'When Ian Smith declared UDI [unilateral declaration of independence] in Rhodesia [November 1965], the country was a major global player in tobacco, but with sanctions their tobacco was under threat.

'In Malawi then, our tobacco was oriental, not the kind that is grown now, so Banda made a strategic move into burley tobacco. People were encouraged to go into large scale tobacco farming, and the banks helped them. There were price controls then in manufacturing, but also in financial services, so the state controlled the interest rates in favour of farming and agricultural loans.'

Professor Kaluwa credits Malawi's growth performance from 1964 to 1980 to Banda's iron grip on economic policy. 'Malawi achieved very rapid economic growth for 15 years after independence, one of the best performances in sub-Saharan Africa. Tobacco was the biggest source of growth. But there were other exportable cash crops – cotton, tea and groundnuts.

'The strategy recognised two key constraints – Malawi was scarce in capital and in skills. The objective was to maximise growth subject to those constraints. Tobacco is a simple processing industry. It doesn't need an educated workforce, so our economy after independence was based on labour-intensive agriculture and uneducated people in the rural areas. It is still a problem.'

But as the 1980s approached, the economy began to falter, as did others across sub-Saharan Africa, and over the next two decades, it slowed down considerably.

It was during this slump that Banda's strategic economic blunders were exposed, argues Professor Kaluwa. 'His development policies recognised the need for industrialisation, but it was state-led, right across the board, in manufacturing, food processing, in banking too. And even though it was never said explicitly, his thinking was that economic growth would "trickle-down" to the poor, that people would benefit from whatever fell off the table.

'Banda also said we were not going to pursue social objectives, including mass education. And by ignoring education, it became a generational problem, we are talking about generations of people in poverty, income inequality that takes a long time to shift. We are still suffering from those strategic blunders and we will continue to suffer for years to come.'

When Malawi embraced multi-party democracy in the 1993 referendum, and elected Bakili Muluzi of the UDF as President the following year, work began to repair the economic and social development damage of the later Banda years.

Supported by the United Nations and Denmark, the government embarked on a national listening exercise and planning process which culminated in the 1998 publication of *Vision 2020*, a 'national long-term development perspective for Malawi.'

In the foreword, President Muluzi declared:

Development planning since Malawi's independence in 1964 has been guided by short-term plans, based on ten-year statements of development policies. This approach has achieved limited social and economic progress, while poverty has become widespread, social services have become inadequate and food insecurity has increased.

And since 1985, when the first person was diagnosed HIV positive, there was a new and terrifying threat to Malawi's national well-being, as President Muluzi acknowledged:

The situation has been aggravated by a high prevalence of hiv/aids, while macroeconomic variables, such as government budget deficits and the balance of payments, have been unsatisfactory. Malawi risks losing some of the progress made if prevailing trends are not changed.

The document made this promise:

By the year 2020, Malawi, as a God-fearing nation, will be secure, democratically mature, environmentally sustainable, self-reliant with equal opportunities for and active participation by all, having social services, vibrant cultural and religious values and a technologically driven middle-income economy.

And it set out how Malawi would achieve per capita income of £770 by 2020, the benchmark of a middle-income country. The government planned to increase the manufacturing sector from 12 per cent of GDP to at least 25 per cent, and to attract more foreign investment and promote exports. It promised to grow the country's tiny mining sector from three per cent of GDP and to increase savings and investment through promoting thrift, the creation of mutual funds and encouraging donors to finance private sector development.

Tourism was singled out as having significant potential for jobs and foreign exchange, if the right infrastructure was in place. The strategy recognised the need for a business-friendly culture, with better access to credit, more vocational training and the encouragement of entrepreneurship. And agriculture, which contributed around a third of GDP in the late 1990s, was centre stage:

Farmers require a multi-dimensional strategy... more land available for

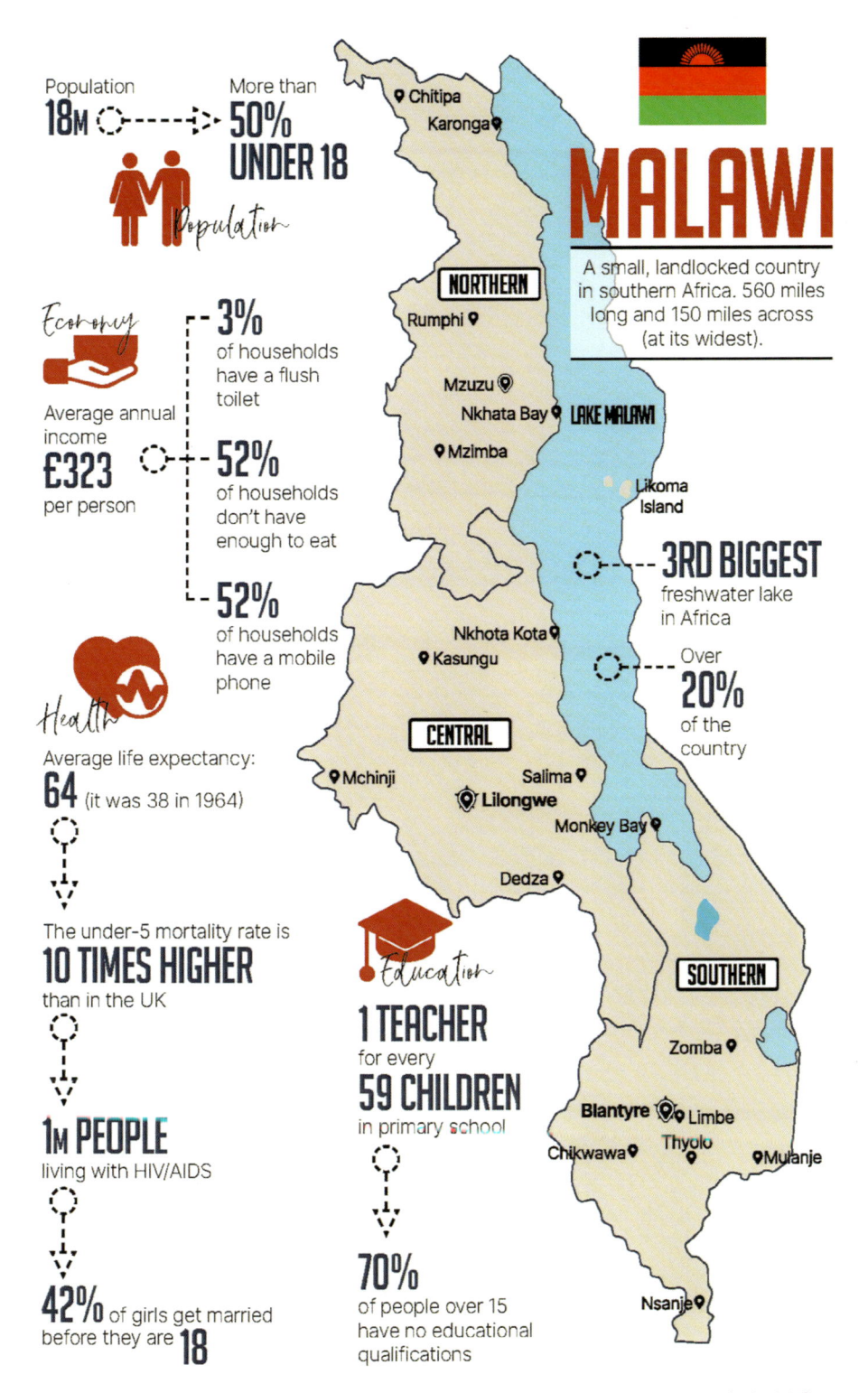

MALAWI

A small, landlocked country in southern Africa. 560 miles long and 150 miles across (at its widest).

Population
- Population **18M**
- More than **50% UNDER 18**

Economy
- Average annual income **£323** per person
- **3%** of households have a flush toilet
- **52%** of households don't have enough to eat
- **52%** of households have a mobile phone

Health
- Average life expectancy: **64** (it was 38 in 1964)
- The under-5 mortality rate is **10 TIMES HIGHER** than in the UK
- **1M PEOPLE** living with HIV/AIDS
- **42%** of girls get married before they are **18**

Education
- **1 TEACHER** for every **59 CHILDREN** in primary school
- **70%** of people over 15 have no educational qualifications

Map labels

NORTHERN: Chitipa, Karonga, Rumphi, Mzuzu, Nkhata Bay, Mzimba

LAKE MALAWI — 3RD BIGGEST freshwater lake in Africa. Over 20% of the country. Likoma Island.

CENTRAL: Nkhota Kota, Kasungu, Mchinji, Salima, Lilongwe, Monkey Bay, Dedza

SOUTHERN: Zomba, Blantyre, Limbe, Chikwawa, Thyolo, Mulanje, Nsanje

Sources: Malawi National Statistical Office, World Bank, Malawi Population-based HIV Impact Assessment   Design: Iain Bunt

Preaching the gospel in Blantyre

Chintali dance performed by women and girls

L: The cycle of life   R: Early years

Students at Senga Bay primary school

Mending nets at Lake Malawi

L: Maize R: Enjoying traditional beer

Ngoni tribe from Mchinji

woman's work

Market day in Chikwawa

L: Plaiting hair R: Preparing relish

Selling toys at Salima

L: Sunset on the road to Thyolo R: Selling tobacco on the auction floor, Limbe

Traditional Beni dance in Mangochi

Village life

L: Washing up R: Voting in the 2019 general election

Helping around the home

Mabvuto Salirana fetches water from a bore hole

L: Party time on the shores of Lake Malawi
R: Laundry day at Lake Malawi

Bill Potani (L) with his mother Debra and sister Eliza at his school

Blantyre dance troupe

Singer Lazarus Chigwandali and his canjo

Everson Mapayani and his local youth group

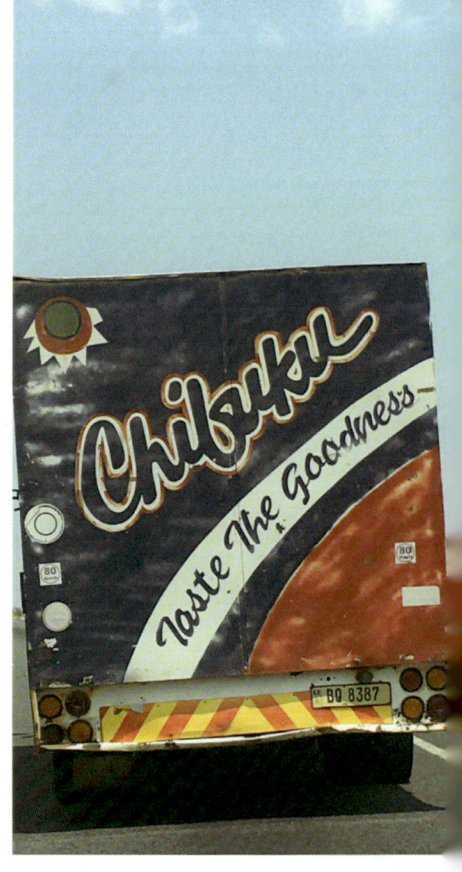

L: Chimwaza Phiri with his daily catch from Lake Malawi R: Chibuku lorry

The Galimoto family outside their Minga home

L: Chitenjes R: Handwashing at Machinjiri maternity clinic

Herding cattle along the lakeshore

L: Rose walking home   R: Jack and Dorothy Juma

UTM dancers on the campaign trail

L: Thoko Nyirenda shopping for clothes in Lilongwe secondhand market
R: Tomato seller

Mzuzu Fashion Week 2019
(photography by Mzati Photography)

First intake of dental students at Malawi's College of Medicine
(September 2019)

smallholders, easier access to farm inputs... preventing land degradation and deforestation... promoting agricultural diversification... enhancing irrigation.

As the document rolled off the printing presses, and Malawi's political, business and church leaders gathered to hear President Muluzi's speech on 31 March 1998 in Chichiri business centre, in the country's commercial heart, Blantyre, a jingle rang round the country's public radio broadcaster, MBC:

Vision 2020
Kukonza Tsogolo
Pofika 2020
Tizakhale pa bwino
Osayang'ana m'mbuyo
Dziko ndi lathu ili...

Or:

Vision 2020
Planning the future by 2020
Let's get on well.
Don't look back.
The world is ours...

On Wednesday 31 July 2019, 21 years after President Muluzi promised 'a technologically driven middle-income country', the National Planning Commission – the body in charge of the preparation and implementation of Malawi's development – convened the first meeting of a 41-member panel to advise the government on the successor to *Vision 2020*. And its chair, leading economist, Naomi Ngwira, who advised the framers of the original document, pronounced *Vision 2020* a failure, not least because it has not achieved its central mission of increasing per capita income to £770. The latest figure, for 2019, is £323 per person, while more than half (52 per cent) of Malawians live below the country's own poverty line of MK 137,400 (£145) per person a year.

Ngwira said, 'the implementation... was not in magnitudes that were required to achieve the desired results of the plan. So even if certain things might have been done, they were inadequate to achieve the quantum expected.

For instance, if Malawi wanted to be a middle-income country, it meant there were supposed to be certain types of investment to achieve that. Unfortunately, these were not done.'

And she argued that there must be a generational shift if the new plan, dubbed *National Transformation 2063*, to align with the African Union's *Agenda 2063*, was to succeed where Muluzi's had failed. 'There is a need for young leaders that must be placed at various levels... to move this country forward... Those of us with a lot of experience can just support them,' she said.

Professor Kaluwa brings 45 years' experience as an economist, including a PhD from Edinburgh University, to bear on the challenges facing Malawi over the next few decades. He is clear what the government's strategic priority should be.

'Education first,' he states with emphasis. 'One of the problems is that education spending does not get politicians re-elected, it requires too many resources.

'My next priority is economic infrastructure. Good transport links are essential. Take rail for example. We had a good rail system, but even the World Bank say it was hijacked by gangsters to move traffic back to road haulage.'

Almost all freight, from tobacco to plastic goods from China, is transported by road, despite only a quarter of the country's 15,500 kilometres road network being fully paved. During Hastings Banda's rule, rail was the main method of transporting goods, but the network collapsed through lack of investment.

In 2017, Central East African Railways, which is owned by a consortium including Brazilian coal giant VALE, started restoring the Nacala railway line from Moatize in Mozambique as it passed through Malawi. This offered landlocked Malawi a freight link to ports in Mozambique and a spur to Zambia. However, vandalism and damage from heavy rains have dogged the project, and the line is not expected to be fully operational until 2022. An exasperated Professor Kaluwa says that the government has not realised its full potential.

He explains, 'VALE gave Malawi a concession to use the train capacity for next to nothing – but nobody in Malawi is using this capacity – the government has not sold it to the private sector. A well-used rail system would be transformational, fundamental – the cost of being landlocked would be reduced.'

He then points to Rwanda as a country that has overcome its geography to attract foreign investment. 'They are nowhere compared to us in terms of natural resources, but they are succeeding because of investment in education, in the people. Volkswagen are going to establish a plant there. Why? Because there is an educated, IT-literate workforce.'

And the professor, whose home in Zomba sits below one of the most beautiful plateaus in the continent, agrees with *Vision 2020*'s dream of a tourism industry.

'Yes, tourism is my other priority. All the resource, the revenue we need for investment in education, we could get from tourism. And we need to make it easy for people to visit, we need to be competitive in tourism. We shouldn't bother with visa fees. Just zero. Just come here and spend money! Tourists will spend more than $75 [the entry visa fee for visitors]. Malawi will be better off if we lower the barriers to entry into the country.'

He is not convinced that another ambitious strategy in the mould of *Vision 2020* will have much impact on Malawi's economic future. 'There are already too many plans and strategies,' he says.

He is certain about one thing, however, and that is that the current generation of political leaders need to make way for a new one. 'With a good leader, we can do a lot, even with our economy right now. There's a whole train of people in that mode. We need fresh people, to start over.'

And he points to nearby Tanzania as an example of how important effective leadership is to economic and social development. 'It is one of the most impressive examples,' he says. 'It was one of the rottenest economies around. Its socialist system depressed wages in the public service. My wages were considerably higher than my Tanzanian counterparts. So people found their way to use the public service positions to do their own private business. It's called the "second economy." But President Magufuli has changed things considerably. Business is not as usual. So, to me, in 20 years, anything can happen.'

In the 20-odd years since *Vision 2020* was optimistically received by a hopeful population and supportive donor community, much has indeed happened to Malawi, yet little has changed. Muluzi's successor, President Bingu wa Mutharika introduced a remarkably successful fertiliser programme that gave the country a secure food supply and boosted exports.

His sudden death in 2012 ushered in Malawi's first woman head of state, and only Africa's second. President Joyce Banda's short-lived tenure ended in disgrace in 2014, after she was implicated in a notorious scandal, nicknamed Cashgate, where around £25 million – perhaps even more – was stolen from government coffers over six months. One of her cabinet ministers and several civil servants were jailed, while donors such as the UK and Germany withdrew direct budget support to the government in protest. Mrs Banda now spends much of her time in the USA.

The fifth President, Bingu's brother, Peter Mutharika, who beat Banda in 2014 and won the disputed election of 2019, ushered in a degree of macroeconomic stability, at least according to the World Bank. He achieved this largely by maintaining high interest rates to reduce inflation and by better financial discipline in government.

China has made its presence felt in recent years, investing in large infrastructure projects such as a new parliament building and national football stadium. Bright young Malawians are offered generous scholarships to study medicine and engineering in Chinese universities, and trade between the two countries is buoyant, if rather one-sided. According to the UN, Malawi's exports to China in 2017 were £32 million (5 per cent of total exports), while Malawi imported nearly nine times more (£288 million), mostly fertiliser, phones, second-hand clothes and metals and machinery.

Malawi's population has more than doubled in the last 30 years and is now around 18 million people. More than half live below the poverty line, and there are millions affected by malnourishment. Inflation has settled in single digits and the exchange rate is fairly stable. But the cuts in direct foreign assistance after Cashgate have contributed to higher government borrowing, with the overall national debt now at around 60 per cent of GDP and rising, and the pandemic will only make it worse. The country remains heavily dependent on donor aid for its most basic public services, such as health and education. The impact of climate change and decades of deforestation and soil degradation are damaging the agriculture industry.

As Dr Kaluwa bemoans, there are a plethora of plans and strategies to guide Malawi's development, each offering similar solutions to the country's stubborn poverty. The front covers may vary but the message is consistent. Malawi's economy needs macroeconomic stability and tighter control over public spending and borrowing, as well as better regulation and stronger governance to tackle corruption and attract investment. The government must invest in the infrastructure required by business and industry, from electricity and roads to affordable credit and a favourable trading environment. It should provide access to quality education and training, while at the same time reducing the birth rate and putting in place resilient systems to cope with shocks such as severe weather, poor harvests and disease.

And, above all, it needs to diversify and modernise its main industry, agriculture. In particular, as global demand for tobacco drops, Malawi has to find an alternative to the cash crop which has been the mainstay of its economy since the Buchanan brothers exported the first two bales of Virginia tobacco, grown in the Shire Highlands, in 1894.

But is there a single alternative to the now noxious weed?

CHAPTER 11

Addicted to tobacco

MALAWI IS A nation of farmers. Almost everyone, from the President to the poorest villager, has a plot of land which they cultivate. Agriculture defines Malawi.

'Not everyone grows food in Malawi,' laughs Gifted Galimoto (43), a porter at Bwaila Hospital in Lilongwe. 'But almost everyone. Me, I have to grow maize and beans, it is the only reliable way I can have food for my family. The prices in the shops go up too often, so I grow maize. And beans that I can sell to pay for school fees.'

Just as the Galimoto family depends on farming for food and cash, so does Malawi. Agriculture accounts for 27 per cent of the country's GDP, over 90 per cent of rural households own or cultivate their own land, and the one million poorest people grow food, not to sell, but simply to survive.

Two crops are the mainstay of Malawi's agriculture industry. Tobacco, on which the country's economy is built, and maize, which sustains life. But both are under threat. Maize from climate shocks and pests like the fall army worm. Tobacco from declining global demand.

'I will put it in this way, the slowdown in consumption in rich countries has affected the production volume, not only volume, but income, as the price has dropped,' explains Felix Thole, Chief Executive of TAMA Farmers Trust, formerly the Tobacco Association of Malawi, which was formed in 1929.

Sitting in his Lilongwe office, surrounded by shiny brochures, newsletters and annual reports, he exudes an air of cheery confidence, but his words belie him. 'The buyers won't pay the same price', he says. 'Farmers are still trying to produce, but are now looking at other value chains, but it is proving difficult, and because of those problems the farmers are still sticking to tobacco.'

And he lists off the crops that have been, at one time or another in recent years, touted as the 'new tobacco', the elusive cash crop that will save Malawi's economy.

'Farmers have tried a lot of things,' he shrugs. 'The country is producing a lot of soya beans, we also produce beans and groundnuts. On a smaller scale, we have tried sunflower seeds. And in the past three or four years, we have found a market in India for our pigeon peas, but now there are too many, so that market is now a problem.'

The tobacco industry, which was commercialised by white settlers in the last decade of the 19th century, is over one-tenth of Malawi's GDP. It makes up more than half of the country's exports, bringing much needed foreign exchange. And it is believed one million people depend on tobacco for their livelihood. Little wonder, then, that Malawi is often described as the world's most tobacco-reliant economy. It mainly produces burley tobacco, a high-quality leaf with a high nicotine content. It is the tobacco that gives iconic cigarettes such as Marlboro and Camel their robust flavour, and is the world's second favourite tobacco, after Virginia.

The industry began in the late 19th century, when European settlers took control of large swathes of tribal land to plant the cash crop. The market expanded in the decades after the Second World War, when Malawian smallholder farmers, mostly in the central region, began to grow tobacco. Today, it is those peasant farmers that make up the bulk of tobacco growers. They join together in farmers' clubs to sell their produce during a season that runs from the end of April to mid-September each year.

Growing tobacco is hard work, as Cuban anthropologist Fernando Ortiz describes:

> The tobacco grower has to tend to his tobacco not by fields, not even by plants, but leaf by leaf... Everything having to do with tobacco is hard work – its cultivation, harvesting, manufacturing and sale, even its consumption.

Nor is it very profitable, for the farmers at least. A 2016 study showed that the harvest from one acre of tobacco only produces a profit of £61, compared to an average of £270 for other crops.

Understanding Malawi's tobacco industry is hard work too. It is a web of intertwining companies, associations and clubs, from global giants such as Philip Morris to the local transport companies that bring the bales of tobacco to Lilongwe and Blantyre to be sold.

The 2019 Tobacco Industry Act was a recent attempt by the government to bring some transparency to the market, introducing new rules for monitoring price, quality and contracts.

'It brings much needed sanity to the tobacco industry... the key foreign exchange earner for our country,' said the then minister of agriculture, Joseph Mwanamvekha, when outlining the new law at a press conference. 'The sector creates employment opportunities to many Malawians and all stakeholders should rejoice for the passing of this bill,' he said, with a final flourish.

The market is overseen by the Malawi Tobacco Commission, which sets production quotas based on market demand, and the bulk of the leaf is sold at auction. Since 2006, growers can also sell their tobacco through a contract arrangement, but this is still a relatively small market. And there are only a handful of buyers, a 'cartel' according to some critics. One of the largest is Limbe Leaf, which is part owned by the Press Corporation, the successor to Hastings Banda's state-owned company, Press Holdings Ltd. Limbe Leaf and the other buyers process the tobacco by removing its stalks, before sending it to Durban in South Africa, from where it is shipped all over the world to be turned into cigarettes.

But for how much longer? Cigarette consumption in high-income countries such as America and the UK has dropped significantly. In the last three decades, it has more than halved in the UK, to only 15 per cent of the population. And as the global market moves east – China smokes 40 per cent of the world's cigarettes – there is a growing demand for oriental tobacco, a lighter, sun-dried plant grown in Turkey, India, and increasingly in China.

Where does that leave Malawi's burley tobacco industry? 'I am hopeful for the future,' says Mr Thole. 'I will tell you why. We are the oldest and biggest institution dealing with tobacco, but last year our AGM endorsed significant changes. We are now looking into those other value chains for our members, not just tobacco, and not necessarily crops. The reality is that tobacco is not all that much supporting our members' livelihoods. Yes, tobacco is still an important crop, but we have a second wing, looking at other value chains, it could be crops, it could be livestock.'

And he recalls a joke he made at a recent meeting of national tobacco associations in South Africa. 'Zimbabwe, Zambia, we were all there. I told them they should come to Thyolo [in southern Malawi] where the farmers are growing crocodiles for their meat.' He laughs, 'Imagine, crocodile farms.'

And to emphasise his point that tobacco is no longer TAMA's sole concern, despite its 90-year history, he says, 'As an association we need to look at the whole agriculture sector, not just tobacco. So, we have changed our name, we have rebranded. We are now TAMA Farmers Trust. And TAMA, the acronym, is not standing for Tobacco Association of Malawi, it is just TAMA. We have a new constitution too, because we recognise that while tobacco is very important, we need to look ahead. We are able to read the global situation, we need to move with the changing times.'

And those changing times could feature Malawi Gold, allegedly the best cannabis in the world. As more high-income countries legalise marijuana, there is a growing global demand for cannabis, both for recreational use and for medicinal purposes. And the hemp variety of the plant has many industrial uses.

The fibre from its woody stem has been used for centuries to make rope, sails and cloth, and oil from its seeds is the basis for a range of products from soap to paint. In the mid-1930s, Henry Ford even built a car from hemp composites which ran on fuel from the plant, but it foundered when, in 1937, America banned all varieties of the cannabis plant, including hemp, in its war against 'reefer madness'.

But Felix Thole is hopeful that industrial hemp will soon become a lucrative cash crop for Malawi. He explains, 'It has been on trial for the past year or so here. A Malawi company, Invegrow, is doing it. I understand the trials have been successful, so colleagues are waiting for the go-ahead from the parliament. The moment it is approved, it will be on pilot for two years or so, to a few farmers.'

And he is confident that the confusion between recreational cannabis and its industrial cousin will not stop it getting the go-ahead. 'Yes, people have confused it with Indian hemp – *chamba* – that has been grown in Malawi here, illegally, for many years. People grow it in the hills. But industrial hemp is a valuable crop, so this could be a straightforward move from tobacco to hemp.'

Mr Thole is also optimistic about new ways to use the traditional tobacco leaf, as he explains. 'Solaris Tobacco has just completed a successful trial for using the plant to make bio-fuel and hopes to pilot it during the 2021–22 growing season. The normal process for tobacco is to remove the seed, because you are only after the leaf. Farmers have to remove the topmost part, so it doesn't form seeds, because the nutrients will go into the seeds. So they cut that, so the nutrients are concentrated in the leaf. But for bio-fuel, it is the opposite. It is the seed that you want. They are crushed to get the fuel. So, it only takes a small change and the economic prospects are similar.'

Whether Malawi will become a cannabis-reliant economy rather than one dependent on tobacco remains to be seen, but the search for reliable cash crops to replace tobacco will only intensify over the next decade as the global tobacco market changes.

One thing is certain – there is very little prospect that country's appetite for maize will dwindle. Maize has been the country's staple crop for nearly 200 years, since it was introduced to East Africa by Portuguese traders. Over three-fifths of the population, in the cities as well as the villages, grows corn, with that figure rising to more than 70 per cent in the populous southern region.

In a good year, Malawi produces more maize than even *nsima*-loving Malawians can eat. In a bad year, the government has to import corn, or depend on international aid to feed everyone. In 2005–06, almost five million people needed emergency food aid, a crisis that prompted the newly elected President, Bingu wa Mutharika, to introduce a fertiliser and seed subsidy scheme for the poorest farmers. International donors, including British and US national aid agencies, were sceptical about Mutharika's plans, critical even, but production doubled within a season, and Malawi was able to feed itself once again, even export grain.

According to Jeffrey Sachs, director of the Earth Institute at Columbia University, 'Malawi had pointed the way to a new Green Revolution for Africa.'

The revolution stalled somewhat in recent years as the scheme became mired in corruption and maladministration. In response, the new government has launched a modernised scheme, the Affordable Inputs Programme, which sets a fair price for a 50kg bag of fertiliser.

Gifted is a typical urban farmer. He lives with his extended family in a village on the southern outskirts of Lilongwe. He moved there 20 years ago after his father died of HIV/AIDS and his mother Clara was forced to return to her home village.

'We came from Mzuzu,' he recalls, 'and we had grown up in town, but now we had to learn how to be farmers, like my mother's family had been. We had no money, and no work after my father died, so we had to grow our own maize.'

Clara was a reluctant farmer. 'I enjoyed being a town wife,' she says quietly. 'But I had no choice, I had to pick up a hoe and plant maize and beans if we were to eat.'

At 67, and HIV positive, Clara could be forgiven for spending her days sitting on a reed mat outside her village home, watching her sons tend their few acres of land, but she still works in her garden. 'Yes, I still hoe the ground,' she says. 'It gets harder, but it keeps me alive.'

Gifted got 17 bags of maize flour from his last harvest, almost twice the national average of ten bags. 'They are 50kg each, so we have enough to feed us and we sold some. We also grew some groundnuts and beans.'

He says the biggest challenge in growing maize is around planting time. 'We have to do it all within two days, so the plants grow up together the same size. That means we get up at four in the morning to start work, on an empty stomach, and work through until three or four in the afternoon. It is tough, but we have no choice.'

He doesn't want his 14-year-old twin sons, Comfort and Collins, to be farmers, even part-time ones like him. 'I surely don't want that, that is why their education is so important, so that they can get a job where they don't need to farm.'

But the majority of Malawians do not have a choice. In the rural areas, where the majority of the population live, almost everyone works the land. Only the very young or very old are exempt.

While maize is the staple crop, pigeon peas are popular in the southern region, and groundnuts in the central belt. Sweet potatoes and cassava are widespread, and most people will grow some form of relish to serve with their *nsima*, such as bitter green leaves, tomatoes, cabbage and onions. If they have a surplus, they will take their tomatoes or cabbages to the nearest trading centre to sell, or sit by the side of a road, hoping a passer-by will stop.

Tobacco and maize may be the country's two most important crops, but the country produces several other cash crops, including tea, coffee, cotton and sugar, as well as pulses and beans. Overall rice production has been increasing for most of the last 40 years, but farmers, mostly in the north and along the shores of Lake Malawi, struggle to fully exploit both the home and export market. There is enormous untapped potential for growth.

One group of farmers, the Kaporo Smallholder Farmers Association, has been more successful than most at selling its fragrant Kilombero rice, thanks in part to the energy and foresight of the association's chairman, Howard Msukwa.

'Our district, Karonga, is home to the best rice in the country,' says Howard. You can plant our seed elsewhere in Malawi, and it will not taste like our Kilombero rice. It is the soil, we think.'

But it is a partnership with a Scottish non-profit, JTS (Just Trading Scotland), that has boosted exports in the last decade, as Howard explains. 'Our 6,000 farmers grow the rice, we process it and send it to Scotland, where JTS pack and market it. It has been a very productive partnership.'

'Our farmers – half are women – can earn up to MK 300,000 (£315) each harvest. That means they can pay school fees for their children, and if you go to a village, the chances are that the houses made of burnt-brick, with solar, belong to our farmers.'

The rice recently won a prestigious award as the most ethical rice on the market. But that comes at a cost, as Howard explains. 'Our rice is the best, but that means it is more expensive than others. So it is more difficult to market.'

He is hopeful that a new national focus on rice will help him and his farmers increase production, and, crucially, find new investment and markets. Malawi joined the Coalition for African Rice Development in 2018, which aims to double rice production on the continent to 50 million tonnes by 2030. The Japanese government, through JICA (Japan International Cooperation Agency), its international development agency, has expressed an interest in helping Malawi's rice farmers, and Prime Minister Shinzo Abe recently promised that 'Japanese technology can play a key role in innovation which is key to agriculture.'

'We will see,' says Howard, who has a healthy scepticism of global strategies.

As in every facet of Malawi life, from its economy to its one million orphans, there is no shortage of plans for the agriculture sector. The government of Malawi's own Growth and Development Strategy (MGDS III) has seven targets for 2022, from increasing diversification to improving food security. There is a national agriculture policy, a national investment plan and a national irrigation policy, master plan and investment framework.

But these plans are nothing without resources. The World Bank has joined forces with the African Development Bank to co-finance the irrigation of the Shire Valley, in the south of the country. The southern region is the country's most populous area, with eight million people. It is also the poorest part of Malawi, and the most susceptible to climate shocks such as flooding and famine.

The European Union has committed tens of millions of pounds to ten districts across the country to help farmers get access to finance and better markets and to improve farming methods. Irish Aid, perhaps not surprisingly, is supporting Root and Tuber Crops for Agricultural Transformation in Malawi, while the Japanese are supporting the national rice development strategy and the UK is investing heavily in climate change adaptions. But the question remains whether Malawi's agriculture industry is sustainable in the long-term.

It faces many challenges, including weather shocks, poor soil, a limited irrigation system and technology that has barely changed in two centuries. Gifted Galimoto and his mother prepare their land with the same type of handmade hoes used by their ancestors before colonial times. Farmers struggle to get credit, and the degraded soil requires fertilisers for most crops to grow successfully.

With its population projected to almost double by 2050, there is simply not enough land to go around. The average farm plot size in the central region is less than one hectare, and in the more populous south it is only half a hectare. But with its future economic growth, and the very survival of 18 million people, dependent on a successful agriculture sector, Malawi simply cannot afford its farmers to fail.

CHAPTER 12

Business life

EVERYONE IN MALAWI does business. Village women grow tomatoes and beans in the small patches of land next to their homes, which they take to the nearest trading centre to, hopefully, sell for a few hundred *kwacha*. Young men attach a rudimentary seat to the back of a bicycle and gather in small groups at strategic spots, offering a cheap, if rather precarious, taxi service. Those lucky enough to find some capital open a stall, or even rent a shop, and set up business selling everything from hairdressing services to coffins. Even middle-class professionals, those few fortunate Malawians who have found a secure post with the government or an international aid agency, supplement their salary with a business.

Thoko Nyirenda, a nurse for 30 years, and now the owner of a private health clinic and pharmacy in Lilongwe's Area 25, has tried her hand at almost everything.

'I have made sausages, cakes and jam. I have bought bundles of shirts which I sorted and sold round offices. I have raised chickens to sell for their meat,' she recalls. 'I used to go to Tanzania by bus to buy household goods, such as food warmers. It would take me three days to get there,' she smiles, rather grimly. 'Everyone in Malawi does business. Most have to sell something to eat and buy soap and school fees. Me, I had to do it to help pay for our three children to go to school, and then university. It is how Malawi works.'

While there is clearly no shortage of enterprise in Malawi's informal economy – which the International Monetary Fund (IMF) suggested recently could be worth an extra £1.5 billion a year – the country's formal business environment is far less vibrant. To understand why, you have to look at Malawi's economy since independence in 1964. Back then, agriculture, farming and fishing made up around half the economy, with services accounting for almost 40 per cent, and manufacturing and construction, the bedrock of any properly functioning economy, lagging woefully behind at just over 10 per cent.

Today, farming has shrunk to 26 per cent, but industry – which covers the energy utilities as well as manufacturing and construction – has increased only slightly, to 13 per cent. Services – which encompass everything from tourism to banking and hairdressing – are now the dominant force in the domestic economy. But with a large trade deficit of £250 million a year, services are not going to provide Malawi with a route to even modest prosperity.

Private sector growth, especially in the micro, small and medium enterprise (MSME) sector – businesses with up to 100 employees – is the answer, suggests Tione Kaonga, Principal Consultant for UMODZI Consulting, Malawi's leading business development consultancy.

'Business is the engine of growth,' he argued recently, 'because it supports and forms the productive base of any economy… but as in the case of other African countries, the private sector here faces many challenges. There is lack of consistency in policy implementation, for example the government interferes in the operation of liberalised markets. There is a poor allocation of resources to MSMEs, and a focus on production, while paying little attention to market linkages. Financial institutions have not been spared blame either, as their high borrowing rate cripples MSMEs. And donors have also been criticised for promoting dependency on aid, through handouts.'

And he criticised business itself, saying that the private sector has 'failed to seize various opportunities availed to it, and has shown a lack of innovation and competitiveness at both local and international market levels.'

There are an estimated one million MSMEs in Malawi, generating about a quarter of economic activity. The majority, 59 per cent, do not employ anyone, with the remainder employing just over one million people – a sixth of all jobs. The importance of this sector has, according to Tione, led key donors to 'reconsider their commitments and efforts to this most important sector' in order to tackle the terrible effects of high unemployment, over-population, food insecurity and climate change.

'Malawi's major bilateral donors, the UK and the UNDP [United Nations Development Programme], have designed special programmes which, if properly adopted, could assist in graduating the country's poor economy to a middle-income, and competitive, one,' asserts Tione.

Mabvuto Salirana is one of the million small business people on whom his country's future depends. At 43, he earns a decent living as a Lilongwe taxi driver, enough to pay for his three children's school fees and to have built his own home, after 20 years of renting. He even manages to save 'maybe MK

20,000 to 30,000 a month, the rest is feeding the family,' he says.

But when he failed his MSCE in his final year at secondary school, he was concerned about his future.

'I was worried,' he recalls. 'I was thinking that my future would not go well, because if I pass my exams, I thought I would have a good job. Luckily, two years after failing, I got a job as a transport officer. It was a small company, five cars. My job, I can say, was like a foreman. So, I worked with him for four years and during that time I got my driving licence. When the owner died, the company went down, but because I had my driving licence, someone called me to drive his minibus. I drove it for one year. I enjoyed that. Then I went with someone as a taxi driver for one year.'

Then came the breakthrough he had been waiting for, as he explains. 'I had saved around MK 80,000 – my first capital – so I bought some tobacco with it. I remember it was five bales, the heaviest was 110kg, down to about 70kg, and I sold them for MK 380,000 (£400). So that was enough money at the time to buy a small car, so I started my own business,' he explains.

Today, he drives an imported Japanese car, which cost around MK three million (£3,160), and he has a large number of regular customers.

'Business is like a chain,' he says. 'If people know me, they recommend me to somebody else. It is about contacts, sharing numbers. If you are friendly and reliable, people will recommend you. They say to their friends, "If you are going to Malawi, maybe you can call Mabvuto." Many people call me from America, the UK, many countries.'

Mabvuto's enterprising and diligent approach to his business has paid dividends. 'I went from my first capital – MK 80,000 – to buying more expensive cars, and a plot of land, where I have built two houses, one for my family and one to rent.'

And he has ambitions for future growth. 'If I have more *kwacha*, I will buy another piece of land, and build a small house where I can live, but it depends on getting more money. I am also thinking I could buy another car and employ someone. Or buy a two-ton truck and employ a driver. People could hire it for bricks, sand and the like. It is a different side of my business I suppose.'

Mabvuto has built his business without any outside help, but he thinks his government and the banks should help more.

'For a start, the government should construct more roads in the rural areas and townships, so that people can find it easier to supply their produce. And poor people need more loans to start their own business. Just now, to find a loan to start a business is too difficult. You need security, but if you have nothing, how can you offer that? It should be easier for people to get maybe MK one million from the bank. But even if you do get a loan, the interest rate is too high.'

And he describes how his only attempt to finance his growing business failed. 'I have never had a loan from a bank. I tried once. They asked me, "Do you have houses?", but at the time I had nothing. So they said, "If you have no house, no plot of land, you cannot get a loan here." I said, "Thank you, goodbye," and worked to save the money.

'But for the rich people with three or four houses, if the bank asks the same questions, they can give you MK 20 million. You are already rich, you have the chance to borrow more. It is too difficult to change the life from poor to better and better to rich.'

It's a pessimistic view that was echoed by the Malawi Confederation of Chambers of Commerce and Industry in their response to the government's budget statement in the autumn of 2019.

In a damning indictment of the country's business environment, they took out a full-page advert in Malawi's two national newspapers to set out the six key challenges facing business growth. They are, in no particular order, inadequate and erratic electricity supply; uncertainty in economic and regulatory policies; the quality and cost of telecommunication services; high levels of government borrowing; corruption; and, echoing Mabvuto Salirana, they emphasised that the cost and availability of long-term finance was stifling business development.

And they went further, saying that the six challenges had:

> contributed substantially to worsening the business environment in Malawi and have led to private sector not responding to government calls for business expansion and new investment.
>
> If government is serious about delivering on its budget theme and objectives, it must earnestly champion generation of electricity… stop formulating policies that tamper with private sector operations without honest consultations, and most importantly not only be rhetoric (sic) about fighting corruption but be seen to be on top of its fight to the conviction of the general public, the business community included.

The titans of Malawi's economy, the 16 companies listed on the country's small stock exchange, as well as a handful of large privately-owned companies, such as the Mulli Brothers' sprawling empire, do not need to take out a newspaper ad to speak to senior government figures. They just pick up a phone. Big business and politics have been intertwined since the country's modern economy and governance structures were established by white settlers in the last decades of the 19th century.

Malawi's first corporation, the Africa Lakes Company, was set up in 1878 by a group of Scottish businessmen, initially to co-operate with the small band of missionaries already settled here, and to help combat the slave trade by introducing legitimate commerce. And of course, to make a profit. It focused on retail, transport and plantations, and its original Mandala House base in Blantyre, built in 1882, is the country's oldest building. Today, it houses an art gallery and café and is home to the Malawi Society of Archives. The company survived independence, only to collapse in 2007 after an unsuccessful foray into IT.

Malawi's biggest indigenous company had its origins in the newspaper industry. In 1961, three years before independence, the MCP, led by Kamuzu Banda, set up Malawi Press Ltd to publish a weekly newspaper, the *Malawi News*.

After independence, Banda's government took control of large tracts of land from white farmers. Some was given back to rural farmers, but most of it was given either to the MCP or to Banda himself. In 1969, he consolidated ownership of the land and the publishing firm into a new company, Press Holdings. This company was to be the vehicle for Banda's personal wealth, and for much of country's economic growth during his 30-year rule. At one point, Press had 17 subsidiary companies and links with another 23, and it had interests in every business sector, from supermarkets to telecommunications.

It almost collapsed in 1983 and, with it, Malawi's fragile business sector. A rescue package was put together by the donors, including the World Bank, and on 27 February 1984, a new company, Press Corporation, was incorporated. This was wholly owned at the time by the Press Trust, a charity set up by Banda the previous year, to 'act on behalf of the citizens of Malawi.'

A year after the restructuring, Press returned to profitability and, in 1998, the company was floated on the London Stock Exchange. Today, it remains Malawi's biggest business. Banda's charity, Press Trust, owns 45 per cent of the shares, while Deutsche Bank has 22 per cent, Old Mutual (a South African insurance company) has 15 per cent, with the rest split among ordinary shareholders. It has a controlling stake in the National Bank of Malawi, a

20 per cent stake in Castel Brewery (formerly Carlsberg), and has interests in telecommunications, tobacco, energy, property, fish farming and steel processing, as well as owning outright the ailing People's supermarket chain. It's 2018 annual return showed a seven per cent growth in revenues, and a profit for the year of MK 37 billion (£39 million).

But does Press Corporation's dominance of Malawi business life stop other smaller companies from expanding? And what would happen if it were to collapse, as it almost did in 1983?

Even a cursory examination of Malawi's economy suggests that it has a long way to go if it is to reach middle-income status by 2035, an achievable target according to Thomas Chataghalala Munthali, Director General of the National Planning Commission.

He suggested recently that it is only over-population that has kept Malawi near the bottom of the world's poverty league tables since independence. He said, 'Simple evidence shows that Malawi would be a middle-income economy with a person earning $1,000 from less than $400 by 2035 if population was growing at replacement levels, or basically having around two children per woman.'

The economic evidence suggests otherwise. While manufacturing in countries such as Rwanda and Ethiopia is growing apace, in Malawi it makes up only nine per cent of total output, its lowest share since records began in 1975. Productivity has stalled across every sector, including agriculture, where it is no higher than the levels it reached 20 years ago. Yet the country is dependent on farming products for around 90 per cent of exports. Little wonder the country has a big balance of payments deficit. Imports in 2017 were 36 per cent of GDP, but exports totalled only 29 per cent. Malawi has to spend over £190 million a year importing fuel and diesel to keep the country moving. And it spends almost the same importing second-hand clothes (£38 million) as it does on cars and buses.

Leading economist Professor Ben Kaluwa can barely hide his frustration when he considers Malawi's immediate economic future. 'Elsewhere in Africa, there has been a move away from tariffs – trade taxes – but not here, we have not been compliant. We have not even lowered our tariffs for our regional partners. We are too rigid, because we think we need revenue from that source. But what we need is more trade with our neighbours.

'Regional trade is the key for us, but we lose out because of our refusal to comply with regional trade agreements,' he adds, citing a fall-out over the textile trade. 'The South African Development Community (SADC) introduced the MMTZ protocol – it involved Malawi, Mozambique, Tanzania and Zambia, the least developed countries within SADC. Under the agreement, MMTZ countries would export duty free into other SADC countries, but our government torpedoed the agreement, as it didn't like the revenue losses from trade taxes. So many local companies lost out because of the stubbornness of the government.'

Or as Export.gov, an American organisation that advises companies on global trade, puts it:

> The SADC Free Trade Area took effect in January 2008 although certain members, Malawi, Mozambique, Tanzania, and Zambia, are still implementing their scheduled tariff phase down. Despite Malawi's membership in these organizations, to date intraregional trade has not been a strong component of Malawi's exports.

At some point during their first visit to Malawi every visitor, whether an aid professional, a businessperson or a traveller, will ask, 'Why is this country not full of tourists?' Malawi has everything a regional or international tourist could ask for, from the white sandy beaches of Lake Malawi to a choice of small, but well-run, game parks. Its people are renowned for their hospitality, and the country has never experienced war or serious conflict. The number of visitors was increasing, until the coronavirus pandemic stopped international travel to Malawi. There were 870,000 visitors in 2018, more than four times the number who came in 1995. Over three-quarters came from elsewhere in Africa, with 12 per cent from Europe and six per cent from the Americas. But most come with their job – fewer than one-third cited holiday and other personal reasons for their visit.

Frank Johnston, the man who dreamt up Malawi's now famous slogan, the 'Warm Heart of Africa', is sceptical whether tourism offers much hope for future economic growth, despite the sector being the country's third-biggest foreign exchange earner, after tobacco and tea.

'The Malawi Government does nothing at all now to achieve a well-planned tourism industry, and what little it does permit… is often sociologically and economically questionable, with very few true national returns. No proper understanding of the industry has, in the nation's history to date, been gained or passed on to the wider population.'

Frank arrived in Malawi in 1972, fresh from a successful stint in Cyprus, where he had helped develop the island's tourism industry. As he recalls, his job was to do the same for Malawi. 'I was the de facto director of tourism.'

His initial contract was for three years, but he and his wife Maria loved the country so much that they settled here. 'Maria and our four children are Malawian passport-holders,' he says. 'At MK two million (£2,100), I can't afford one,' he laughs, wryly.

He says his proudest achievement as tourism chief was creating a marketing department to promote Malawi, and a fund to support it 'derived from expenditure in hotels and restaurants.' His biggest frustration came when the fund was cancelled in the mid-1980s because the money was 'abused by individual ministers, and some very unwise marketing expenditure by civil servants.

'Tourism promotion was seen to be non-productive, and that view has been allowed to prevail ever since. Little wonder we commonly see the headline "Malawi, Africa's best-kept secret" – this comes directly from an inactive tourism ministry.'

Frank explains that the modest growth in tourism in recent years comes from two sources. 'Wildlife and business conferences. Any significant international tourism is into the wildlife parks and reserves, and the islands on the lake. Such concentrated tourism is the direct opposite of my early intentions and has been regarded by some as latter-day apartheid. Tourists are drawn, correctly and with reason, by a Malawi portrayed as the home of personal warmth and friendliness... but they effectively pay heavily to be kept apart from Malawians, and I know many visitors are disappointed by this.'

He is, however, cautiously optimistic. 'If the tourism ministry was better funded, had some expert help to guide them through appropriate online marketing channels, and had a general entrepreneurial eye to opportunity, Malawi could have a sensationally different industry in two or three years.'

But he thinks things will have to change significantly if Malawi is to achieve middle-income status any time soon, as he explains. 'It will need to find true democracy instead of cherry-picking democratic practice elsewhere for individual political advantage at high levels.'

And he agrees with the head of the National Planning Commission on the impact of a growing population which has seen Malawi grow from four million in 1964 to 18 million today. 'The population growth has never been well addressed. Few, if any, countries, let alone one of the poorest, could respond well, even to just the health and education needs of an exploding population. And it seems to many that the huge inequalities could be a recipe for certain civil strife, if not soon, within a generation.'

SECTION 3

The people's culture

CHAPTER 13

The lake of stars

THERE ARE FEW sights more evocative of Malawi than its lake.

Carefully captured images of the hot, red African sun bursting over the water in early morning, or the twinkling lanterns of fishermen trawling the fresh waters in the ink-black night, dominate tourist brochures, aid workers' blogs, even government policy papers. The lake is Malawi and Malawi is the lake. Just as Malawians say they have not eaten that day if they have not tasted *nsima*, then they will tell visitors to their beautiful country, 'You have not seen Malawi if you have not seen the lake.'

It is a magnificent sight, stretching almost the full length of the country's eastern side. It is 363 miles long, 50 miles across at its widest spot and up to 700 metres deep. It is the third-largest lake in Africa and the ninth largest in the world. And many say it is the most beautiful. Sitting on the white sands of the northern lakeshore, near where early Scottish missionaries taught the Tonga people arithmetic along with the gospel, it is hard to disagree.

The shore is fringed with a variety of trees indigenous to Malawi, such as *mulombwa*, used to build the fishermen's dugout canoes. Boys from the nearby villages run naked through the water, fully at ease, for now, with themselves and their environment. The water is home to the world's biggest collection of cichlids – colourful freshwater fish – and is considered a global biodiversity treasure. Lake Malawi is, quite simply, an African paradise.

The first recorded description of the lake was slightly more prosaic. It was written by a Jesuit priest, Father Mariana, in 1624, nearly 250 years before Dr David Livingstone more famously described it as 'the Lake of Stars'. King Philip IV of Spain and Portugal asked Father Mariana, a Catholic missionary based in Sena, on the Zambesi river in what is now Mozambique, to find out more about a 'great lake' (Lake Malawi), which had been mentioned eight years previously by a Portuguese trader, Gaspar Bocarro. The king was keen to find a safe route to Ethiopia, one that avoided the Turks who controlled all the ports in the Red Sea. At the time, it was believed that the great lake in the centre of the continent (Lake Malawi) stretched all the way up to north Africa.

Father Mariana wrote:

The lake begins some distance south of Maravi, where the River Cheri [Shire] flows from it...

Maravi lies between the lake and Zambesi. The country beyond it is quite thickly populated with heathens...

Its width is between four or five leagues more, for at certain places one cannot see the opposite shore. From there onwards information is lacking since the cafres [people of southern Africa] neither travel nor trade by water.

He goes on to describe the people who live by the lakeshore:

It is said that they have no lack of maize or meat, and even less of ivory, which they offer for sale in abundance, and at cheap rates; a useful point to keep in mind for someone willing to organise this [journey].

They also say that there is no lack of dugouts which, by the addition of a raised plank, should suffice to take a person anywhere.

But he concluded that, while he was 'prepared to do whatever sacred obedience orders me to,' exploring the full length of the lake would be neither comfortable nor safe. 'That much is clear from the common and more serious diseases from which all those suffer who travel... hereabouts,' he warned.

It was those diseases, malaria in particular, that plagued David Livingstone's exploration of the lake in the mid-19th century, and then almost decimated the team of Scottish missionaries who followed in his wake. Livingstone was convinced that Lake Malawi would lead him to the source of the great River Nile, so between 1859 and 1863 he visited three times, becoming the first European to sail on the lake in 1861. He mapped in detail the western side of the lake, and sent back to the UK reports of the slave trade that had scarred this part of southern Africa for decades. And it was on this lakeshore, two years after Livingstone's death in 1873, that the first party of Scottish missionaries landed.

'They followed the map Livingstone had left them,' says Reverend Maxwell Banda, sitting in his home, only a few hundred metres from where the missionaries set up a mission in 1881. Now retired from his senior management role with the Livingstonia Synod of the CCAP, 65-year-old Rev Banda is still active in local and national life. And he is an expert on the history of his people, the Tonga and his church.

'The Scots wanted to settle at the lakeshore, so they went straight to Mangochi. But after a year, one of them, Henry Henderson, decided to move to what is now Blantyre, to settle among the Kapeni villages.'

He goes on, 'The rest of the Livingstonia party stayed for five years, then they abandoned the area. The reasons? This was an Islamic area, and the reception was not good. And the disease, malaria, was killing them. Once they decided to move, they followed the route of Livingstone and reached Bandawe [on the northern shore, near Chintheche]. There they met Malenga, who had earlier met Livingstone.'

And it was here too, living among the Tonga people on the lake's northern shore, that the Scottish missionaries, led by Dr Robert Laws, found a more willing audience for their evangelising. But first the preachers built classrooms, as Rev Banda explains.

'Dr Laws said, "Okay, we will not start with evangelising per se. We will build schools and teach the gospel alongside education." The Tonga people are an open people, and they found this schooling a good thing, and eventually many young people grasped what this is all about, and many became Christians.'

The Livingstonia Synod of the CCAP still has a strong presence in the area today, but a row of white crosses, engraved with surnames such as Swiney and Fraser, and one that simply says 'Baby,' is a stark reminder of how hostile the first European settlers found the environment.

'Christianity and education flourished. But the area was inhospitable for white people,' explains Rev Banda. 'The heat. The malaria. Many died, so in 1894, 13 years after he arrived, Dr Laws is forced to look for another place, away from the lake.'

The lakeshore may have proved too dangerous for northern Europeans, but recent research suggests Lake Malawi was a home to the earliest humans. The lake lies in a valley formed by the opening of the East African Rift, and scientists estimate that a lake basin began to form here about 8.6 million years ago. In 1991, a team led by Professor Friedemann Schrenk unearthed a fossil jawbone at Uraha, on the north-western shore of the lake. This discovery, named *Homo rudolfensis*, proved to be the earliest known relic of the Homo genus – modern humans – and is estimated to be 2.4 million years old.

In a podcast interview in 2016, Professor Schrenk recalls the find. '*Homo rudolfensis*, as you say, was the first member of the human genus, and the special thing at that time was actually the age of this find. Because until then, the genus Homo was maybe two million years old, then suddenly she was half a million years older. And this first-time member of the human species has already used tools – this is actually included in the definition of the genus Homo.'

He goes on, 'I think this knowledge about the early phase of humanity could really contribute to a new understanding of history in Africa.' And perhaps of Malawi, which, following Schrenk's find, could claim with some confidence to be the cradle of humanity.

The first modern humans to settle by the shores of the lake were the Akafula people, a wandering tribe of copper-skinned pygmies who made the lakeshore and its arable highlands their home for thousands of years before being displaced by Bantu people, the Maravi, who had migrated from the north.

The Maravi harnessed the power of the lake, perfecting the art of making dugout canoes which are still carved in the same way today. In the 15th century, the ivory trade with roaming Portuguese traders made the Maravi chiefs rich, and for 200 years their kingdom stretched across southern Malawi, northern Mozambique and eastern Zambia. It started to break down into smaller groups during the 17th century, and when the Yao people from Mozambique arrived on the southern lakeshore at the turn of the 19th century, they found it easy to displace the Maravi (mostly of the Chewa tribe), who moved further inland. The Yao were slave traders, who converted to Islam after prolonged contact with their Arab collaborators. Over decades, they stole thousands of people from the shores of Lake Malawi to sell in the slave markets of Zanzibar.

When David Livingstone arrived in Nkhotakota, the heart of the slave trade in 1861, he described the area as 'an abode of lawlessness and bloodshed... literally strewed with human bones and putrid bodies.' Livingstone met twice with Jumbe Salim bin Abdullah, the local ruler, but while the two signed a treaty in 1864, ostensibly ending the slave trade, it didn't last. Twenty-five years later, an elderly Jumbe signed a lasting treaty with Harry Johnston, then British consul in Mozambique, just as the slave trade was coming to an end. Two years later, Malawi came under British 'protection'. And in 1895, Johnston, by now Governor of the new British Protectorate, captured Mlozi, the last of the Yao slave traders, in Karonga, the most northerly settlement on the lake, and ordered his hanging.

Today, the Yao people live peacefully alongside their fellow Malawians, and the first President elected after the introduction of multi-party democracy in 1994 was Bakili Muluzi, a Muslim Yao.

During the colonial era, according to Michael Mutisunge Phoya, co-author of *Malawi: Lake of Stars*, the lake was 'valued more for its beauty and tourism potential than practical usage.' After independence in 1964, President Hastings Banda took a different approach. Realising a dream he had while in Gweru Prison during the independence struggle, he ordered the construction of the M5 road, known by all as the Lakeshore Road. Today, it winds its way from the Balaka district in the south on to Salima, then through Nkhotakota and Chintheche before reaching Nkhata Bay. It bends west into Mzuzu, Malawi's third-biggest city, then back along the lake and up to Karonga, which sits on the northerly tip of the lake, only 40 kilometres from the border with Tanzania. This road opened up new markets for the lake's abundant fish stocks, and for the first time, fishermen were properly connected with traders in towns and cities across the country.

By the 1970s, fish made up 40 per cent of Malawians' annual protein consumption, with each person eating around 14kg of fish a year. The most popular fish was *chambo* – a species of tilapia – and it is said its plentiful stocks helped fuel Malawi's population growth, a near-doubling in 20 years, from 3.9 million in 1964 to 6.9 million in 1984.

But by the mid-1990s, over-fishing had started to take its toll. In 1997, the government introduced a closed season programme to protect Malawi's *chambo* during their peak breeding time in November and December. Restrictions on the size of fish caught and the gauge of fishing nets were introduced. Poisoning or blasting fish out of the water was banned, and village beach committees were set up to ensure close seasons were observed.

'Since the closed season is implemented during the peak breeding season of the major species of commercial value, it helps to protect the parent fish as well as the juveniles from fishing nets,' Sloans Chimatiro, Director of the Department of Fisheries, told the *New Humanitarian* magazine in 2004. 'In the long-term, closed season as a management strategy will ensure conservation of species which would otherwise have been endangered by uncontrolled fishing practices.'

Mr Chimatiro's optimism proved premature. Over-fishing persists today, with the *chambo* now under serious threat.

Chimwaza Phiri, who with his friend, Annock Bande, fishes from a dugout canoe off Msondozi beach near Chintheche, understands why there has to be controls on fishing.

'These things that the fisheries people are talking about, "Let's keep our fish, let's protect our fish, don't kill small fish," we understand them. As we tell our children, you know, before we used to catch so many different species of fish, some tasty fish. But they have disappeared, and we can understand why they disappeared, because there was this kind of fishing where they were not protected. Now we have to think about the future.'

He pauses. 'If we keep on fishing unprotected, like we are doing now, fishing small fish... there was this example that the Ripple Africa people [a local NGO] gave one day, when they called a meeting. It attached [to] my heart. They were like, "Imagine if today someone can go to a hospital and start killing all the children who are born there. Do you think there will be people in future?" The answer was no, because people come from children.

'Now we are killing small *chambo*, like our children, what they catch is very small, even now women use nets to catch the fish. They can catch so many of small *chambo*, they can fill a bowl, hundreds just to fill it. But when it is big, one *chambo* would not fit inside the bowl. So we must imagine and think about how many fish do we destroy when we are eating them young. We are destroying many, many fish, instead of eating one, which is bigger, which can feed a lot of people. This kind of fishing is destroying our own future.'

But he acknowledges that the conservation message is often ignored, particularly when there are hungry mouths to feed, and no money to buy meat. He says, 'People can understand, but you see them going back to fish. They have no food, that is the problem. Those who don't have money to buy their needs, they end up forsaking what they have heard. They are, "Aah, this is rubbish, what are we going to eat?" But we know the true fact is what fisheries people say.'

Malawi's fishing industry is divided into three sectors. The ancient tradition of catching fish from dugout canoes or wooden plank boats, as practised by Chimwaza and Annock, makes up 90 per cent of the trade.

These small boats are joined by three trawlers, owned by Maldeco, the largest single supplier of fish in the country. The company is a subsidiary of the giant Press Corporation, and its boats trawl the deep waters in the middle of the lake that local fishermen cannot reach. But according to Dr John Wilson, who has worked on Malawi's fisheries policy for nearly five decades, over-fishing is compounded by uncontrolled illegal trawlers, which often fish at night and close to the shore.

The size of the total annual catch has doubled in recent years, from 96,000 tonnes in 2010 to more than 200,000 tonnes in 2018. Most of the increase has come from a higher catch of *usipa*, a small fish whose breeding patterns mean it cannot be over-fished.

Ornamental fish exports are growing, but remain a niche product, worth only around MK 226 million (£240,000) a year.

Many Malawians, including the government and donors, see aquaculture – fish farming – as the answer to both preserving the lake's precious resources and feeding the 18 million population. Fish farms are not a new phenomenon. From 1908, European settlers raised rainbow trout for sport, and in the 1950s, the British Colonial Office introduced small-scale fish production in the northern region. The government's 2019 *Annual Economic Report* claims the sector has grown from a few hundred ponds in the 1970s to around 10,000 today, operated by 15,000 local fish farmers, producing around 9,000 tonnes of fish in 2018, compared to only 2,500 tonnes in 2010.

But according to a 2018 report, written by team of international researchers, led by Moses Limuwa from Mzuzu University, Malawi's fish farming industry still has a long way to go before it reaches its full potential. They wrote:

Despite efforts from the government and NGOs, fish from Malawi's farms are still mainly for household consumption by the farmers themselves and the surplus is sold locally.

The government's support for fish farming is challenged by a high vacancy rate in the Fisheries Department. Additionally, most fish farming efforts have failed to continue beyond the funding lifespan of developmental projects by NGOs and development agencies, keeping adoption very low.

Indeed, fish production remains lower than other developing countries, which started aquaculture long after Malawi.

They cite several reasons as to why fish farming is not the panacea it is sometimes sold:

The fish farming food system is faced with production challenges – especially accessing fingerlings, formulated feeds, and extension services – even though the fish farmers have access to water and land.

And they point out that climate change is a big risk to future production, in particular, recent changes to rainfall and temperature patterns which have seen drought and flooding destroy crops, including fish produced in ponds.

Just as the lake has played a central part in the country's life from the time when our human ancestors first used rudimentary tools to forage for and prepare their food, so it is essential to Malawi's contemporary development and its progress from low- to middle-income status. Malawi relies on the lake not only for fish, but for water to power its hydroelectric power stations – over 90 per cent of the country's electricity depends on Lake Malawi and its only outflow, the Shire River. The lake provides the water for most of the country's irrigated farming production, from rice to coffee and tea. And the lake's water system is essential to maintain the country's delicately balanced eco-system.

Water levels have varied dramatically over the centuries. Between 1390 and 1860, the lake was around 150 metres below its current level, and inadequate water management and climate change now threaten the lake's future viability as the country's reservoir. And with rivers in Tanzania contributing 41 per cent of the lake's water inflows, decisions taken by its government on irrigation schemes and water management will directly affect the people of Malawi.

Decisions taken in the boardrooms of global oil companies may also have a significant impact on the lake in the future. Since the 1970s, there have been sporadic studies to find whether there is oil and gas in Lake Malawi, as well as elsewhere in the country. Six exploration licences were granted in a two-year period from 2011, including three covering the whole lake and two in the land surrounding the Shire River. The sixth is in the north-west of the country.

In 2018, two of the licences for exploration inland were returned, 'following their failure to find partners with whom to share risks associated with exploration…' declared the Ministry of Natural Resources, Energy and Mines in a newspaper advert looking for new bidders. But, insisted the Ministry at the time, both companies submitted reports which 'clearly indicated the likelihood of finding commercially viable quantities of petroleum.'

A fact that worries Chimwaza, and many others whose very lives depend on the lake. 'Of course, we had heard about that [oil]. It would hurt us, so it must just stay where it is,' he insists.

And he is not reassured by a promise made by President Peter Mutharika in 2017, when he said, 'If we decide to drill oil in the lake, we will ensure we use clean, on-shore modern technologies that will prevent oil pollution on our lake which we value most.'

Chimwaza shrugs. 'Politicians. It would damage the lake badly. All the money would go to Blantyre, Lilongwe, wherever, outside, but we would lose a lot in the lake. Our health, our life depends on the lake.'

His pessimism is borne out by examples from across the world, from Venezuela to Nigeria, where the discovery of oil has led, not to shared prosperity, but to widespread corruption and an increase in poverty. This phenomenon is known as the 'resource curse,' a point well made by American commentator, Rachel Maddow, in *Blowout*, her recent blistering critique of the global oil industry. She writes:

The basic problem is that oil doesn't happily coexist with other industries upon which you might build a reasonably stable national economy... oil infrastructure is often environmentally destructive, which thereby screws up other economically productive things.

And she warns that it 'sets the stage for grand-scale corruption of the political class.'

Lake Malawi has provided Malawians with the basic elements of life for thousands of years. Its great beauty, its huge variety of fish and the immense power of its water, could, if carefully managed, be the key elements of an economic strategy that will raise the country from the bottom of the world's poverty league. Or, like the terrible years when its shores were littered with the abandoned corpses of Malawians, slaughtered by the slave traders, the lake's economy – oil this time instead of people – could prove to be the nation's downfall.

CHAPTER 14

Tribal traditions

THE REVEREND MAXWELL BANDA is comfortable with his country's dual personality.

'We all live in two worlds,' he asserts. 'A villager holds on to his traditional beliefs while going to church on a Sunday. And we all hold on to our tribal identity as well as being a Malawi citizen. Two worlds, ancient and modern, together.'

Rev Banda has spent most of his life ostensibly in the modern world. Now officially retired, and living back in his home village at Bandawe, a short walk from the shores of Lake Malawi, he can look back on a long and distinguished career with some pride.

He was one of the country's first theology graduates, he led the Livingstonia Synod's Church and Society committee for many years, where he campaigned for social and economic justice, and he was a member of Malawi's Electoral Commission for four years, from 2012. He is also a proud Tonga and vice chair of *Mdauko wa a Tonga*, his tribe's cultural organisation.

'Almost every tribe has one,' he says. 'Since the coming of the missionaries, they did well in providing us with education, with the new religion, I have no problem with that.

'But what they did wrong was to suppress our culture and tell us everything cultural was bad – you could not dance, the cultural dances that we inherited from our ancestors, these were evil and so on. The missionaries turned their back on everything that was African culture, so you had to begin doing things the European way. If you go to a wedding you do it the European way, if you go to a burial ceremony, you do it the European way, so a lot of good things were lost. And so it was a matter of saying, what can we retain that was practised by our forefathers. We want to promote our Tonga way of life.'

The Tonga is one of the smallest tribes in Malawi. The 2018 Census details 12 tribes, from the biggest, the Chewa, with six million members (34 per cent of the population), to the smallest group, the Sukwa, with only 93,800 members. There are 310,000 Tonga, with the majority living in their traditional homeland along the northern shores of Lake Malawi.

The Tonga's history is intertwined with that of their Chewa brothers and sisters. The biggest Bantu tribe to settle in Malawi was the Chewa, but the origins of the Tonga tribe are lost in history. However, tradition suggests that they, like the Tumbuka tribe who are also from the northern region, came from the land north-west of Malawi.

'We came along with the wave of Chewas coming from the Congo,' says Rev Banda. 'They trekked through to what Malawi's central region is now. We Tonga went north. We are related somehow, at least that is what they [the Chewa] claim, that we had all migrated from the Congo.'

As Kondwani Bell Munthali, one of Malawi's leading journalists, asserts in his guide to customs and culture – *Malawi: Culture Smart!* – the people of Malawi are made up of a 'mosaic of African cultures.'

The Chewa tribe, who by the 16th century had established the Maravi kingdom, and the smaller Bantu tribes, such as the Tonga, the Nyanja and the Mang'anja, were joined in the early 19th century by the Yao people from Mozambique, by marauding Ngoni warriors from South Africa and finally by the Lomwe tribe, also from Mozambique, who came to southern Malawi in the early 20th century as migrant labour to work in the European plantations. Other ethnic groups include the Senga, the Lambya and the Nkhonde – a pastoral tribe whose home is the Karonga district, the most northerly part of Malawi, which borders Tanzania. The Lomwe has grown to become the second biggest tribe, with more than 3.3 million members. The Yao are next with 2.3 million, and the Ngoni are nearly two million strong.

As Kondwani explains, contemporary Malawi reflects this range of influences:

> Dress, dance, mask language and traditional festivals all reflect waves of migrating tribes – those fleeing Shaka Zulu's reign of terror in the south (Ngoni), Swahili Arab slave traders in the east, and Bantu from central Africa.

He goes on:

> Other cultural influences come through the slave trade routes, contact with the Portuguese and Indian traders and British missionaries who fought slavery...

And he asserts that despite there being more than ten tribes, Malawi has remained 'uniquely peaceful.'

In fact, the country's first head of state after independence in 1964, the authoritarian President Hastings Banda, declared that as far as he was concerned, 'There is no Yao in this country, no Lomwe, no Sena, no Chewa, no Ngoni, no Tonga; there are only Malawians. That is all.' He then proceeded to promote his fellow Chewa above other tribes, putting paid to his stated ambition of one Malawi, one tribe. And he declared that the Chewa language, Chichewa, was to be the national language, with English as Malawi's official language, an edict that still stands today. The Tonga and Tumbuka people hold on to their own Bantu-based languages but move seamlessly from Chitumbuka to Chichewa in a single conversation. 'We speak Tonga at home, Chichewa outside and English at school and business,' explains Maxwell. The Ngoni and Lomwe languages have all but disappeared.

And every tribe has its own traditions, from the food that they prefer to grow and to eat, to their laws of inheritance and burial rites. The Ngoni were renowned for three things, says Maxwell. 'They liked hunting and eating meat, they liked marrying many women and they like drinking beer,' a cliché that many say still holds true today.

One of the customs that the Ngoni brought with them from South Africa, and that they still celebrate, is their marriage traditions. Unlike other Malawi tribes, where families are built through adherence to matrilineal customs, the Ngoni are patriarchal. A woman moves to her husband's home village after marriage, in a procession called *umthimba*. Cattle is still used as a girl's dowry, even when the prospective bride is a sophisticated city woman, as Thoko Nyirenda explains. Her daughter, Vilerani, who works for one of the country's leading insurance companies, is planning her marriage to Moses, an auditor in an international accountancy firm, but tribal traditions almost stood in the way of their romance.

'Moses was brought up by his *agogo* in a village in the north. She said that Vilerani was worth many cows, too many that she cannot afford them. And if she cannot pay them, *agogo* said they cannot get married. It can be so frustrating, because the young people do not accept the dowry custom, but the older people still do, and their opinion matters. His *agogo* could have stopped their marriage,' she shrugs, 'but that is their tradition. We are very happy she didn't.'

The Yao tribe mixes its ancient rites with those of Islam, their predominant religion. During the 19th century, the Yao, who migrated from the northern Mozambique, made their living as ivory and slave traders along the shores of Lake Malawi.

One of the most powerful Yao chiefs, Makanjira, adopted Islam in the 1870s, after regular contact with Swahili Arab traders, and his people followed suit. Islam was a particularly attractive religion because, unlike Christianity, its converts were not asked to give up their ancient traditions such as polygamy.

As Augustine Msiska wrote in the first volume of the 1995 *Society of Malawi Journal*:

Islam as a faith and way of life did not interfere with the traditional beliefs and customs of the Yao people just as was the case wherever it spread. If anything, it merely modified or made slight changes to some of the local customs.

Today, the Yao Muslims observe the most significant Islamic festivals, such as Ramadan, while continuing to practise ancient rites such as circumcision of boys when they reach puberty.

One of the most striking and colourful elements of Malawi's tribal customs are traditional dances. Every visitor to Malawi will, at some point, be treated to a dance display, and the programmes for political rallies, cultural events, even state occasions such as the inauguration of a new President, always include dancers. Three of the biggest tribes, the Ngoni, Chewa and Yao, see teaching young people their ancient dances as a way to preserve Malawi's culture.

In an interview in *The Nation* newspaper, Miliyoni Leveni, a Yao from Mangochi, explains why learning his tribe's traditional dance, *Beni*, is so important. 'I normally teach the youth basic steps of the *Beni* dance, which I feel good and proud to do. It is my hope that these young ones learn and take our traditions to another level. I have been a *Beni* dancer since 1955, and all this happened because someone taught me how to dance.'

The male dancers wear a costume based on an army uniform, to reflect the Yao's reputation as the *askari* – the policemen or soldiers of Malawi. And the dance is supported by four different types of drums, which guide the dancers' steps. 'They bring out the *Beni* sound,' explains Mr Leveni, 'The dance is normally a dance of happiness, and is performed at *chinamwali* (initiation ceremonies), weddings and chiefs' coronations.'

The Ngoni's dance is *Ingoma*, and like the Yao's *Beni*, has its own costume, described in *The Nation* by Group Village Headman Mkwangwala of Ntcheu district. 'We have our own dressing code. It is made from animal skin, and is unique,' he says. He agrees that dancing is the best, perhaps only, way to preserve his tribe's unique culture in the 21st century. 'We want to share the knowledge with the young ones, and at the same time share it with the world.'

Perhaps the most striking of all Malawi's tribal traditions is *Gule Wamkulu*, the dance performed by the Chewa tribe, often at funerals. *Gule Wamkulu* dates back 500 years, and despite the efforts of Christian missionaries to ban the tradition, as Rev Banda described earlier, it has survived. But today, the performances are as much entertainment for tourists as they are for moral teaching.

'It is our identity, and we want our culture to go beyond us,' says village headman Mlesi from Salima. 'When we die, people should be able to know our heritage, which is why we involve youth in the dance.'

The *Gule Wamkulu* was officially recognised by UNESCO in 2008, and is performed by *virombo*, men who are members of the Chewa's secret society, also named *Gule Wamkulu*.

Chewa society is matrilineal, and traditionally married men played a marginal role in daily life, so this brotherhood offered a way for them to find a common bond and meaning within their tribe. Today, the cult members are still responsible for the initiation of young Chewa men into adulthood, and *Gule Wamkulu* is always performed at the end of each initiation ceremony. It is also performed following the July harvest, and at weddings, funerals and the installation, or the death, of a Chewa chief.

The dancers wear costumes and masks made of wood and straw, and these represent a range of characters, from wild animals or spirits of the dead to slave traders, as well as more modern symbols such as cars. According to UNESCO, each figure plays a particular, often evil, character, and is used to teach moral and social values. The dances entertain and scare in equal measure.

Traditional dances have also been embraced by politicians as campaign tools, to the concern of many who see the promotion of ancient traditions, not as a way of preserving Malawi's culture, but as means to encourage nepotism and tribalism. When Malawi embraced multi-party democracy in 1994, after 30 years of authoritarian rule, its new constitution guaranteed tribal rights. 'Every person shall have the right to use the language and to participate in the cultural life of his or her choice,' it says in Chapter 4, Section 26. A further clause provides that 'every person shall have the right of freedom of association, which shall include the freedom to form associations. No person may be compelled to belong to an association.' Twelve years later, the first ethnic organisation was established by the Chewa people. The Chewa Heritage Foundation was set up with the 'aim of preserving customs, values and tradition across the nation.'

In 2008, the then head of state, President Bingu wa Mutharika – a Lomwe – founded the *Mulhako wa Alhomwe* group. Its aim was to 'expose children and people from other tribes and countries to the ethnic customs such as dance, drumming, storytelling, poetry, tribal history, arts, crafts, as a means of promoting self-esteem, creating and preservation of the Lomwe tribal customs.' Some commentators were fearful that the new group was simply a political vehicle to ensure that the Lomwe people prospered over other tribes. Their disquiet was compounded by a report in the influential online newspaper, *The Nyasa Times*, where a leading member of the tribe boasted, 'It is our time to enjoy ourselves and have all good things. Others will also have their time and leadership goes to their homes.'

Since 2008, other groups have been set up. The Mzimba Heritage Association promotes the Ngoni way of life, the Karonga-Chitipa Cultural Heritage Festival is for the Nkhonde people and *Mgumano wa Asena na Amang'anja* was set up by the Mang'anja and Sena tribes.

Rev Maxwell Banda dismisses the suggestion that these cultural organisations are mainly concerned with political power and patronage. 'There were bad things in our culture which needed to be thrown out, but you need to retain the good things. People without a culture are almost dead. Our traditions help us be who we really are. They bring us together. Our peaceful values, or respect for each other. How you raise children, life's rites of passage, from conception up to death. Our African rites of passage. They are important to us.'

Others are more sceptical. Leading law professor, Danwood Chirwa, writing in the newspaper *Nyasa Times* in 2017, said that while the tribal associations had a role to play promoting cultural diversity, there was a danger that they encouraged discrimination based on ethnicity. 'Mobilisation along tribal lines is intrinsically exclusionary and often results in discrimination based on ethnic or social origin, language or birth status.' he added.

He also argued that tribal associations allowed elites to exploit ethnic differences for political gain. He explained, 'The political problems Kenya has faced in the last decade have arisen largely from the predominance of tribal pacts in national politics. Tribal associations also serve as a means of distributing and entrenching tribal systems of patronage.'

And he had a warning for Malawi. 'Evidence abounds in Malawi of the troubling links between tribal associations and politics, patronage and tribalism. Every government since 1964 has linked itself to a particular ethnic group, whose culture and people it has promoted. The MCP government raised the Chewa above all other ethnic groups. Muluzi's government promoted the Yao, although he was generally pro-south in general. The DPP [Democratic Progressive Party] government has tended to promote the Lomwe.'

He went on. 'In general, the tribal association linked to the ethnical group of the incumbent President enjoys greater patronage and disproportionate state support. This not only includes the amount of state resources that are given to the association, but also the increased recruitment of its members to public positions.' And he concluded that the inevitable politicisation of tribal associations made them 'a uniquely improper means of facilitating socio-economic and cultural development in Malawi.'

It is hard to see how the Tonga's tribal association is 'improper.' Rev Banda explains that one of its main aims is to preserve the country's natural environment. 'If you go around the rest of the country, you will see that everywhere, trees have been cut down and the land is almost bare. But if you come to Nkhata Bay, to our land, there are trees around. We have told our people, since time immemorial, that nature is good for us. It supports us, that is the message we need to share with our fellow Malawians.'

He dismisses any suggestion that the Tonga association could be used for political purposes. 'The Tonga is a small group. And in a democracy, the numbers dictate who becomes the leader.' He chuckles, 'Who has the numbers wins. Even if you don't have the ideas, if you have the numbers, you win.'

The man with the numbers, President Peter Mutharika, who won the disputed 2019 presidential election with a majority of 160,000 votes over his nearest rival, Lazarus Chakwera of the MCP, chose the 2019 Lomwe festival to make an impassioned plea about tribal divisions. Dressed in a pink and red suit, emblazoned with the legend *Mulhako wa Alhomwe,* and clearly unaware of the irony of preaching unity while sporting the colours of the association most recently associated with causing division, he urged Malawians to love one each other.

'Let us not allow failed and frustrated politicians to divide us,' he said. 'Let us not allow tribes to divide us. There is no tribe which is superior to other tribes in Malawi. We are one. Let us love each other.'

The association's chairperson, Leston Mulli, echoed the President's remarks, saying Lomwes will always live in harmony with people of other tribes. 'Politicians want to divide us for their personal reasons, but we are one,' he said.

A year later, the people of Malawi came together as one to vote Mutharika out of office.

CHAPTER 15

In God we trust

THE BILLBOARD ON the road from Mzuzu to Nkhata Bay on the northern lakeshore is unequivocal. 'Breaking news,' it declares. 'Jesus is coming soon.'

There is no clue as to who paid for the unmissable advert which sits on a prime roadside spot, only a Bible verse – Revelation 22:7, which in the King James version reads, 'Behold, I come quickly: blessed is he that keepeth the sayings of the prophecy of this book.'

It seems everyone in Malawi is blessed, in that almost everyone has faith. There are places of worship everywhere, from simple whitewashed mosques and grass-roofed churches to stylish Catholic cathedrals, their stained-glass windows paid for by rich congregations 5,000 miles away. Those who cannot reach their nearest church on a Sunday morning hold simple services in each other's homes. Newspapers offer weekend religious sections, and every meeting, every meal, every school day starts with a prayer.

The 2018 Census lays bare Malawi's faithfulness. Only two per cent of the population say they have no faith (377,000 people), with more than three-quarters stating they are Christian; 2.5 million people are Muslim and nearly one million follow non-Christian faiths. Fewer than 200,000 people describe themselves as adherents of Malawi's traditional beliefs.

'The gospel is not just one unit of human life,' states the Reverend Maxwell Banda, former Moderator of the Livingstonia Synod, part of the CCAP – Malawi's first Christian denomination. 'The gospel is our whole life... An African is religious by birth. It has always been part of life. If we lose religion, we lose life,' he asserts quietly, but with absolute conviction.

Before David Livingstone and the advent of Christianity, Malawi's tribes enjoyed a sophisticated belief system, which included a 'High God,' explains Kenneth Ross, Church of Scotland minister and theology professor at the University of Malawi's Chancellor College. 'This God was perceived as remote and distant. The practice of religion focused more on ancestors and spirits, perceived to be more accessible. Sociological analysis suggests that this form of religion was satisfactory while people lived very locally, with little exposure to the outside world.'

He goes on, 'With the advent of modernity, they needed to make more of the High God, as they sought to come to terms with a much more extensive context. This made both Christianity and Islam attractive as both revolve around the one true God, who is Lord of Heaven and Earth.'

Or, as Rev Banda puts it, 'The traditional religions had one spirit... so Christianity was simply a change, replacing traditional religion with Christianity or Islam. It is the same story, it just developed.'

The first chapter of the story to develop was Islam. The Jumbe clan, traders of Swahili Arab origin, settled on Lake Malawi, near Nkhotakota, around 1840. Their leader, Salim bin Abdullah, converted the local population to Islam, even sending the sons of prominent chiefs to Zanzibar, ostensibly to sell their ivory directly to merchants there, but also to expose them to Islam. Nkhotakota remains a centre of Islam today.

Further south, in the Mangochi area, Yao trading chiefs, such as Makanjira, were converted to Islam while doing business with the outside world, as leading Malawi historian John McCracken explained:

> Converts to... Islam were frequently made in the late 19th century from among people like the Yao... who were in the process of being integrated into the world economy.

Others argue that the conversion to Islam happened, in part, as a reaction to the arrival of white settlers from the 1870s onwards. 'It is probably part of a great scheme of black versus white,' declared a writer in the Universities' Mission to Central Africa magazine, published in 1906.

Whatever promoted the Yao people's conversion to Islam, the new faith was particularly attractive because it did not interfere with their traditional practices such as polygamy. Indeed, initiation rites for adolescents, such as male circumcision, were simply modified to reflect the Islamic teaching and are still practised today, as is polygamy.

Today, the majority of Malawi's two and a half million Muslims live in the southern region. Most are Sunni, and there are around 800 mosques, with a major centre of Islamic teaching in Mpemba, just outside Blantyre. There is little evidence of tension between Islam and Christianity, as found elsewhere in Africa. Eid is a national public holiday, which all Malawians enjoy, and the first freely elected President of Malawi, Bakili Muluzi, was Muslim.

Imedi Jafali, a former councillor who lives in Zomba district, near the lakeshore, is Muslim, and he says Islam and Christianity, 'live together happily, most of the time. When I was a councillor most of the people I represented were Christian, but my faith did not matter to them. Christians are our brothers and sisters, we are of the same blood, so we don't hate each other. There is sometimes a little tension, between Seventh Day Adventist and Islam, and maybe Roman Catholics. It seems these faiths have deep teachings about their religion. But the elders on both sides, from Christian and Muslim, quickly condemn any bad conduct and unite people. And don't forget one of our Presidents was Muslim.'

The introduction of Christianity to Malawi has become the stuff of legend, with Dr David Livingstone as the protagonist. Livingstone is remembered for the respect he showed indigenous people during his explorations of central Africa, and he spoke frequently of his ambition to help the tribes living on the shores of Lake Malawi escape the slave trade, and instead build an economy based on commerce and rooted in Christian values. The first missionaries to heed his call were not, as people often believe, members of the Church of Scotland, but Anglicans from the universities of Oxford, Cambridge, Durham and Dublin. Inspired by Livingstone's lectures on the slave trade, they set up the Universities' Mission to Central Africa (UMCA) and appointed Bishop Charles Mackenzie to lead the first attempt at establishing Christianity in Malawi.

In 1861, Mackenzie set up a small base in the Shire Highlands, near the lake, but within a year, he and three members of his team were dead, killed by malaria. The mission was deemed a 'miserable failure,' and it was to be several decades before the UMCA tried again.

Two years after Livingstone's death in 1873, the first Scottish missionaries arrived in Malawi, determined to continue his life's work. The team, from the Church of Scotland and the Free Church, settled at Cape Maclear, near Mangochi, but as Rev Maxwell Banda tells, their mission proved less than successful. 'First, one member of the team, Henry Henderson, left to set up the Blantyre mission, inland. The rest of the Livingstonia party, led by Dr Robert Laws, stayed for five years at Cape Maclear, before abandoning the area. They managed to attract only one convert. That was Albert Namalambe.'

Albert accompanied the missionaries to their next port of call, Bandawe, 400 kilometres north on the lakeshore, where they were to spend another five years. There, among the Tonga people, they found a warmer reception, and by the time the Livingstonia mission was established in its final location further north, on a plateau 500 metres above the lake, Christianity was firmly established among the Tonga.

'The Tonga had a belief in a supreme being anyway, so the Christian message had resonance,' says Rev Banda. 'The older people were resistant, but the young people were more open and Christianity flourished.'

Dr Laws and his team were able to settle comfortably in their new location with its European climate, and they set about building one of central Africa's first formal education systems, as well as Malawi's embryonic health service. And they began the challenging work of converting the Ngoni tribe. They had migrated to Malawi from South Africa in the middle of the 19th century, settling in the central and northern regions. They were warriors and spent much of their early years in Malawi fighting with the established Bantu population.

'They liked hunting game, they liked marrying more women, they liked drinking beer,' explains Rev Banda, 'So the missionaries said to them, "You like hunting, eating meat, but meat will not be available for ever, but if you allow your young people to be educated, you will eat meat always." It is something they yearned, to them to eat meat was life. It was a simple way of saying education is the route to prosperity. They were interested.'

It was around this time too, in the late 1880s, that the missionaries first got involved in the governance of Malawi, a central role churches and faith groups continue to hold today. Faced with the threat of Arab slave traders, led by Mlozi in the north, and with the Portuguese about to annexe southern Malawi, the missionaries, through the Church of Scotland, successfully campaigned for the country to come under formal British protection.

On 15 May 1891, Malawi was pronounced a British Protectorate and a colonial government established. It didn't take long, however, for the missionaries to clash with the new administration, and according to Rev Ken Ross, they had 'a robustly critical relationship' with the country's new masters. Writing in *Friendship with a Purpose*, he describes how:

> on the crucial inter-linked issues of land, labour and taxation, the Blantyre missionaries consistently took the side of African communities as they faced the pressure of the colonial regime on these fronts.
>
> As a settler dominated economy and an accompanying racist ideology came to hold sway, the Missions stood for African advancement and for

appreciation of the positive qualities of African life and culture.

The primary instrument through which they worked was the vast network of schools that they developed. Through the schools, they cultivated values that implicitly challenged racism and colonialism, and educated the Malawians who, in due course, would form the nationalist movement that led the country to independence.

Two years before Britain took control, the Catholic Church sent its first missionaries to Malawi. Like the Protestants before them, the White Fathers, a predominantly French apostolic society founded in 1868, first settled at the lakeshore, near Mangochi. After 18 months of 'sickness, loneliness, anxiety, without having administered a single adult baptism,' the White Fathers abandoned Malawi in favour of Zambia, where they founded the more successful Mambwe Mission.

In 1901, the Catholic Montfort Missionaries arrived at Nzama near Ntcheu in the centre of Malawi, where they established the first permanent Catholic mission. Like Dr Laws and his Church of Scotland team, they offered education and rudimentary healthcare alongside the Bible. Inspired by their work, the White Fathers returned to Malawi a year later, also to the central region where they set up three missions, at Likuni, Kachebere and Mua. They handed a fourth, Nguludi, to the Montfort Missionaries.

The first Malawian Catholics were baptised in 1904, and in 1937 the first priests, Cornelio Chitsulo and Alfred Finye, were ordained. Today there are four seminaries, including the Inter-Congregational Seminary at Balaka. Mua Mission in the central region is home to the famous KuNgoni Centre of Culture & Art, established in 1976 by Fr Claude Boucher Chisale. Its museum describes the Chewa, Ngoni and Yao cultures and their encounter with Islam and Christianity. It also holds a unique collection of *Gule Wamkulu* masks and other artefacts.

Perhaps surprisingly for a country so long associated with the Protestant Church of Scotland, the recent Census revealed that the Catholic Church is now the single biggest denomination in the country, with three million adherents. But an even bigger group describe themselves as 'other Christians'. This category is a catch-all for members of the plethora of smaller churches and faith groups that have sprung up in Malawi the last few decades. Some, like the Church of the Latter-Day Saints (Mormons), are globally established churches. Others, like the Winners' Chapel, founded in 1981 by Nigerian David Oyedepo, are authentically African. And many are part of the Pentecostal movement, which believes that faith must be a direct personal experience, like speaking in tongues, not something experienced simply through quiet contemplation.

Maggie Banda, founder of WOLREC, a leading NGO, is also a pastor in the Living Cornerstone Church International, where her husband, Kondwani Kathewera Banda, is the bishop. She believes that faith is essential for Malawi's development, particularly in the country's governance.

'One of the things our church is trying to do is to raise a generation of people with integrity. We are trying to use the word of God to preach to people to follow God's instruction, because if you follow God's word, then you will indeed live a life of integrity. When this generation goes into public service, they will remember their principles. Wherever they go, into a bank, public service, become leaders of society, if integrity is in them, they will make sure they are able to use the country's resources in the right way for the benefit of the public.'

And she says that her faith and its values have shaped her professional work. 'WOLREC is a reputable organisation because even though we are not preaching the word of God in WOLREC, the values we encourage in our employees are those based on our faith. Integrity. Justice. Responsibility. The values our country's leaders need.'

Maxwell Banda says the growth of Pentecostal churches is, in part, because mainstream denominations like the CCAP have become more 'European' in their theology and liturgy. 'These self-styled churches tend to read the Bible literally,' he says. 'They put on a show, speaking in tongues for example, and so many people, often with little education, are attracted to this kind of church. They are building a sizeable following, but I am not here to judge.'

But he does point out that they do not offer the same level of social protection as mainstream denominations. 'These new churches do not have the same social services as say Islam or the Catholic Church. That is their weakness, they do not have a strong base, or tradition within communities.'

Others, like Kenneth Ross, worry about the growth of the 'prosperity gospel' in Malawi. The doctrine, popular in the United States since the 1950s, holds that good health and prosperity are always the will of God. A deep faith, married with donations to the church and its leadership, will guarantee a better life.

Rev Ross believes that this is the biggest issue facing Christianity in Africa and Malawi today. 'There is a possibility that it creates a situation where manipulative preachers can exploit the poor, so as to enrich themselves and their organisations. However, the issues of exploitation and abuse do not invalidate the whole thing. The same medieval European Christianity that featured corrupt Popes also produced Francis of Assisi. The same African Christianity that features exploitative preachers has also produced Desmond Tutu.'

The mainstream churches do not promise poor Malawians instant riches, but since Dr Robert Laws opened the first rudimentary school in Bandawe, they have been at the forefront of public service provision. Nearly 30 per cent of all health services, from primary care to hospitals, is provided by CHAM. Churches are still heavily involved in the provision of education, from early years to post-graduate. According to their very detailed website, the Catholic Church in Malawi oversees 1,500 primary schools, 14 national Catholic secondary schools and 127 CDSSs, as well as seven technical colleges, two teacher training colleges and two universities.

Dr Laws, who died in 1934, dreamt of opening a university on the plateau where he built his final and most successful mission. His vision faded with his death, but was resurrected in the early 21st century, and in 2003, the University of Livingstonia accepted its first undergraduates, with the aim of educating students to become 'principled leaders who will transform society for the glory of God.' The CCAP, through its three synods – Livingstonia, Blantyre and Nkhoma – also provides a range of schools and colleges, including some of the country's few facilities for special needs education.

Women's faith groups are the backbone of most Malawi villages, according to Rev Ross. 'They are ubiquitous in Malawi's rural communities, highly visible because of the "uniforms" they wear. Most of them are not at all well off in material terms, but through their shared faith, they discover agency and purpose. In a situation where there is no state provision of social security, it is often the women's faith groups who reach out to the sick, the elderly, the bereaved, the needy. Out of their meagre resources they will visit with a little sugar or flour, as well as the solidarity of love and prayer.'

While churches continue to play a significant role in the economic and social development of Malawi, it could be argued that their biggest impact has been in the political life of the country. The campaign for Malawi to be brought under the protection of the British state in 1891 was the first example of the church's role in shaping the country's political economy and protecting its very existence. The Church of Scotland fiercely opposed the

1953 forced integration of Malawi with Northern and Southern Rhodesia (now Zambia and Zimbabwe), not least because the prevailing orthodoxy in Southern Rhodesia, the strongest of the three nations, was white supremacy. And leading church figures in Malawi and Scotland supported the revival of Malawi's independence movement during the 1950s, which led to the dismantling of the hated Federation and independence in 1964.

But it was a letter from Malawi's Catholic bishops nearly 30 years later that arguably had the biggest impact on Malawi life, and its reverberations are still felt today. The Lenten Pastoral Letter, *Living Our Faith*, was published on 8 March 1992, and was the first public criticism of President Hastings Banda's authoritarian regime since he took power. The statement called for far-reaching social and political reforms and unleashed a national movement that led first to a referendum on multi-party democracy in 1993, then a year later to the country's first free elections, in which the MCP and Banda were heavily defeated by Bakili Muluzi and his new UDF.

Rev Banda recalls the impact of the bishops' letter. 'The government took a strong hand to silence the bishops. Dr Banda made a claim that the Catholics were deliberately destabilising Malawi because they wanted what was happening in Northern Ireland. He claimed the Catholics were jealous of him because he was an elder in the CCAP church. So that is when the Presbyterians took courage and said, "This is not about Catholics versus Protestants, this is about national leadership. We are equally concerned."' Together, the Catholic bishops and the leadership of the CCAP formed Malawi's Public Affairs Committee, known now simply as the PAC. And its membership extended beyond the churches.

'Then we said, it is not about church only, these issues of governance that the Catholics have raised, they affect all of us as Malawians,' recalls Rev Banda. 'So, we appealed to the Law Society of Malawi, you are most welcome to give us your perspective as lawyers. The business community joined too, so it was now a national movement, spearheaded by the churches.'

Today, Rev Banda argues that the PAC is more important than ever to the nation's development. 'The move from autocratic rule to multi-party democracy is very difficult, wherever it happens. In Malawi, it was quite remarkable indeed that the churches and civil society led the discussion and we managed to have a largely peaceful transition. It was quite an example in Africa.

'It remains so that the churches are still trusted by the general population as mediators in crisis. When we speak on behalf of the people, we are listened to, we are credible. We really set a precedent in 1992, which we are building on. Of course, there are pitfalls here and there, but surveys have shown that people suspect traditional leaders, police are not trusted, and political leaders are the worst. But over the years it has not changed here. Church leaders are still perceived as trusted, to be fighting on behalf of the people.'

But despite Malawians' almost unquestioning faith in God, or Allah, Malawi remains one of the world's poorest countries, while more secular nations, as Scotland has become, continue to prosper. 'We will have a better life in heaven,' is a common refrain among Malawi's poorest people, who seem happy to accept that their reward is most definitely not here on earth.

Kenneth Ross is quick to dismiss any suggestion that religion is, as Karl Marx argued in 1844, the opium of the people, preventing them from understanding the causes of their poverty and oppression. He says, 'Malawi is among the poorest countries in the world, and with harsh levels of poverty affecting a large proportion of the population, human dignity is at stake. It is through faith that many Malawians assert their dignity... it is therefore the opposite of an opiate, it activates, empowers and energises people to counter dismal and demoralising circumstances in positive ways.'

Anyone, whether atheist or pious believer, who has taken part in an exuberant Malawi church service will recognise that faith really does empower and energise people. And it most certainly activates people, from the village women who care for the most vulnerable in their community to the members of the PAC, dedicated to and fighting for a fairer, more prosperous Malawi for all its people.

But there is a stirring afoot, with even establishment figures like the Rev Banda impatient for fundamental change. 'Malawi has always been peaceful, with people accepting their lot. But there comes a time when people say enough is enough, we cannot go on like this. I think that time has come.'

CHAPTER 16

Creative forces

DURING THE STONE AGE, the people who lived in the central region of Malawi, near the Mozambique border, started painting images on the large rocks that dominated their landscape. These hunter-gatherers were Malawi's first artists and their red geometric paintings, which can still be seen today, marked the genesis of Malawi's rich cultural life. Malawi's spirit, as expressed in its people's creativity, has survived tribal wars, slavery, colonialism, authoritarian rule and censorship, and flourishes today, not on rocks, but on social media.

And the catwalk. Wezi Mzumara (32) is the co-founder of Mzuzu Fashion Week, a festival of runway shows, cocktail parties and business seminars held every year in Malawi's most northerly city. She credits social media with changing how her generation approach creativity.

'Everyone is digital,' she says. 'That has changed how people think and how people are working in the creative industries. People can see what is happening in Lagos, what they are doing in South Africa, and they think, okay we can also do it.'

Wezi's parents were exiles during Hastings Banda's rule, and she was born and grew up in Addis Ababa. 'I can't speak Chichewa fluently,' she laughs ruefully. 'I speak Amharic, but I do understand Chichewa.'

She studied culture and communications in the UK and returned to her motherland in 2011. 'I didn't know anyone,' she explains. 'And I didn't know how anything worked in Malawi, I didn't know things were so slow. I came with my fast-paced energy, and I was told, "Relax."

'I started designing accessories, made with *chitenje* cloth, bangles and earrings, but there was no market for them here, so I shipped them to the USA. It worked for a year or so, then the market died down because everyone was doing it.

'So, I thought, we have all these beautiful products, but no way to actually market them. And all these fantastic, amazing young designers who also need a market. So, coming from an events and marketing background, I thought, okay, why not do a fashion week. The funny thing is the resistance was coming from within Mzuzu, which is quite a traditional place. They said it was not possible, but we did it and it was a success. We have just finished our fifth year.

'We want the whole country to be fashion forward, for Mzuzu to be the Milan of Africa, and why not? I think we can have a proper fashion industry here, it has huge potential for economic development. Our country could have the perfect blend of agriculture and fashion and beauty. We have the cotton industry, we have honey for beeswax, we could manufacture silk, as we grow mulberry trees, and cocoa too for its butter.'

But Wezi, like many entrepreneurs, struggles to find investors willing to support her ambitions. She says, 'Investment? Nothing. Nobody is interested. We have tried, but they go, "Eeeeeh, fashion... no." They will invest in farming projects, in healthcare, in education, but fashion... no. They don't understand it.'

The sparse economic data available on Malawi's creative industries underline Wezi's frustration. The UK's creative exports are worth around £50 billion a year, with clothing and fashion bringing in an additional £11 billion, but Malawi's creative earnings are minimal. The most up-to-date UN survey shows that the country only exported £690,000 of creative goods in 2014. Tobacco exports that year were worth £492 million, 700 times more. The figures reflect a lack of interest in Malawi's fashion potential.

In her first official visit to southern Africa in 2019, the Duchess of Sussex captured the headlines in a black and white cotton dress. 'Meghan Markle wears patterned dress from ethical Malawi brand,' shrieked one UK newspaper. Wezi is not impressed. 'Mm, that was not a Malawi label,' she asserts. 'They are a UK company that is part of the "ethical" fashion culture, but my question is, are they really ethical? Meghan Markle's dress was £69. How much of that actually went to the person who made it? Very little. Of course, there should be a mark-up, but some are so huge, you have to ask, are they actually ethical? I have kept quiet about the whole thing, but while companies like this one may make some of their products here, they are never sold here. They are not a Malawian company.'

Nzika Arts is a Malawian company owned by Mwai and Sheena Namaona. They are only in their early 30s, but are already veterans of Malawi's fashion industry, as Sheena explains. 'We started in 2006. We did clothing only at first, but the fashion market is dominated by second-hand clothing – *kaunjika*. We cannot compete with that. It is cheaper, and it is everywhere. For us to make a shirt, we need to sell at MK 15,000 (£16), but someone can go to *kaunjika* and get a shirt from the UK for MK 1,000. We cannot compete with that one. So, we decided to diversify. Now we work in the corporate world, doing decoration for events. We did the presidential debates for the 2019 election, and we work with most of the big banks.'

But while their Standard Bank contract pays their rent, their creative soul is rooted in their country's rich traditions. '*Nzika* means citizen, the people,' says Sheena. 'And since we started we have tried to express what it means to be Malawian through our designs. We think about it all the time. We want to produce unique fabrics that are 100 per cent Malawian. The cloth we all use is mostly from Zambia, Tanzania, Nigeria. Now China too. Our home-produced cotton is not of good enough quality. You go to Ghana, to South Africa, they have their own fabrics that immediately identify their culture. We want to produce prints, designs that are authentically Malawian.'

But despite their decade-long success, they too can't find affordable finance to invest in machinery. 'We have the designs, but to make an impact, we need to have a proper production line, one that is sustainable, that will allow us to export. We want mass production, not handmade products. We will get to our dream. We will keep pushing. We have many young designers asking us how we have sustained our business for so long. We always tell them, "Stand your ground, be authentic." You can't go wrong if you are authentic.'

The couple are frustrated by how little attention is paid to Malawi's creative industries. 'The people in power don't really understand culture and its importance to all parts of our life,' says Sheena. 'Our culture is rich, we are a very creative nation, but 150 years ago we were taken over by foreigners. Then in Kamuzu's day, British traditions continued to dominate. Now because of Facebook and Pinterest, people take designs from Nigeria and say they are Malawian. It is just a matter of ourselves discovering who we really are.'

Malawi has always had a rich storytelling tradition, of passing down tales through the generations, creating a cultural tapestry that sustained communities through bad times as well as good. The first published Malawi novel, and one of the first to be published by any African, was *Nthondo*, or *Man of Africa*, by Samuel Y Ntara, a young school teacher from the central region. In 1932, at the age of 27, Ntara entered his 'beautifully written manuscript' in a competition sponsored by the London-based Institute of African Languages and Cultures. His tale of how a young man comes to terms with adulthood and the advent of colonialism won first prize in the biography section. The records show that he used the prize money to buy his mother a cow, a bicycle for himself and he gave one-tenth to his church.

The book was published in the UK in 1934. Today, English copies of *Man of Africa* are very rare, but the Chichewa edition is taught in secondary schools. However, there appears to be little appreciation of its significance as one of sub-Saharan Africa's first published novels.

Malawi's most famous writers made their reputation, and arguably wrote their best work, during the Kamuzu years. Many were poets, like Felix Mnthali, Edison Mpina and Jack Mapanje. Most were victims of Banda's strict censorship laws, where nothing could be published without approval, and many were imprisoned.

Jack Mapanje, renowned across Africa for his poetry, was detained in 1987 and was only freed four years later after international pressure. Today, he lives in the UK. One of his contemporaries, Steve Chimombo, who died in 2015, wrote what is regarded as the best Malawian novel of recent times, *The Wrath of Napolo*. Like Mapanje, his work was heavily influenced by Malawi's oral traditions of myths and legends, where animals and inanimate objects are not always what they seem.

But perhaps the most remarkable story of all is a true one. In 1958, at the approximate age of 18, Legson Kayira left his home in northern Malawi to walk to America. Inspired at school by Booker T Washington's *Up from Slavery* and the story of Abraham Lincoln's rise from poverty to President, he saw 'the land of Lincoln as the place where one literally went to get freedom and independence.' In his autobiography, *I Will Try*, first published in 1965, he tells the story of his two-year journey from his home village in the Chitipa district of Malawi to college in Washington state, then later to Cambridge University in England. Kayira went on to write four novels, which were banned in Malawi, so he could never return to his homeland as he had promised his mother the morning he set off on his epic journey. He died in exile in England in 2012.

Kayira is one of Burton Chirwa's favourite novelists. 'I especially like African writers,' he explains. Burton (46) is the head librarian of Mwaya Community Library, in the Nkhata Bay district. Community libraries are rare in a country where most schools struggle to provide students with even essential textbooks. Burton's was built by a UK charity, Ripple Africa.

The National Library in Lilongwe has a small collection and the Society of Malawi, whose reference library is in the country's oldest building, Mandala

House, has a range of books, many dating from the 1860s and beyond.

'We have 4,588 books here, and 1,836 members,' Burton says, with all the precision of a librarian. The books are mostly novels in English, donated by well-wishers. 'We don't have enough books in Chichewa,' he explains. 'That is one of the reasons why people do not read. They have grown up in areas where there are no books, no libraries. And at home, there are no books.'

English is taught in primary school, but as the majority of students don't finish their primary schooling, it is hardly surprising there is not a culture of reading, or that the writers are largely drawn from the urban middle-class.

Burton is the exception. He has written since he was a teenager. 'I started writing about football matches, then I read books by Chinua Achebe, and I became inspired, so I started writing stories. Right now, I have five short stories, they are in English. I hope to finish a book of them.' He understands why there are relatively few Malawian writers. 'For someone to become a writer, you must read a lot,' he says. 'But because Malawians do not like reading, they do not write. We need libraries like this in every community, so people understand the importance of books and reading.'

While community libraries, stocked with relevant books, could spark a reading revolution in Malawi's rural areas, social media and blogging has spawned a new generation of urban writers.

Nthanda Manduwi (24) is one of the new voices helping to create Malawi's contemporary culture. A tax collector by day, she spends all her spare time 'telling stories of people and places.' She runs an arts collective, promoting young Malawi film-makers, musicians, visual artists and writers. She has published one book, *By the End of Your Teens*, writes screenplays and manages several social media accounts as well as a blog. 'I am peaceable shit-stirrer, I question, and I create things,' she declares on one of her Twitter accounts.

Young women artists like Nthanda are challenging Malawi's conservative culture. Only 30 years ago, under Hastings Banda, women could not wear trousers or dresses that 'went above the knee.' Same-sex relationships are still illegal. And while strides have been made in female equality, Malawi society remains stubbornly patriarchal.

'But our country is changing,' says Nthanda. 'And the creative industries, art, are key to our development. Not only culturally, but economic too.'

When the legendary US soul group, The Temptations, played in the Bingu International Conference Centre in August 2019 to a small crowd of corporate guests and music fans, they were the first major American group to have performed in Malawi. International stars do not include Malawi on their tour programme.

But there is no shortage of home-grown musicians. Lucius Banda, aka The Soldier, is Malawi's best-known contemporary musician. His first album, *Son of a Poor Man,* was released in 1983, and 19 albums later he still pulls in the crowds. The Black Missionaries are the country's biggest band, and their reggae style is much copied by young musicians. Hip-hop artists such as Tay Grin and Maskal are very popular, but gospel music seems to be everyone's favourite soundtrack.

Church services are a joyous weekly event where people dance in the pews and choirs sing gospel, their glorious, unaccompanied voices soaring, it seems, straight up to heaven. Even funerals are a time for singing. Women gather in the *nsiwa* (traditional vigil room), where the body lies for 24 hours before burial, and they sing a constant stream of hymns.

The missionaries who flocked to Malawi in the wake of David Livingstone almost destroyed the country's indigenous music, based on handmade banjos, zithers and drums.

Harry Johnston, Malawi's first British Governor, wrote in 1897:

> There is evidence that before the coming of the white men to these countries, bringing the abominable concertina, panpipes, penny whistle and harmonium, the natives played more musical instruments of their own than they do now, and thought much more of native music.

Indeed, according to Dr John Lwanda, a Lanarkshire GP and expert in the music of his homeland, the missionaries regarded Malawi's music as 'inferior or heathen' and did their best to suppress it. Even today, traditional music is not taught in Malawi schools.

Malawi has never had a major recording industry with big studios and record companies. While popular artists like Lucius Banda and the Black Missionaries can make a living from live shows and do make albums for commercial release, the work of most musicians over the decades was never recorded.

A race is now on to save thousands of tapes from the only outlet that was available for music over many decades, the state broadcaster, MBC. The folk songs, traditional chants, dances and contemporary music of the 1930s up to the '60s were recorded on reel-to-reel tapes in towns and villages all over Malawi. They are now being digitised to save them for future generations.

The sounds of ancient Malawi also influence some contemporary artists, most notably Lazarus Chigwandali, whose potent blend of gospel, punk and traditional folk music has captured the attention of superstars like Madonna. Lazarus (39) has a story to tell, as well as music to make. He is one of 135,000 Malawians with albinism, which means he has no pigment in his skin, eyes or hair. He also has poor eyesight, and skin cancer is a constant threat.

So is kidnapping. In a country where the population glory in their black skin, people with albinism stand out. Their condition is believed to be contagious, and their body parts, bones and skin are highly prized in witchcraft. The United Nations suggest that, in recent years, there have been around 150 cases of people with albinism kidnapped and tortured in Malawi, with at least 18 people murdered.

Lazarus first picked up his canjo – a banjo made from an oil can and bamboo – when he was 15.

'My younger brother, Petro, was ten, and he was more into music than me, so he taught me how to play. Our parents were not educated, they were farmers, so music was something we did to make money, to buy our clothes and things.'

Petro also had albinism, so the brothers found music a useful escape from the sun. 'In the summer, when it got very hot, our skin reaction to the sun was bad, so we had to stay in the shade, we couldn't work in the fields. So we played music to earn a living.

'And our white skin meant we were discriminated against, so rather than go to school, we did music.'

Sadly, Petro died around 1995, when he was only 20, from skin cancer. 'I still miss him,' says Lazarus. 'We wrote music together and we made new music all the time. After he died, I had to start doing it on my own. Now I can write a song within a night. My music is mostly to do with things I come across, our culture, our church, and I write about albinism. My story is different, and people want to listen to songs about it.'

Until 2018, Lazarus was a street busker, playing outside a burger bar in a Lilongwe shopping mall. A chance encounter with a London-based Malawian, Spiwe Zulu, led him to a partnership with Johan and Esau of The Very Best – the successful duo who mix Malawian music with Western dance and hip-hop – and a documentary of his life, which was first shown at New York's Tribeca Film Festival in 2019. Not to mention a friendship with Madonna, who co-produced the film.

'I remember when I first met her in Kasungu. We had dinner together, our whole family, and she danced to my music. It was a dream, because she is one of the most famous musicians on earth, and here I was hanging out with her.'

Lazarus is hopeful his musical career will continue to grow, and not just for his own personal success. 'When I started playing music, I had no idea where it would take me to. I never thought any of this would happen, but music is helping to change perceptions about albinism, it is inspiring those people who didn't have any chances.'

Malawi's national football team, nicknamed the Flames, can be a source of inspiration too. Football is Malawi's national game, some would say obsession, and the Flames are the fragile repository of the population's hopes and dreams.

Gifted Galimoto and his brother, Wales, are typical fans. They live in Minga, a village on the outskirts of Lilongwe, and while both work – Gifted is a hospital security guard and Wales a truck driver – the cost of attending a match is too high for them. So, they listen on the radio or watch at their local bottlestore.

'Everyone follows the national team,' says Gifted. 'When we are doing well, the mood of the whole country is lifted. I still remember in 2010 when the team managed to beat Algeria 3-0 in the Africa Cup of Nations. It was the biggest moment.'

Malawi's top-flight league has 16 teams, but according to Gifted, there are only four major clubs. 'Mostly people follow Nyasa Big Bullets, Mighty Be Forward Wanderers, the Silver Strikers and Civil Service United.'

And everyone has a favourite English side. 'Yes, the Premier League comes first, then La Liga [Spain]. As well as being expensive, there is a lot of violence at our local games, fans fighting each other, even fighting the officials.

'So, we are very comfortable watching the English league in the bottlestore, and we just follow the local results on the radio.'

Children play football from a very early age, and not just boys. Increasingly, women and girls are playing too.

'There are regional leagues, for the north, south and central regions,' explains Wales. 'And the schools have teams too. We watched Minga girls last week, unfortunately they lost. But our women's national side is good. We have beaten Mozambique, Botswana and Uganda recently.'

Malawi's women's netball team is even better. The Queens are currently ranked number six in the world, but the sport has suffered from a lack of proper investment in the past.

Former Queens' captain Emmie Waya-Chongwe told *The Nation* newspaper in 2019 that the team required more resources. She said, 'Apart from not having proper development structures, the Queens lack ample time and adequate funding for preparations ahead of high-profile competitions. The Queens are among the least supported teams on the continent. It is a big psychological torture to expect players to perform to their level best when they have left no food in their homes due to meagre allowances. It is important for stakeholders to think about improving the players' welfare.'

President Chakwera has promised to build a national netball complex, as well as employing 800 sports coaches in schools. Gifted welcomed the move. 'It is better to put money into netball than football. We give a lot of money to football. The last government even wanted to pay billions of *kwacha* for two new stadiums in Blantyre for privately-owned clubs, for the Big Bullets and the Wanderers. It is all about politics. We should be pumping money into netball. They are putting us on the map.'

And sport unites the country in a time when regional and tribal tensions threaten to divide its post-independence stability.

'Most of our best footballers are from the north, but no one worries about that,' says Gifted. 'In everything else you have to think about where you are coming from, but whether you are Chewa or Lomwe or Tumbuka doesn't matter in football. What unites Malawi is football. It is the only thing that unites us.'

SECTION 4

A young democracy

CHAPTER 17

Colonialism to aid

ON THE EVENING of Saturday 23 January 1915, John Chilembwe fought his way into Malawi folklore. The US-educated Baptist preacher led a ferocious attack on one of the large farming estates run by the country's British colonial masters, an act of reckless and violent rebellion by a man now regarded by many as one of the first heroes of African nationalism. Speaking in advance of the rebellion, he urged his supporters to 'strike a blow and die, for our blood will surely mean something at last.' This was the only way, he declared, 'to show the white man that the treatment they are treating our men and women was most bad and we have determined to strike a first and a last blow, and then all die by the heavy storm of the white men's army.'

Magomero estate, like all the large, white-owned plantations that had sprung up in southern Malawi since the 1880s, was dependent on local labour, including thousands of Lomwe refugees who had fled neighbouring Mozambique, where the Portuguese had imposed a harsh forced labour regime.

Malawians were forced to live and work on the European plantations, paying rent – *thangata* – on their modest huts, not with money, but with their labour. The families had no security of tenure, and if any man dared to look for work elsewhere, they faced eviction. The *thangata* system, as it became known, was regarded by many Africans as nothing more than slavery.

Magomero estate was run by Alexander Livingstone Bruce, the grandson of David Livingstone, who only a few decades previously had done much to open up Malawi to the outside world, largely in a spirit of friendship. But it was another family member, William Jervis Livingstone, thought to be a distant relative of the missionary explorer, who was brutally murdered by Chilembwe and his small band of men on that fateful evening, which also saw an assault on the headquarters of the African Lakes Company in Blantyre.

During the Magomero attack, William Livingstone was decapitated, and the following morning John Chilembwe preached a sermon with his victim's head on a pole as a backdrop to his homily. The rebellion was short-lived. Within a fortnight, 36 rebels had been captured, convicted and executed, with many more, including Chilembwe, killed by security forces while on the run. Three Europeans died, including Livingstone, but the legacy of the Chilembwe Rising lives on.

'Chilembwe's was the first Central African resistance to European control which looked to the future, not to the past,' wrote George Shepperson and Thomas Price, authors of the major work on the rising, *Independent African*. It was aimed at 'founding a nation rather... than restoring the fortunes of the tribes,' was their conclusion.

Today, 15 January is a public holiday in Malawi, in honour of John Chilembwe. His face is on the country's largest banknote (MK 2,000), and he is revered as one of the country's few national heroes.

Shocking though the uprising was, the British colonial government studiously ignored Malawian demands for liberation, and it was to be a further 49 years before Malawi finally gained its independence in 1964. The road to freedom was a rocky one, particularly when, in 1953, the British unilaterally created the Federation of the Rhodesias and Nyasaland, which united Malawi – against its people's will – with Zimbabwe and Zambia. The establishment of the hated Federation unleashed a mass political movement, strengthening the Nyasaland African Congress (NAC) which had been established in 1943.

The movement coalesced around Hastings Banda when he returned home from the UK in 1958, and the NAC became the MCP. Angered by the months of civil disobedience that followed, the British colonial government declared a state of emergency on 3 March 1959. Within hours, white troops of the Royal Rhodesian Regiment opened fire on a group of unarmed Malawians in Nkhata Bay. At least 20 people were killed, and many more were injured. In the days following the massacre, another 30 or so Malawians died as the British fought to control the situation. Thousands of Malawians – including Banda and the MCP leadership – were detained without trial.

Faced with a furore in the House of Commons, the British government set up a Commission of Inquiry under the chairmanship of a senior judge, Patrick Devlin. His findings, published only five months after the Nkhata Bay massacre, were devastating. One sentence on the report's first page effectively signed the death knell of both the Federation and colonial rule in Malawi:

> Nyasaland [Malawi] is – no doubt temporarily – a police state, where it is not safe for anyone to express approval of the policies of the Congress

party, to which before 3 March 1959, the vast majority of politically-minded Africans belonged.

Banda was released from prison in April 1960, and the MCP won a decisive victory in national elections held a year later. The British conceded the principle of African majority rule, and on 6 July 1964, Nyasaland became the independent state of Malawi, with Banda its first Prime Minster. In 1966, Malawi became a republic, with Hastings Banda as President. Malawi was now free to develop on its own terms.

But its new government – which quickly descended into an autocracy, with Banda declaring himself life President in 1971 – inherited an economy that was, at best, marginal. Agriculture had not flourished in the 73 years of British rule. There was very little industrialisation, while essential infrastructure – roads, energy and communications – was practically non-existent. Public services, such as health, education and social welfare, were largely provided by religious missions, much as they had been for the preceding decades. It was one of the poorest countries in the world.

Today, in the sixth decade of independence, little has changed. Malawi remains poor and its economy underdeveloped, despite being a peaceful, welcoming nation, free from the bloody conflict that has characterised much of sub-Saharan Africa since the 1960s.

It is a paradox that has puzzled many, including Malawi expert, Dan Banik of the University of Oslo, who wrote in 2018:

> I am often asked… why Malawi is lagging so far behind its neighbours in terms of development and poverty reduction.
>
> Indeed, many Western analysts have even begun to propagate the idea that Malawi is unique. For example, I have heard colleagues state: 'There are developing countries, and then there is Malawi,' implying a sense of hopelessness that characterises the country's development trajectory.
>
> All this points to a paradox: despite peace, political stability and consistent support for democracy, a majority of the country's 17 million people has not witnessed radical improvement in their living standards.

This is despite significant investment from international donors. In 1994, the year that Malawi embraced multi-party democracy, aid reached a peak of 41 per cent of national income. In 2018, it was still around a fifth of Malawi's annual

GDP, at one billion pounds. The biggest single contributor in 2018 was the USA, with £340 million. Malawi's former colonial masters, the British government, spent around £85 million – and the country remains one of the biggest recipients of UK aid relative to its population outside the world's war zones.

City streets are clogged with shiny, off-road vehicles boasting the logos of every conceivable international aid agency, from the World Food Programme to the World Bank. And alongside the bilateral donors and global institutions, thousands of international charities and NGOs, from giants like Oxfam and Save the Children to partnerships between individual churches in Scotland and Malawi, offer support.

But still Malawians remain poor. It is an issue that exercises the mind of some of the country's leading thinkers, people like Henry Chingaipe, a political scientist and economic researcher, who is a member of the advisory panel drawing up the government's new long-term strategy, *National Transformation 2063* – the successor to *Vision 2020*.

'The philosophy of aid is a good thing,' he muses in his Lilongwe office, surrounded by a team of young researchers. 'But the devil is in the detail. The donors in this country, until recently, had been very bad at problem analysis, very, very bad. My reading of the situation is that from the late 1980s to the early 2000s, nearly all the official donors took it on themselves to be agents of the neo-liberal agenda. They did not do very good problem analysis of any of the sectors they wanted to help, they came with ready-made solutions, sort of looking for problems where they could attach their answers.'

Henry is describing the 'Washington Consensus,' a concept adopted by, among others, global institutions such as the IMF and the World Bank, and which formed the basis of aid to low-income countries for nearly two decades. There were ten themes in this theory, hammered out in plush Washington, DC offices, including fiscal policy discipline and the avoidance of large deficits; privatisation in sectors such as energy and water; deregulation of rules that were deemed to restrict competition and competitive exchange rates.

'The donors then were too ideological,' asserts Henry. 'They wanted to deregulate, to privatise, but they did not think about contextualising the application of their ideology. And so, they misled people, particularly our government at the time. President Muluzi was elected in 1994, and he was very receptive to the big donors, he didn't really do much hard thinking. The challenge came when Bingu was elected in 2004, but by then it was too late, we had been set on a particular path, and to change course is not easy.'

President Bingu wa Mutharika came to power in 2004. Malawi had suffered a severe drought in 2001, and in the subsequent famine upwards of 3,000 people died. As Mutharika entered office, another drought was underway. The new President, a former World Bank economist, did what was later described as a 'brilliant' thing, and announced that his government was going to subsidise Malawi's millions of smallholder farmers to buy a small amount of seed and fertiliser.

Writing in *The New York Times* after the President's death in 2012, Professor Jeffrey D Sachs, director of the Earth Institute at Columbia University, praised Mutharika's approach:

> This was to be a smart subsidy. Rather than simply lowering fertiliser prices for all... the government gave a voucher ticket for a small fixed amount of fertiliser and seed per household, thereby disproportionately benefiting the poor.

But, as Professor Sachs goes on to describe, the donors were not happy:

> The donors were aghast, scandalised. Didn't Malawi know that farm subsidies were bad, indeed 'prohibited' by the donor community?
>
> The head of Britain's Malawi assistance programme actually told me that Malawi's peasants (presumably by the millions, though this was only implicit) should leave Malawi for other countries rather than be supported by 'unsustainable' subsidies. I told him that his idea was tantamount to a death sentence for a vast population.

Mutharika ignored donor resistance and used his government's own meagre revenues to introduce a modest subsidy programme. Production doubled within the first season, and Malawi went on to be a food donor when famine struck other countries in the region.

As Professor Sachs pointed out, once the programme began to show success, donors embraced it. Some even began to fund it:

> More importantly, many other African countries began to follow Malawi's lead, and thereby to achieve breakthroughs in farm yields and food production for the first time in their modern history. Malawi had pointed the way to a new Green Revolution for Africa.

He went on to recall a conversation that illustrates the unabashed arrogance of many donors:

Around 2009 there were rumours, fortunately false, that Britain would withdraw its support from the donor programme. I called one of the UK government's lead development advisers. The adviser, a very congenial person, told me in all innocence, 'No, of course we won't stop funding it. The subsidy programme was our idea.'

'I had to laugh,' wrote Sachs. 'Such is the way with success.'

International aid has helped Malawi succeed in the fight to control HIV/AIDS, which, only two decades ago, threatened to overwhelm the country's fragile health service and decimate its economy. It is now one of the few countries or regions on track to meet UNAIDS' '90-90-90' target, with almost everyone with HIV knowing their status, getting treatment and – crucially – being well.

Dan Namarika, former Principal Secretary for Health in the government, was one of the first students to complete their entire medical training in Malawi. 'The reason I chose medicine was because of AIDS,' he told UNAIDS in 2019, 'I couldn't believe there was an illness like this with no cure. I remember the first case in my neighbourhood. It was a lady who succumbed to AIDS after a chronic illness. I have had family members that have died. My long history has been impacted on by AIDS,' he said.

Mr Namarika attributes Malawi's successful response to HIV in large part to high-level political commitment and leadership, as well as considerable investment from donors. He explained, 'Besides policies being made at the highest levels of government, we also have ministries other than health involved, such as the treasury, gender, education and local government; we have civil society, the faith-based sector, cultural leaders and technical assistance from development partners, such as UNAIDS.'

If the fight against AIDS is a successful model of co-operation between donors and Malawi, the relationship is not always as productive.

In an argument over monetary policy during President Mutharika's second term, he again clashed with the country's biggest donors, including the UK.

In 2011, Britain's senior diplomat, Fergus Cochrane-Dyet, was expelled after a leaked document revealed he had described Mutharika as 'becoming ever more autocratic and intolerant of criticism.' In response, the major donors withdrew direct budget support to the government of Malawi, channelling money instead through organisations on the ground, prompting Mutharika to tell them to 'go to hell.' Following his sudden death in April 2012, Malawi's first woman President, Joyce Banda, was appointed as head of state and 'normal relations' were resumed, but the honeymoon did not last long.

When details of the Cashgate scandal erupted in 2013 – which saw £25 million stolen from government coffers in a six-month period – the donors once again withdrew their direct financial support. The World Bank restored direct budget support in 2017, primarily for agriculture, but most donors continue to bypass government departments. 'The UK does not provide direct financial aid to the government of Malawi,' reads a recent UK government briefing note. 'We work with the government, and in support of national priorities, but do not currently plan to provide direct support through government financial systems.'

Donors have found alternative ways to support development. There are sector working groups to co-ordinate aid distribution, and structures such as the World Bank and UNICEF's Education Services Joint Fund ensure that the money is invested on the ground. And the government is still involved in designing programmes.

Henry Chingaipe is convinced that Malawi should be more assertive when it comes to aid. 'Look at Kenya and Ethiopia,' he says. 'They are rising African countries, and Rwanda, even with their democratic deficit. These countries are so clear what they want aid for. They will come to the table, ready to negotiate with the big donors, and they will tell them, "We don't want that, this is what we need." They will actually tell them, "If you can't budge on this one, then keep your money, we don't need it." Our Malawi counterparts are not as assertive. At a negotiating table, they will not put up a case, they will quickly sign up as long as it is bringing money.'

But his frustration lies more with the multilateral institutions and new bilateral players such as China and India. 'Organisations like the World Bank offer mostly loans, only about 25 per cent of their investment is a grant. China is all loans. So is India. For them, international development is a business. They want to make money, that is all. This is a perspective our government has not quickly grasped. A few times, I have had the opportunity to speak truth to power. I have said, you know what, international aid is not a charity, it is an instrument of foreign policy. I tell them, some agencies and countries are in the business of lending money. They are looking for customers. We should always ask ourselves, "Do we need this money?" We are spending on behalf of the next generation.'

As Malawi's population continues to explode – projections suggest it will almost double by 2050 – it is difficult to see how Malawi can become less reliant on aid. The country's tax base is low, its institutions are inefficient, and the haphazard supply of electricity, water and telecommunications hamper growth.

Lewis Kulisewa, a former employee of the British government and an expert in trade and exports, recognises that while aid is important, it is not sustainable in long-term. 'It is a sticky one. When an aid portfolio is controlled by a foreign government who decides how the money is spent, it is a bad thing. We need to do more trade. That is where we need assistance, to help build our capacity in trade and exports. The aid programme continues to focus on consumption, not production.

'I agree that that the HIV/AIDS programme has been a huge success, but that is because the people of Malawi had to engage with it. There was a specific need. But our needs cannot be perpetual if we are to grow as a country. It is like Bingu's fertiliser programme, farmers need to be able to graduate from the scheme. We should be saying, "Help me set up the industries, they will be running after a few years, then you can withdraw." But that needs a leader who can pull in the donors, says here is our plan, and asks which bit can you support.'

Since independence, international aid has probably contributed more to Malawi's development than the 70-odd years of British colonial rule. Under-fives' mortality has improved significantly and life expectancy has increased – the average life expectancy for a woman in at independence in 1964 was only 38 years, but is now 67. And the country has met the challenge of HIV/AIDS with resilience, becoming one of the biggest success stories in sub-Saharan Africa. But extreme poverty persists, and the majority of the population live lives not very different from those of their ancestors when the first Europeans settled along the shores of Lake Malawi.

Farming remains the mainstay of Malawi daily life and its economy, as it was in 1915 when Chilembwe rose up. Yet neither the colonial government nor the international donors have been able to stimulate sufficient growth in agriculture to support Malawi's exploding population and move it towards becoming a middle-income country.

A truth that Bingu wa Mutharika understood only too well. As Professor Sachs points out in his *New York Times* tribute to the late President:

However many missteps he [Mutharika] may have made in the last years, his positive legacy remains historic.

He was the first African President in recent years to face down the donors by insisting that Africa can and must feed itself, especially by helping smallholder farmers gain access to the vital inputs they need to raise their productivity, diversify their production, and escape from poverty.

And as Mutharika himself said in a blistering speech only weeks before he died, '...they [IMF officials] are just arrogant, undermining what a black man can do. They think that because they are Westerners, they know everything.' The history of Malawi since 1859 proves they do not.

CHAPTER 18

Governing Malawi

MALAWI'S FIRST WRITTEN constitution came into force on 6 July 1966, the day it became a fully independent republic, with a President as head of state.

Thirty years later, after it had been re-written to reflect the advent of multi-party democracy, an eminent law professor, Peter Mutharika, welcomed his country's progress towards good governance.

'For a period of 30 years, Malawi has been subjected to a one-party dictatorship led by Dr Hastings Banda,' he continued. 'Supported over the years by the West because of its anti-communist rhetoric, the Banda regime found itself abandoned with the ending of the Cold War and the collapse of apartheid in South Africa. Pressure from internal and external groups led to a referendum on the one-party state in June 1993 which the Banda regime lost and to the first multi-party elections in May 1994 which the regime also lost.'

He went on: 'a major characteristic that underlies the new constitution is an attempt to address the excesses of the Banda regime, while at the same time creating a document that gives a democratically elected government sufficient powers to rebuild the country and to create a new political order.'

That man who wrote these optimistic words went on to become Malawi's fifth President, first elected in 2014, and again in 2019 in an election that was mired in controversy with allegations of rigging and intimidation.

In the immediate aftermath of what became known as the 'Tippex election', because of the liberal use of the correcting fluid by poll workers, many Malawians feared that their young democracy had become forever mired in corruption and tribalism.

Mutharika, younger brother of Malawi's third President, Bingu wa Mutharika, won only 38.6 per cent of the national vote, exposing a national divide along tribal lines that seemed entrenched.

Speaking a few weeks after the disputed election, Lewis Kulisewa, a long-time observer of the Malawi political scene, was despondent.

'The south voted for him, that is why he won,' he explained. 'It is the most populous region and is home to almost all the members of the Lomwe tribe. We are the country's second biggest ethnic group and make up a fifth of Malawi's population.

'Like me, the Mutharikas are Lomwe, and his party, the DPP, is now associated with the Lomwe. Our politics and our problems seemed to be entrenching around tribes. It is not good.'

Twenty-five years after multi-party democracy was successfully introduced to Malawi, it appeared to many that political progress had stalled, mired in patronage and corruption, the country controlled by a generation of old men determined to hang on to power at any cost.

But a new generation of Malawian politicians and civil society leaders were determined to live up the constitution's ideals, even if Mutharika was not. Malawians took to the streets in their thousands in protest, led by the Human Rights Defenders Coalition, while the main opposition parties – the MCP and the United Transformation Party (UTM) – challenged the election result through the courts.

On Monday 3 February 2020, the five High Court judges of a specially convened constitutional court, led by Judge Healey Potani, gave their verdict.

For nearly 12 hours the nation was glued to the radio as the judges took turn to read from their 500-page report. In a clearly argued, legally robust judgement, the court declared that the presidential elections were null and void because of irregularities in the ballot.

They criticised the Malawi Electoral Commission for its failure to oversee the election properly, and in a decision that stunned the country, they announced that there must be a new election for the head of state within 150 days.

They went even further, demanding that the country revert to the 2014 presidential team until the election – keeping in place the incumbent, Arthur Peter Mutharika, and restoring the former Vice President, Saulos Chilima, who had resigned to become leader of a new opposition party, the UTM.

And they instructed parliament to follow Malawi's constitution and amend the Parliamentary and Presidential Elections Act to require future winners to achieve an absolute majority of 50 per cent plus one votes.

News of the historic judgement was greeted with enthusiasm across the world. Writing in the influential Washington-based online newspaper, *The Hill*, award-winning author K Riva Levinson wrote that Malawi was 'now swept up in the most important political revolution to hit Africa in the last two decades.'

She lauded Malawi's 'activist generation' who, she argued, had learned that protecting the integrity of the ballot was crucial in the defence of democracy, and she praised the judiciary which had put 'national interests ahead of narrow political agendas'.

As cheers rang out in every city, town and most of Malawi's villages, the country's political elite struggled to take in the import of the decision.

It 'inaugurates the death of democracy,' declared President Mutharika, who at nearly 80 years old, faced a second gruelling election campaign within a year.

But the majority view was one of hope – and pride that Malawi's young democracy, only 26 years old, was showing a belief in the rule of law that many other, far richer, countries did not.

Speaking to *The Nation* newspaper a few days after the judgement, Professor Danwood Chirwa of the University of Cape Town dismissed Mutharika's comments as 'the words of a person who has benefitted from illegality and now is embarrassed that he's been exposed.' He went on:

> Far from his claim that the judgement inaugurates the death of democracy, the verdict in fact heralds a new dawn – of democratic renewal and of respect for the will of the people.
>
> The system under which he rode to power is deeply flawed, built on a tribal and corrupt substructure. He could be scared that that substructure has been cracked and a new one that is forward-looking, inclusive and progressive has been set in its place.

On Tuesday, 23 June 2020, as the coronavirus pandemic threatened to overwhelm the world, including Malawi, the presidential elections were re-run, with few international observers and much reduced resources. But it was peaceful and well-organised, with a very respectable 65 per cent turnout.

The result was clear. Dr Lazarus Chakwera, leader of the MCP, was elected as the sixth President of the Republic of Malawi with 59 per cent of the popular vote, and his running mate, Dr Saulos Chilima, head of the UTM, became Vice President. Peter Mutharika left the presidential palace for his lakeside home and retirement.

In his first State of the Nation address to the country's parliament, on 4 September 2020, President Chakwera told the assembled MPs that the people were tired of the human causes of their impoverishment.

'They are tired of electing people to public office who use public funds for personal enrichment, not public service. They are tired of a civil service overrun by the rabble of unprofessional cronies who are neither civil nor of service.'

He went on: 'They are tired of Parliament sessions that produce budget after budget to pay for the status quo without changing it. They are tired of hospitals without care, schools without desks, families without food, roads without tar, homes without electricity, communities without water, courts without justice, crops without markets, markets without capital, skills without jobs, jobs without wages and wages without value. They are tired of the biting long winter of economic hibernation.'

The country's parliament, housed in an imposing but soulless structure, purpose-built with a loan from the Chinese government, has passed an impressive list of laws since 1994. Aided by international experts, Malawi's 193 MPs have debated and passed scores of bills on a range of topics, from freedom of information, gender equality and violence against women to decentralisation, fisheries conservation and the registration of births and deaths.

But as President Chakwera observed, little has changed in people's daily lives. A view confirmed by Dr Henry Chingaipe (46), a Cambridge postgraduate, who spends most of his professional life examining the state of governance in his country.

Henry believes there has been a failure to translate well-written laws into effective public services or the creation of the right conditions for sustainable economic growth. And that one of the main reasons why Malawi's politicians have largely failed is their reluctance to embrace new ways of thinking.

'They don't want ideas that challenge conventional wisdom and threaten vested interests,' he says. 'Our main pre-occupation just now is to try and get decision-makers to rely on evidence. At the moment, a lot of public policy decisions that are made are really just based on whims, perceptions and vested interests. Very little of it is driven by data, or analysis on how to address issues in the long-term. Tony Blair had that inclination, to develop evidence-based policies, though on occasion he would distort the evidence,' he laughs. 'That's the politics.'

He also says that the people have a responsibility to help improve their country's governance, as much as the politicians. 'We still have a lot of our people who behave, or their attitude towards political power and authority, is that they are really like subjects, rather than citizens of a modern state. Their understanding of the state is still sub-optimal. Everyone strongly believes the elections are the way to go in choosing leaders. But a large proportion of our people still see the President as their father. He is the country's chief. So, they expect certain things on the basis of that relationship, and I think the expectations engineer and fuel patrimonial politics, patronage. It is not that democracy is bad, it is just that we did not sufficiently build the systems and prepare the culture that is necessary. So, the attitudes towards political power and the state are still stuck in the past. Very much so.'

Visit any Malawi village, where the majority of the people live, and as a stranger, the first person you should meet to explain your business is the village headman. The ethnic groups that lived in Malawi before colonialism each enjoyed their own sophisticated governance structure, based not on multi-party elections and liberal democracy, but on tradition and inheritance.

This form of traditional leadership is still very much alive today, as Dr Boniface Dulani, senior political science lecturer at Chancellor College, described in a recent podcast.

'We have four levels of traditional leadership in Malawi,' he said. 'The bottom level is the village heads. Essentially these are local leaders that govern small areas, mostly, at least in theory, with people belonging to the same ethnic group, a group of clans.'

These headmen are in turn governed by a group village headman and presiding over this collection of local leaders are the Traditional Authorities – the chiefs, as Dr Dulani explained.

'The group village heads… are overseen by a higher level of Traditional Authority (TA), this is the level called chiefs. The word chief, one has to be careful how you use it, as it means exclusively the Traditional Authority.'

The group village head and the TA are no mere ceremonial remnants of Malawi's past, as he set out. 'The two levels, the Traditional Authority and the group village head, also play a quasi-administrative role in the development and local government structures… they identify development needs at the local level and feed those into the government's planning system.'

Malawi has a single tier of local government, comprising four city councils, three municipal and town councils and 28 districts. Each of the 28 districts is sub-divided into Traditional Authorities, each with its own chief or TA. Like Europe's ancient aristocracy, including the British Royal Family, Malawi's Traditional Authorities are hereditary institutions.

'We have different inheritance practices depending on ethnic groups,' pointed out Dr Dulani. 'In patrilineal societies… the traditional leadership is passed on through the male side, whereas in matrilineal societies, the inheritance of traditional leadership is through the matrilineal line.'

And presiding over the three tiers of local leaders – village headman, group village head and TA – are each tribe's paramount chief.

'Technically they are tribal kings, so we have seven,' explained Dr Dulani. 'In our studies, we find a lot of ordinary Malawians don't even know who their paramount chief is and even when they do, when you ask them what the role of the paramount chief is, they really have no clue. This is understandable from the point of view that the paramount chief is someone who is so distant from the normal person. Most deal with their village headmen, their group village heads.'

Or their Traditional Authority. TA Makinjera is the community leader for around 45,000 people in the Salima district, near the southern shores of Lake Malawi.

Sitting in the compound of his home, with a small group of villagers in the background, discussing plans for a new school block, the Yao chief explains his role. 'I was 30 years old when I became the successor to my grandfather. I am the TA from my mother's side, and I have been chief for nearly 30 years.

'Chiefs have an important role to play. We rule a lot of people and our main job is to settle disputes, any quarrels over land, money, fighting or stealing. First, people go to the village headman, then the group village headman, to the senior one. If he does not understand it, they will come to the TA. I am the final person.'

Chief Makinjera, like all traditional leaders, is a quasi-government employee. 'I get an honorarium, it is about MK 35,000 (£37) every month, group headmen get around MK 5,000 (£5), the village heads MK 2,500.'

He enjoys his role, but his judgement is not always welcomed, as he explains. 'Some decisions are challenging, and some people will say you have not done well, so I tell them to go to the court or the council to seek a judgement.'

He adds, with a smile, 'Usually they will find the council or court's decision is the same as I have judged. I work closely with the courts, the council and the police. For example, when someone has stolen maize or something, we don't deal with that – they are sent to the police. Or if someone has beaten someone, we don't take that case, it goes the police and the court. Any case that involves blood.'

As well as deciding disputes, chiefs will agree local by-laws, on everything from child marriage to fish conservation. TA Makinjera is currently working with his fellow chiefs on a by-law to restrict the hours that local video shops can show films.

'We want to close the day shows, so the children go to school instead of watching films,' he says, 'And set a time when they finish at night, around ten o'clock. Long ago, chiefs would decide the local laws themselves, but now because of this democracy, we send them to the council, where the law is approved and comes back to my Traditional Authority as a by-law.'

While Dr Dulani recognises the important role traditional leaders continue to play in Malawi's civic life and its development, he fears that these ancient structures damage contemporary democracy.

'The state feels less pressured to provide services that it is supposed to provide because the traditional leadership takes on that role. If you look at the justice system, courts are far apart in this country and very remote to most ordinary people. Even when people go to these courts... they are considered to be alien... they are not the kind of concepts of justice that most ordinary people would have.

'The traditional leaders practise and offer a kind of justice that makes sense to an ordinary person. Unfortunately, it also means that the ordinary people don't have to put any pressure on government to provide the services, because they are already there, at least in some form.'

But it is the hereditary nature of Malawi's community governance that he finds most problematic. 'Traditional leadership is by and large hereditary, and I think our political leaders have, over time, tried to adopt some of the traditional leadership characteristics so that people look at them as these leaders.'

He suggests that because chiefs have their role for life, some politicians believe that they too should be able to stay in office until they die, particularly, as Henry Chingaipe points out, an elected head of state is often seen as a country's chief.

Dr Dulani believes this attempt to blend tradition with contemporary forms of leadership has a very negative effect on the development of democracy. 'If democracy has to grow, then the traditional leadership might have to die,' he suggests, provocatively.

Maggie Banda (46), one of Malawi's leading civil society figures, whose NGO, WOLREC, campaigns for legal, social and economic justice for poor women, believes that corruption, not chiefs, is one of the biggest threats to Malawi's nascent democracy and its development.

'Corruption has got worse since multi-party democracy,' she says. 'It is really difficult for people to get services from government. Every public service that people need is a hassle. There are even allegations that when people go to government hospitals, sometimes they are told to pay something so that they can be assisted.

'When there are allegations of government ministers or public officials being involved in corrupt practices, we should see something happening. The government should be able to say what they are doing about it. They should institute an investigation, come up with a report and tell us, the nation, that we have investigated the allegations, and this is what we have found. Then the public would be able to judge correctly whether there was corruption or not, but hiding everything, the names, what they were involved in, it raises a lot of suspicions.'

Malawi's Anti-Corruption Bureau (ACB), established by an act of parliament in 1995, is mandated to prevent and investigate corruption, but with its limited resources it has struggled to make an impact.

Speaking at an event to mark the 2019 International Anti-Corruption Day, ACB Director, Reyneck Matemba, said that as well as funding challenges, the bureau does not receive enough support from the public.

'We are aware that some members of the public have stopped tipping us on suspected cases of corruption because the public perception is that ACB drags its feet to investigate and conclude cases. Ideally, to meet public expectations and send proper warnings to would-be perpetrators, we need to expedite investigations, followed by proper court processes which should end in conviction. That way, Malawians would be convinced that we are fulfilling our duties,' he said.

Henry Chingaipe agrees that corruption is a major threat to Malawi's development. 'I know of no public sector in the world that has been as wasteful as ours. Up to one-third – and this is a very conservative estimate by the Auditor General – 33 per cent of the national budget was "wasted" through theft and corruption.'

He is convinced that, until Chakwera's election, there was a conspiracy among senior figures in the government to maintain a 'slush fund' of national resources, ripe for plunder, as he explains. 'The figures the Finance Minister used for government revenue were always estimates and these were not based on the actual tax collection of recent years. The Auditor General audits government expenditure, but not revenue. So, for example, the story of Cashgate, our biggest scandal in recent years, is this. In one quarter, for example, the Finance Minister estimates he needs MK 50 billion. The Malawi Revenue Authority –

the tax agency – delivers MK 58 billion. What does the government's Budget Director do? He says, "Okay, we have the money for this quarter, and there is eight billion left over." And who knows about this eight billion?

'To get the money out without a vote [in Parliament], the Budget Director looks at the tourism department. It is funded for the month, so he transfers MK four billion to an accomplice in tourism. It is processed, cheques made out, and then the transaction deleted. They take the cheques to the Reserve Bank and cash them.

'The case goes to court. What does the accountant for the tourism department tell you? "M'Lud, I was funded my full amount, and this is my expenditure report. I can testify that my money was never stolen. I got as requested. I spent as mandated." This is your key witness, and he is saying no money was stolen. Do you still have a case? You don't. That was Cashgate.'

The scandal, which broke in 2013, was the biggest in Malawi's history, and implicated senior politicians, civil servants, even the then-President, Joyce Banda. The Budget Director, Paul Mphwiyo, survived an attempted assassination. Ralph Kasambara, a former Attorney General and adviser to Joyce Banda, was sentenced to 13 years in prison for his part in the murder plot. He is currently free 'on bail.'

Latest estimates suggest that up to £213 million has been systematically looted from the people of Malawi by politicians and civil servants over a much longer period than just the Cashgate episode, where an estimated £25 million was stolen in just six months. The scandal destroyed what little trust citizens had in their political elite. People will shrug and say, 'They are all corrupt, look at Cashgate,' and more recent events suggest politicians and civil servants had not learned the hard lessons of 2013. In the summer of 2019, an inquiry by the Ombudsman, Martha Chizuma, found the Ministry of Agriculture and Ministry of Finance guilty of maladministration and mis-procurement. The report revealed that the government had borrowed £38 million from India to buy farm machinery for 'poor farmers.'

Only a third of the equipment was distributed to smallholders, with the majority of tractors and maize machines sold at rock bottom prices to 'powerful and influential people within government and political parties.' The two civil servants in charge issued a public statement 'apologising' for the debacle, and were later charged, not with corruption, but for making the apology too late.

And, in what appeared to be a blatant misuse of government money in November 2019, the then Vice President, Everton Chimulirenji, claimed MK

100 million (£105,000) for a month's 'urgent expenses'. Newspaper reports suggested he used some of the money to pay for the Dubai honeymoon of the Ngoni King, Inkosi Gomani. To date he has escaped censure.

Little wonder then that most Malawians agree with Maggie Banda and Henry Chingaipe that corruption is damaging Malawi's future. An Afrobarometer survey, published in 2019, showed that 72 per cent of Malawians thought corruption had got worse, much higher than the African average of 55 per cent. The police were seen as the most corrupt institution, with the President next. Less than half thought that ordinary Malawians could make a difference in fighting corruption, with most fearing retaliation if they reported it.

But Henry Chingaipe believes there is another, less obvious, reason why Malawi's progress stalled.

'The tragedy of this country is the missing middle,' he says. 'Look at the private sector. We have a few big companies, then people eking out a living as vendors. There is very little in-between. We don't have the small to medium size enterprises. In society in general, we have a very tiny middle-class and millions of poor people. We, the educated middle-class, stand guilty in this country for the kind of democracy we have, and the level of economic development we have. We have failed this country.'

He cites water tanks, solar power and private education and health care as symptoms of a selfishness that lets the state off the hook. 'What are we, the middle-class, doing? We are becoming states in our own right. We provide for ourselves the goods and services the state should be providing. I am sending my children to a private school because I cannot send them to a public school. I have installed a water tank. Blackouts? Everyone is running back-up solar power. The middle-class is happy because they have been able to take care of themselves and they don't see the people in the villages. And so it is very easy for the political parties. They say, "Let's just deal with the masses, we will give them fertiliser and maize for their vote." Those of us with ideas and the agency to challenge the status quo and turn this thing around are complicit.'

And he cites the riots of 2011, which saw 19 people killed on one terrible July day, as proof of his theory. 'The main reason why everyone rose against the government, and effectively killed the President [Bingu wa Mutharika] with pressure, was because there was no fuel. The middle-class needs fuel to get around. So, they went up in arms and the government was jolted into action. When the middle-class gets angry, the government acts.'

But Henry remains resolutely optimistic about governance in his country.

'The old men are going,' he says. 'Perhaps it's a blessing in disguise, but there had been very little assimilation of younger people, my generation, into politics. The old men kept us away, but now they are going, we can maybe get back on track.'

CHAPTER 19

Justice for all?

ALEXANDER GALIMOTO REMEMBERS every detail of Wednesday 23 January 2019.

'I wasn't feeling too well when I woke, but I was less than two months into my new job, so I had to go.'

Alexander (27) was the administrator at a private health clinic in Lilongwe's Area 44, an attractive residential suburb. After years of study, interrupted by a lack of funds and depression, he was relieved to have found a salaried position, even such a relatively junior one.

'But I was the most senior person there that day,' he recalls. 'The owner, a Malawi Indian, was in hospital. It is a small clinic, only three years old. As soon as I got into work, I was told some visitors wanted to see me. I didn't know then that they were police, they didn't have a uniform. We had a good chat, but I was quite busy, they were taking my time, but I had to be polite.'

Then his life shattered. 'Boom, they said, "We have a search warrant. What are you keeping in your dispensary, your stores?" I was pretty new, everything was in place, so I was like, no problem, do your job. They started to look and then found out we had malaria drugs, some syringes they suspected had been stolen from public hospitals. We also had some gloves.

'They said I should explain how these things got here. I said, "I'm just new, I haven't acquainted myself with how everything got here." But they didn't care. They said, "You are the senior person, you should be able to explain."

'I said we should look in the files to see what has papers and what has not. There were a lot of papers, it took a lot of time and I tried to make them wait so that we were done looking. They were getting impatient, so they said let's go to the station. I didn't like it, we argued a bit, but police being police, they tried to show some force, authority, so we went.'

What Alexander did not know at the time was that the officers were part of an operation led by Malawi's Drug Theft Investigations Unit. Estimates suggest that the country's public health service loses 40 per cent of its drugs through theft.

'I remember I wasn't putting on a top, it was a cold day, I was trying to tell them I wasn't feeling alright, they didn't care. They got me in a cell. It was already late, around 4.00pm or 5.00pm, so people were knocking off, nothing would get done that day. I stayed that night in the police cell.

'Morning came, that was my first time sleeping in a police cell, it was hell. I wasn't thinking about sleeping without a blanket. It was the thought that I'm in police custody that was killing me. I never slept.'

His second day in police custody passed by slowly.

'They called us for statements for the police reports and told me around ten in the morning that I was going home today. I was hopeful. I didn't stress. I was innocent, I hadn't committed any crime, I will be let go. I waited, and by the time it was 2.30 in the afternoon, I was stressing. The reality hit me. I slept there a second night.'

On Friday morning, his brother, Gifted, arrived to tell him that he was going to court, that the family had borrowed money for a lawyer, and that he would get bail.

'Whatever happens in this case, it will happen from home,' Alexander remembers Gifted telling him. 'Then we get to the court somewhere around 1.30 and the magistrate wasn't there. I just felt sick.'

Alexander's nightmare was about to get much worse. As he had made a court appearance, even in the absence of the magistrate – who had, unexpectedly, taken Friday afternoon off – he could not go back to the police cell. He was going to spend the weekend on remand in Lilongwe's notorious Maula Prison.

Maula Prison is infamous across the world. A life size mural of its crowded conditions covers one wall of the Legacy Museum in Montgomery, Alabama, which honours the 4,000 African Americans who were victims of lynching. The Maula mural is used to show how little conditions for black prisoners have changed since slavery.

Malawi's prisons are overcrowded. The official capacity of the system is 7,000, but the number of inmates is at least double that figure. A 2018 survey by the Inspectorate of Prisons revealed that at the time of the report, Maula Prison had 3,026 inmates. It was built 50 years ago to house 480 men. The number of detainees on remand, or pre-trial, has dropped from nearly one-third in 2005 to 18 per cent in 2019, thanks largely to temporary camp courts which hear cases around the country. But this welcome progress was no consolation to Alexander as he prepared to spend his first night on a concrete floor, sleeping next to strangers.

'I remember I almost cried that day,' he says. 'Maula Prison is seen as the worst place to ever be at – there are criminals, murderers, people who've done drugs, done the worst. Of course, there are innocent people there, but most of them are people who have done the worst. I go there knowing it's Friday, and there's Saturday, Sunday, until Monday…' he trails off. Some memories are just too painful.

'Monday came, it was going to be okay, I thought, surely the magistrate is fine now. But around 3.00pm, I was told the magistrate isn't feeling alright again. It was then I stopped expecting anything. I remember feeling on the Tuesday morning, nearly a week after the police came to the clinic, to stop hoping. I was cool, not expecting anything, whatever happens let it happen. I never expected this in my life, ever.'

Alexander was released six days after he was arrested for a crime he did not commit. Wesley Namasala, the lawyer Alexander's family hired to help him navigate his way through Malawi's criminal justice system, shakes his head in frustration. 'That is how it is here in Malawi,' he says.

Wesley set up his own firm, Wilberforce Attorneys, in 2017. 'I want my firm to grow, so I am happy to do criminal law, though some firms will do only corporate work.

'Building your reputation is key. People need a good lawyer, not a thief. Here there are people who are very successful lawyers, but only because of their corrupt ways. Before certain magistrates, where the corruption mostly is, you know you have lost as soon as you see them, they are attached to certain law firms. You know you will have to appeal to a higher court. Mostly, these kind of lawyers are politically connected, but what happens when the government changes?'

Wesley says the other big challenge facing Malawi's judicial system is a lack of personnel, which in itself leads to corruption. 'Until recently, we didn't have the required number of High Court judges. Here in Lilongwe we only had five judges, they were dealing with all matters pertaining to the entire central region [7.5 million people]. So all the criminal appeals from Ntcheu, from Kasungu, from Mchinji, came here.

'It was a huge burden on these five judges, and it gave room to corruption. If you filed a document to get a date for an appeal, some people would give something to court officials to get to the top of the pile. It was a challenge, there must be political will to tackle it. Corruption happens in every country, but here it is everywhere. These things get reported in the newspaper, but nothing gets done. The corruption becomes normal. Everyday.'

Wesley's shrugged acceptance of corruption within the judicial system is echoed by Alexander's brother, Gifted, himself a victim of false allegations of theft several years ago.

'The drugs in Alexander's case were worth MK 8,000 (£8.50). If he had offered the two officers MK 10,000, they would have left him alone. That is how it works,' he says matter-of-factly.

Maggie Banda, whose NGO offers, among other services, free legal advice and representation to women, is as pessimistic about Malawi's justice system as Wesley and Gifted.

'Yes, there are allegations of corruption. Even the police, in the courts,' she says. 'Malawi is a mess indeed, because the court, the judicial system is ideally supposed to be the one corruption free, the one still standing proud. But now you find that even the court system itself cannot be trusted. It is a major concern, because you find that this is the last resort for people seeking justice. Citizens think, "I can go to court and get justice," but if the court is also part and parcel of the corrupt system, then there is no justice here. There is no hope.'

Maggie Banda's organisation, which she founded in 2006, was set up to help women find their way round a legal system described by the former EU Ambassador to Malawi, Marchel Gerrmann, as too 'formal and complex'.

'The EU notes with concern that justice is very expensive in Malawi and therefore out of reach for many Malawians, who are poor, disadvantaged, hence vulnerable,' he said at the 2018 official launch of the Chilungamo Project, a joint programme between the EU and Malawi's Justice Ministry, which runs to 2024.

Chilungamo means justice in Chichewa, and the project, worth MK 38 billion (£41 million), hopes to improve the judicial system through interventions that will reduce prison overcrowding, retrieve stolen assets and improve access to justice for the most vulnerable citizens.

'It is much needed,' says Maggie Banda. 'The main reason I set up WOLREC was because I thought there was a missing element in terms of access to justice for women and girls. I had been working in an organisation that offered legal aid for women, but then the organisation stopped doing that, because they thought it was more interesting to work on advocacy issues rather than legal aid provision.

'I felt there was a gap, because women would come to the office and would just be told to go to the government's legal aid office – now called the Legal Aid Bureau. They wouldn't really get the required service or advice because legal aid here is understaffed and under-resourced. In the end, I saw women had nowhere to go to access justice.

'We started off in that direction, saying we were providing legal aid and advice. But soon I discovered that the women coming to us also had financial problems. For example, if a woman was undergoing a divorce, then the next issue was about survival. There was a need to address a need for financial justice for women. Now we look at justice from three angles: legal justice, social justice and economic justice.'

Maggie's organisation – which is supported by a range of international donors, including Dan Church Aid, the Royal Norwegian Embassy and the UK – offers a lifeline to women at their most vulnerable.

'We receive a range of cases, but the most common ones are domestic violence, divorce, issues of child maintenance.'

More than a third of women in Malawi experience physical or sexual violence. Nearly half of girls (42 per cent) will marry before they are 18, and Malawi ranks 116 out of 153 countries listed in the World Economic Forum's 2020 *Global Gender Gap Report*.

'Things have improved since 2006, when I set up WOLREC,' says Maggie. 'More and more women are becoming knowledgeable. They are more aware about the laws that exist to protect them.'

But while she acknowledges that Malawi now has the legislative framework in place to secure gender equality and justice for women, she insists the outlook is not particularly positive. 'It is not good. The government says they have come up with laws, and yes there are laws, there are so many gender-related laws, but they are not being implemented. And we still have harmful social and cultural practices, where people hide behind culture and tradition to violate women's rights. There was an attempt to come up with an HIV/AIDS Act where they were going to address the issues of social and cultural practices, but up to now it has not been enacted. We have the Gender Equality Act of course, that prohibits harmful practices, but again, implementation has been poor.'

She goes on. 'There is also the Prevention of Domestic Violence Act and the Deceased Estates and Inheritance Act, all these progressive pieces of legislation. Even our constitution talks about the right of women to live a violence-free life, but implementation remains a challenge. Sometimes it seems there is no political will for change, because even the line ministry that is supposed to be advancing issues of gender in Malawi is heavily under-resourced.'

And she points to the recent allegations of rape by the police during the 2019 post-election demonstrations. A report by the NGO-Gender Coordination Network (NGO-GCN) claimed that police officers in Lilongwe had 'raped women, defiled self-boarding girl students, tortured people and looted private property.'

'There is so much impunity,' says Maggie Banda. 'People can do anything and get away with it. If there was political will at the highest level, we would by now [November 2019] see the perpetrators being brought to book. But the government has not spoken, the President himself has not spoken, which I find very disturbing. He is a UN 'He for She' champion. He should have come out and condemned the violence. But nothing. You wonder if they are really interested in equality, in justice.'

There seems to be very little political will to make life easier for Malawi's LGBT community either. The country's penal code prohibits 'carnal knowledge against the order of nature' and acts of 'gross indecency.'

Men in a same-sex relationship risk up to 14 years in prison and women five years, but since 2012, when President Joyce Banda suspended – not repealed – the laws that criminalised homosexuality, very few people have been arrested.

In 2016, however, a High Court order suspended the moratorium, pending a judicial review by Malawi's Constitutional Court. That review has still to take place, and according to a 2018 report by the global NGO, Human Rights Watch, the uncertainty has encouraged 'private individuals to attack LGBT people with impunity, while health providers frequently discriminate against them on the grounds of sexual orientation.'

It goes on to say that:

Lesbian, gay, bisexual and transgender (LGBT) people face routine violence and discrimination in almost all aspects of their daily lives.

Police often physically assault, arbitrarily arrest and detain them, sometimes without due process or a legal basis, at other times as punishment for simply exercising basic rights, including seeking treatment in health institutions.

Beatrice Mateyo, a gender activist, told France 24 recently that the government tends to ignore the issue. And she says her country's religious conservatism has played a major role in the continued hostility to the gay community.

> We are seen as a God-fearing nation, so society tends to skew towards religion where you are seen as a sinner... And if you are of a different sexuality, then you are perceived as a sinner... [People] will rather remain in the closet – hidden.

Human rights are front and centre in Malawi's 1994 constitution. It sets out commitments on every aspect of life, from personal freedoms to property, culture and language, equality and the rights of women.

'Every person shall have a right to recognition as a person before the law... have access to any court of law... the right to an effective remedy by a court of law,' promises the constitution.

Malawi's judiciary was established in 1902, when the British colonial government set up the High Court, modelled on the British system. Even today, judges will wear wigs like their counterparts in the UK. The Supreme Court of Appeal is the country's highest appellate court, with the High Court next in line. Then come the 'subordinate' courts: Child Justice, Industrial Relations and a network of magistrate courts. Since 2011, there has been legislation in place to establish a network of local courts to handle minor disputes, some of which are currently settled by chiefs.

The introduction of these innocuous sounding tribunals faced significant opposition, however, as there were fears that they were similar to the traditional courts introduced by Hastings Banda during his dictatorship. Banda used his local justice network to punish political opponents, and immediately after the introduction of multi-party democracy, the much-hated local courts were suspended.

The new government seems determined to make progress in reforming the judiciary and rooting out corruption. President Chakwera, in his first State of the Nation address, said, 'The Executive is too powerful, the judiciary too underfunded, the Legislature is too subservient, and all three are too corrupt. That is what Malawians elected me to correct'.

And despite limited resources he has promised, among other reforms, to increase the number of High Court judges, establish a Probate and Family Division as well as a Financial Crimes one, and he set a goal of having a Senior Resident Magistrate in all 28 districts by 2022.

Eighteen months after his arrest and weekend of hell in Maula Prison, Alexander Galimoto still has the threat of prosecution hanging over him.

'It is still there,' he says. 'I had to report for bail every Monday, and after about 11 times, the guy told me I could come once every two weeks. Then he told me, you are being honest, coming every time, so you can come once a month. I still go once in a month. I can choose the day I want.'

Alexander was arrested by officers taking part in a one-off operation to highlight the government's commitment to tackling drug pilferage, and so it now seems he may never find justice.

'I have been told that now the project is over, the Malawi government can't fund these people, with transport allowances, to come to the court,' he explains. 'Someone told me the only time I will get back to the court to prove my innocence is if they are doing this project again. So maybe next year? I don't know what will happen.'

His brush with Malawi's under-resourced justice system has left him feeling differently about his country.

'It made me learn a couple of things,' he says. 'Firstly, corruption is everywhere. I saw it when I got to the cell, I saw it when I got to Maula, I saw it everywhere. Things can't be made better easily, because everybody is corrupt. We were not allowed to have phones in the police cell, but people had phones. How do they get them? Police officers come and give them the phones, they are paid to do that. Even at Maula, people had phones – how can it be possible? Because they are conniving with police officers, prison warders, they bring them – anything they need is possible.'

And he no longer has faith in the justice system. 'I don't trust the police anymore. I used to think when I had problems, I will call the police and they will help me out, but you can't trust anyone. The courts, the same thing.

'The day I got into the cell, there were some other people with a similar case. I slept there but they got out. I asked what happened – they paid some magistrates, it happens everywhere. They are all rotten. The police, the courts, we trust them to protect people, they are trusted to enforce justice, but they don't do any of that. It is very sad.'

CHAPTER 20

Village to city life

'PEOPLE USED TO eat together. In our language, Tonga, we call it *mphala*. But that thing of cooking together and then eating together has completely ended,' says Chimwaza Phiri.

At 43, he was born after independence and before multi-party democracy. The village way of life in Malawi has certainly changed, but only slowly. Many aspects of his childhood were not much different to that of his grandparents, and their parents before them. Some parts of his five children's lives, though, are much more comfortable.

'When the Europeans came, there was no money, no cash. Very few people went to school. Communication, travelling far was hard. Even when I was a child no one drank tea, now everyone does,' he says. 'The village life my grandparents and parents had was dependent on going to the farm, to grow food to eat. As long as there was *nsima* at home, then we were fine.'

Eighty-four per cent of Malawi's 18 million population live in villages. These small settlements of a few hundred people are scattered far and wide across Malawi. Each village is self-contained but connected to their neighbouring communities through family and tribal links. A sophisticated governance structure, which echoes the tribal governments of the past, links each village headman with their chief, the TA. And classroom blocks, one-room churches or mosques, or the shade of an acacia tree, provide a meeting place for the community. The village is the heart of Malawi life. It is where everyone came from and where everyone hopes to be buried.

To reach some villages, you have to drive two hours through the bush in a 4x4. Others are hidden high up in the mountain ranges of the north and the south-east. The lakeshore is home to hundreds of thousands of people, their villages nestling beside tropical beaches. There are villages on the edge of towns and cities, and as urban migration increases, some of these will become slums. And there are hundreds of villages right beside the main tarmac roads that connect the country.

Chimwaza, like his mother before him and her mother, was born in Msondozi village, close to the small town of Chintheche, in the Nkhata Bay district of northern Malawi. He is lucky. He has a full-time, paid job as a caretaker for two holiday homes owned by a Blantyre family. Most people work only in the informal economy, growing crops on their farms – which are often smaller than a hectare – or fishing in the lake. Sometimes both.

'The biggest change I have seen is in our houses,' offers Chimwaza. 'Now you can see there are many houses with iron corrugated roofs. They even have cement on the floor, though most don't have any paint or plaster inside.

'But when I was younger, the houses were built with fresh bricks, without burning them. Most were like that. In fact, trees were used to build houses. A man would cut straight poles and make a wall, divide rooms, make a window, design it like a house using the poles. These houses could not be very big. One or two rooms. At that time, the duties of a woman were to collect the moulding soil to plaster the poles, and because many people could not afford to buy cement, the floor was soil. The roof was grass. It was the duty of the woman also to collect the grass.

'People still live in houses like that. In our village, there is a small one with a grass roof and it was built ten years ago, they do last. But when people get money, they spend it on building a house with burnt bricks and iron sheet roofs. We are changing from the old life to the new one.'

The change from the 19th century to the 21st is evident by the occasional satellite dish that sits proudly atop a corrugated roof, but hardly anyone is able to power South African cable television or a fridge. Only three per cent of rural households have electricity, compared to nearly half (42 per cent) in the urban areas.

And just one in 200 village households has a flushing toilet. Chimwaza laughs, 'Yes, half our community has a toilet – I mean a pit latrine – there is another half that does not. They have to go into the bush. The health people try and educate people about that, but it is a big problem.'

So much so that gaudily painted billboards boasting, 'No open defecation here' are scattered along the Lakeshore Road. These are put up by international charities, proud of their achievement.

'Yes, I have seen,' says Chimwaza. 'But when you live in a village where the soil is really sandy, you cannot dig a deep hole for a toilet, so you have to use an open space.

'Where I stay, almost everyone has a toilet. A toilet will last about five years, if you dig it deeper, six or more feet. The hole is covered with trees, then more soil, but the termites will eat the trees, and after some time you will find it has collapsed. And there is a small wall to keep it private. When it is full, I will cover it, and dig another one.'

Food is cooked outside, on traditional open fires made with three stones. Despite efforts to persuade women to use mud stoves to protect both Malawi's dwindling forests and the women's health, the majority of people use the same method to cook *nsima* as their great-grandmother did.

But as Chimwaza says, extended families no longer eat together, at least in his village. 'Now it is only two homes who do that,' he says. 'In most of the houses, it is just the parents and the children eating together. We have become more like white people,' he laughs. 'We still share food, salt, whatever, but everyone eating together encouraged people to become very lazy. Or greedy. A greedy person would get a good fish, a *kampango* [catfish] from the lake, tell his wife to cook it, and keep it in the house. Then they would just cook cassava leaves for the relish and take that to the *mphala* [communal meal]. So it is stopping now.'

Chimwaza is pessimistic about the future of village life. He may be one of the few in his village to have running water, and his children enjoy free primary education, but he says life is much worse than when he was young.

'Village life is breaking down. Now it is just families depending on their own. And if there is a weakness in the family, it means everything will be weak. The village. And the country.'

Alexander Mwakikunga, the former Mayor of Mzuzu, was brought up in a village in the Karonga district, but moved to the capital city, Lilongwe, in 1986 to study. Six years later, he moved back north, where he has stayed.

He has no sentimental memories of village life. 'I lived in the village in my childhood, and the town as an adult. I am the product of both lives.

'Life in the village is hell. Even in terms of basic needs, if you are sick, you first want to go to a hospital, but you have to go to a dispensary. At the dispensary, the only person who is there is the health service assistant who often doesn't even know the basic information about medicine. He will just say, "This is malaria," and give you Panadol. He has not done the tests. He just says, "You are feeling warm, it must be malaria." And sometimes he doesn't even have Panadol and says you should go and buy this from the local shops.

'As for education, in the villages the education standards are very low.

Here, in the city, you can go to a private primary or secondary school – even the government primary schools in town are much better, because the teachers are better.'

But he acknowledges that life in a city is just as difficult as the village if you are poor.

'Yes, I will take both as challenges,' he agrees. 'If you are poor and live in the town, it is hell. If you are staying in the village and you are poor, your life is also hell. At least in town, somebody might give you some piece work and you earn some little money, if you are hard-working that is. In the village, nobody is going to give you some piece work. But at least 90 per cent of the people in the village own some land, so they can eat. If you live in the town, the chances are you might not have the land, so you need to find work to find money.'

The most recent Household Survey supports Alexander's assertion that village life is tougher than urban living. Nearly a third (32 per cent) of urban teenagers enrolled in secondary school in 2017, compared to only 11 per cent of rural children. Village households are three times more likely to experience a malaria-related death, and women in rural areas have an average of 4.7 children, against three for urban women. And 69 per cent of villagers say their food consumption is inadequate, with 59 per cent claiming their healthcare is sub-standard too. Only one-third (35 per cent) of city and town dwellers think their health care is poor, while more than half (58 per cent) have plenty to eat.

Across the world, urbanisation is happening at a phenomenal rate. According to UN Habitat, half the world's population now lives in cities, and this is projected to increase to two-thirds by 2050. The share of Malawi's population living in urban areas has progressively increased, from six per cent in 1964 to 16 per cent (2.8 million people) today. According to the government's long-awaited urban policy document, published in April 2019, Malawi has been one of the most rapidly urbanising countries in the world. And while the rate of growth is expected to slow down, the UN forecasts that the country will be one of the top ten fastest urbanising countries from 2018 to 2050.

Malawi's four main cities – Mzuzu, Blantyre, Zomba and the capital, Lilongwe – certainly have a long way to go before they are teeming metropolises like Addis Ababa or Nairobi, but they are all experiencing significant growth and migration from the rural areas. The fastest growing city is Mzuzu in the north, an urban centre that did not even exist 70 years ago. It was established by the British Colonial Development Corporation (CDC) after it decided to develop tung tree plantations in the nearby Viphya grasslands. Tung oil was a quick-drying agent used in paint and was much in demand after the Second World War.

Writing in *The Society of Malawi Journal*, Sir Cosmo Haskard, a former District Commissioner in the colonial administration, describes the city's beginnings in 1949:

> A small township was laid out at Mzuzu by the CDC with a substantial headquarters office block at the crossroads in the centre of the settlement.
>
> Workshops, stores and housing were constructed. An airstrip was cut out of the woodland alongside a new road to Ekwendeni, and Beaver aircraft of Central African Airways inaugurated a service which linked Mzuzu several days a week to the rest of Nyasaland [Malawi].

Today, the city has a population of at least 220,000, with around 60 per cent living in 'unplanned settlements' without proper access to water, sanitation or power. A profile of the city by UN Habitat points to economic challenges such as an overly high dependence on public sector jobs and small-scale trading activities, inadequate infrastructure for small and medium enterprises (SMEs), and weak land-use planning and regulations. The City Council is responsible for Mzuzu's physical planning and economic development, as well the provision of local services such as water, sanitation and refuse collection.

But even the government acknowledges that councils do not have the resources to manage their cities properly. The urban policy document points out that local government faces challenges that:

> relate to human resources (quantity and quality of relevant personnel), low level of financial resources at the local government level and weak urban finance mechanisms/institutions that will support infrastructure investment.
>
> As a result, there is a mismatch between the rate of urban population growth and infrastructure and service provision.

Or, as Alexander Mwakikunga points out, 'it sometimes feels impossible. The budget in 2019 is around MK 2.9 billion (£3 million), but it is just not enough. We are a growing city, people come from the rural areas, looking for white collar jobs in town. And we now have a branch of the Reserve Bank,

Auction Holdings [a tobacco trading company], and of course the University of Mzuzu, so it is a young population too.'

Alexander, who was mayor from 2017 to 2019, says one of the biggest challenges is managing land-use. 'We do have a structure plan, so if you want to build a house you are supposed to prepare drawings for the council and get them approved by the Planning and Development Committee. Many people ignore that, particularly in the high-density areas. There are a lot of squatters, people will just build shacks to live in. The city has changed, it is much busier, but that has come at a price. Crime has gone up, and the high-density areas are a mess.'

Mzuzu City Council's revenue comes from a range of sources, including an annual grant from central government, service charges and local property taxes, or rates. But, as Alexander explains, the relationship between taxpayers and the council is often fraught. 'The business community drive the city and the council's economy, so it is imperative that we are close to them, but unfortunately we didn't serve them well, so they were not as co-operative as they might have been. It is the same with property owners. We are supposed to provide them with refuse collection, but we didn't do that, so we failed them. And we are supposed to provide good access roads, like in Blantyre and Lilongwe where they are tarmac, not dirt. But we didn't do that either. I am not surprised that they say, "You want us to pay rates, but you are not providing us with anything in return, so why should we pay up?"'

Despite the challenges, he is excited about his city's growth. 'When I came in 1992, there were very little services, there was no electricity at all on the eastern side of the city. I think that there was one person, and he was a member of the ruling party, who had electricity. Now we are connected. And we have a central hospital. The university. A bigger airport. It is much better.'

And he is thrilled by the growth of Mzuzu's arts and culture sector, even if he rarely enjoys its spirited night life. 'We have a real hub in the Old Town, there are many clubs there, it is very lively. There are many young musicians, and we now have Mzuzu Fashion Week too. But I am getting older now, I would much rather be dozy and stay at home in the evening,' he laughs.

Over 350 kilometres south, in the heart of the central region, sits Malawi's capital city, Lilongwe. Now the country's most populous city, with around one million people, it faces the same challenges as Mzuzu.

Visitors to Lilongwe often don't stray outside the city's administrative centre or the luxury hotels built for the regular influx of aid workers and international consultants, but here too the majority of the population live in informal settlements, with few or no services.

In her introduction to the National Urban Policy, the then Minister of Lands, Housing and Urban Development, Dr Jean Kalilani, warned that Malawi currently does not have the capacity to provide the 'shelter, infrastructure, services and jobs' needed for the growing urban population. She went on:

> This has created a number of challenges in cities and urban centres which include: urban poverty, urban sprawl, informal settlements, environmental degradation and weak urban resilience to climate change, disasters, risks and shocks.
>
> As a result, the country is struggling to attain sustainable urbanisation which is key to achieving sustainable development of its cities and urban centres.

She concludes, somewhat forlornly, 'It is my hope that this policy will be translated from paper commitment to implementation so that Malawi can attain sustainable development.'

For most Malawians, whether they live in an urban township in a shack with one room and no running water or toilet, or in a village hut with a borehole three kilometres away, daily life is a challenge. Their government has a plethora of policies, strategies and vision statements, setting out how the country can 'attain sustainable development.' The urban policy document lists 18 policies and pieces of legislation, from the 1994 constitution to the National Meteorological Policy, that if matched with sufficient investment and enough human resources, would indeed transform the country's fortunes. But, as former President Mutharika acknowledged, Malawi has always been good at planning, less so at delivering change.

'There is no point in planning if we can't implement what we plan,' he said at the National Planning Commission in November 2019. 'For a long time, this country has always been good at planning. We have always had good ideas. But implementation has often been our problem.

'I want Malawi to move from a low-income country to a middle-income country. Let us remember that our ultimate goal is to create wealth and improve the quality of life for Malawians. In the end, every community in Malawi should have these seven essentials – sufficient food; clean water; a health facility; electricity; access to a tarmac road; a good secondary school and a community technical college. The question is: how do we create wealth to make Malawi a middle-income economy?'

That is the question that everyone asks. How does Malawi change from the old life to the new? Only time will tell if the new government has the answer.

SECTION 5

Whither Malawi

CHAPTER 21

A hopeful future

SITTING IN A wing-backed chair in the cavernous lobby of a five-star hotel in downtown Blantyre, Edyth Kambalame is every inch the 21st century professional woman.

'I have 4,000 followers on Twitter,' she laughs. 'That's Malawi. We love communicating, and everyone knows everybody. Our oral tradition works on social media. Our culture is about sharing stories, telling each other stories. So digital media is going to be very influential in Malawi.'

Edyth is one of the most senior women in Malawi's growing media industry. At 38, she is at the top of her profession. She is deputy editor of one of the country's two leading national newspapers, *The Nation*, working 12-hour shifts to produce a daily print edition, as well as keeping the online one up to date.

Malawi has had a lively media scene since the 1880s, when the Scottish missionaries published *Kalilole* (Mirror) for their Malawian converts in 1881, soon followed by an English-language church newspaper, *Life and Work*. In 1895, the first edition of *The Central African Planter* rolled off the presses. Today, that newspaper, first produced by two white settlers, RS Hynde and RR Stark, is *The Daily Times,* making it one of sub-Saharan Africa's oldest publications.

During President Banda's 30-year dictatorship, *The Daily Times* and its weekend edition, *The Malawi News*, were his master's voice, alongside the MBC, the state broadcaster, which still dominates the airwaves today. The Censorship Act of 1968 ensured that citizens only read, or heard, what their government wanted them to, and nearly 1,000 books were banned. Writers went into exile or were jailed. Towards the end of Banda's reign, as his grip on power waned, journalists began producing special interest magazines, focusing on sport, business and women, and with the advent of multi-party democracy, more newspapers arrived on the scene, mostly published by politicians.

The Nation, owned by Aleke Banda and first published in July 1993, is the only one to have survived beyond the heady early days of freedom.

'We now sell around 13,000 copies a day,' says Edyth. 'But most people don't have the financial muscle to buy a newspaper every single day. They have to choose between *The Times* and *The Nation*. They can't afford to get both. And the print media is elitist because of cost and because it is in English... If you go to where the average Malawians live, they will not buy a newspaper.'

They will, however, listen to the radio, from MBC and the BBC's World Service to the plethora of private and community radio stations on offer, including Zodiak and Capital FM. Middle-class households boast satellite dishes, picking up South African cable television as well as Malawi TV stations. In almost every village and township, people will crowd into video stores to watch Nigerian films or European football matches for a few *kwacha*. As Edyth says, Malawians love stories and they love social media.

Mobile phone ownership in Malawi is growing, despite the relatively high cost of airtime and data. The 2018 Census shows that 52 per cent of households have a mobile phone. The messaging service WhatsApp is by far the most popular platform, used by villagers and city dwellers alike.

'Everyone is on WhatsApp,' says Edyth, 'And at The Nation we are always looking at ways of being innovative. The impact of digital is not as bad as it has been on the UK print media. We have time to think about how to make online the go-to platform. We have time to work out how to make digital work.'

As she finishes her cappuccino and prepares to go back to her office, Edyth ponders the future of her country.

'I think Malawians are getting more empowered, despite their poverty, despite literacy challenges,' she says. 'The majority of Malawians know their rights now, they know what is going on, they know that short-term handouts don't do us any good. Our democracy is still young, only 25 years old. People need to understand that we have the power, that politicians work for us, that they are not our bosses, not our chiefs. I think we are moving towards the time where people understand it is our government, our money, our resources. That is a good thing.'

She stops for a moment. 'I have always said Malawi needs a revolution, for the status quo to change. Democracy is a living thing. It develops. But I am optimistic for the future,' she finishes with a smile.

Some people believe that revolution came on Tuesday 23 June 2020 when Lazarus Chakwera, leader of the MCP won the re-run of the presidential election.

Malawi won plaudits from around the world for its remarkable display of democracy during a global pandemic. A report by Washington think tank Freedom House showed it was the only country where democracy got stronger in 2020, compared to 80 where it weakened, with the rest staying the same.

Vera Kamtukule (38) is one of the people responsible for making sure that the ballot ran smoothly. She took leave from her job as Chief Executive of the Malawi Scotland Partnership, a civil society network, to organise a country-wide team of independent poll observers.

'I used all my savings,' she says. 'I recruited 350 people, all professionals in their field. There were no outside auditors, like BDO. What happened was that for the first time Malawians were saying this is our country, we don't need people from outside, these are our elections.

'In 2019, the international observers said the election had been free and fair, when it was not. So I took three weeks' leave from the office to mobilise and train people to observe the elections as professionals. And this election was not corrupt.

'What you saw in Malawi was the citizens delivering a credible election, by ourselves, which is so important because democracy is meaningless if it doesn't belong to the people.'

A few days after the election, Vera was shocked to get a phone call from the new Vice President, Dr Saulos Chilima, offering her a cabinet position as Deputy Minister for Labour.

'It came out of the blue,' she laughs, recalling the conversation. 'But what can you say when your Vice President asks you to serve. You have to say yes.'

The Tonse Alliance – the coalition between MCP and UTM – went into the election with a promise to create one million jobs in its first year of office, a pledge that had to be broken within weeks of Chakwera taking office.

'My ministry cannot create jobs,' explains Vera. 'But we can create the environment for job creation, so we are working on a blueprint for that. Our plan will be responsive to the job market. Look at small business, we have so many of them. Now if we could focus on just 250,000 of them, and each were to create a job over the next year, that is huge progress.'

She is determined to improve vocational training in Malawi. 'There are huge numbers of young people entering the job market every year,' she says. 'But many of them are not job-ready, they lack the skills that are being demanded by those that are providing the jobs.

'The problem is that here in Malawi we have placed a very low status on vocational skills, the training provided by TEVETA, our skills agency. We consider someone who graduates from university as being more skilled, when very often they are not.'

Her boss, Vice President Saulos Chilima, has no shortage of qualifications. His CV is a glittering testament to a successful career in the private sector. An economist by trade, with a PhD in Knowledge Management, he worked for Unilever and Coca-Cola before joining Airtel Malawi, where he rose to be Chief Executive. During his time in charge, the company grew from 375,000 customers in 2006 to 2.8 million by 2012.

Standing in his private office in Lilongwe a few weeks before the historic election, the Vice President contemplated his country's future.

At only 47, he is relatively young for a senior Malawi politician. He says he gave up business for politics in 2014 because of a 'call to national duty'. 'Some told me politics was difficult,' he said, 'but I opted to set aside my private sector career to respond to the call, to see if my expertise, the knowledge that I had acquired over many years, could be used to benefit many more people than just myself.'

He was straightforward in his assessment of the challenges facing the new government. 'I wish we had the luxury of saying this [is] priority number one, number two, number three. Unfortunately, we don't. Food security is an issue. Health is an issue. Unemployment. Education. Security. Gender is an issue. They need to be dealt with in tandem.

'But if we say, "let's try and do some prioritisation", we need to deal with food security once and for all. We must make our agriculture sector work properly.

'We also need to do away with avoidable diseases, through better health and education. Then you would begin to look at young people, the empowerment of women. We must develop our human capital.

'And for all of this to work, you must have good governance as the centrepiece. We need to get rid of fraud and corruption. The judgement showed the rule of law works here.'

The successful corporate boss who cites Coca-Cola's business model as an inspiration is also a classic Keynesian. At times of trouble, and Malawi's economy is most certainly suffering, Chilima believes the government should borrow to invest in the country's future.

'We have to find a way of jump-starting the economy. One way is a loan fund, for the people who already have a business, invest there, so their businesses will grow and they employ more people. Invest in the village banks, the co-operatives where people lend to each other to support economic activity.

'Invest in infrastructure, and the construction sector absorbs a lot of people immediately. They need suppliers, and they need to eat. The chain continues.'

'We have a simple promise,' he said. 'We want a happy nation, to be a middle-income economy where people enjoy three meals a day,' he says. 'And we can do it.'

Economist Dalitso Kubalasa has spent his career thinking about where Malawi is coming from and where it is going. He graduated from Bunda College of Agriculture (now LUANAR) in 2000 with a degree in agricultural economics. His first job was in micro-finance, then he joined a new organisation, the Malawi Economic Justice Network, ending up as its Director. Today, he is the Southern Africa Regional Director for IM Swedish Development Partner, a leading international aid organisation.

He ponders Malawi's fate as one of the world's poorest countries. 'This has been the million-dollar question I have been grappling with,' he says. 'The irony of Malawi is that it is sitting on a lot of wealth.

'The policies and statements are like a sing-song: "Agriculture is the backbone of the economy." We have all the factors of production we need. We have the land, even with some scramble because of population growth, but we still have it – and very rich land. But it's not been managed well. We are not even a quarter of the way to the potential it should be yielding.

'Then we have the other factor of production, labour. Yes, we have a growing population, but we can choose to be progressive and harness the potential of a young population.'

And he shrugs as he bemoans Malawi's crowded policy landscape. 'We are policy-rich, implementation-poor. The policies that we have, they are really good on paper, but it remains just on paper.'

But he is hopeful that the new administration will make an impact, where others have failed. 'The start seems promising', he says, 'especially with the Vice President (Dr Chilima) championing mindset change and public service reforms. And it is worth noting that he is now Minister of Economic Planning and Development and Public Service Reforms, as well as VP.'

Dalitso is clear where the country has failed. 'Education,' he says, echoing Dr Yonah Matemba and economist Dr Ben Kaluwa. 'It is the biggest way to set people on the path to be a productive workforce, but the majority of children are left by the side.

'In 1994, we had free education – but what was accompanying that policy so that we sustained all that to the end of Standard 8? We have 97 per cent enrolment in Grade 1, but then we seem to lose interest, we have massive dropouts, girls especially.'

The figures bear him out. Only half of children enrolling in Standard 1 will complete their primary school education.

'When they drop out, where do they go?' asks Dalitso. 'Nobody really seems to care. It's a collective responsibility, beginning with the parents. It's a conscious decision they are making for their kids. This is a vicious cycle that has so many tentacles and is becoming a huge nightmare. So, education is one of the most binding constraints. You deal with it and you solve a number of other things. But because it is not happening, it's a fire-fighting exercise.

'Primary education is a system failure. The teaching and learning materials are not there, the teachers are not there and not motivated, the classrooms are not there. So it becomes overwhelming. But we don't have to just give up. The best way to deal with things is one at a time. But you get the sense of a defeatist approach, maybe the system is giving up.'

Malawi's over-burdened systems now have to cope with Covid-19. 'It is an irritating pandemic breaking out in the middle of another, far more serious political pandemic of poverty, political impunity, corruption and cronyism,' says Dalitso. And he says it has increased pressure on the new government. 'It is a like a nightmare coming in the middle of a very good dream.'

The Reverend Maxwell Banda, who has campaigned for better governance all his adult life, has decided to pass the baton on to Dalitso and Vera's generation, the people who grew up after multi-party democracy was secured. 'I am only 65 years old,' he says. 'But my thinking is not as sharp as it used to be when I was in my 40s.'

He goes on, 'In a democracy, it's a game of numbers. The youth population is 60 per cent, and those in power now fear them. It began in the 2019 election. The young people's vote was quite a big chunk. And it is growing. I am very confident that come the next ten to 20 years, the young people are going to completely take over. The demographics are changing. The Speaker of the National Assembly is not that old, she is in her late 40s. And the Vice President, Dr Chilima, is still a young man, so you can see more young people are getting involved in politics and in governance. A better Malawi is coming.'

He argues that progress will come with the empowerment of women and girls. 'All along, our history was that education was a preserve for men, not many women were encouraged. It was thought they were good enough for the kitchen, but now educational opportunities are opening for women.

'And there are lots of movements that are discouraging early marriage. When perhaps a girl becomes pregnant, then quickly she is encouraged to go back to school. So, such mechanisms will allow more and more women to be in school and to finish. After all it is proven that if you educate a woman, then you educate a nation, in the sense that if a mother has gone to the end of primary school, then there are greater chances that her children will do better than herself. Hopefully in future, more women will have attained at least a primary education, and therefore their children will become better, and so Malawi will become a better place because illiteracy will have been wiped away. Once that happens, there are greater chances that development will accelerate. Illiteracy is one of the reasons why poverty is taking centre stage.'

Rev Banda's advocacy for women is Maggie Banda's lifelong work. The founder of one of Malawi's leading NGOs, she once considered a career in politics as her contribution to her country's development.

No longer, as she laughingly explains. 'For me, I will continue in the church and civil society. I see a lot more potential to change and help people there than in politics. I think you cannot always make an impact as a politician, so working in an NGO and working in the church, I think I am making more of an impact than I would be in politics.'

She welcomes the new government. 'Since their victory, we are no longer living in fear, because under the previous regime, people were frightened to speak out. That is not the case now, we are free to criticise.'

And Maggie, who is a founding member of the Women's Manifesto Movement, formed in 2019 to promote better policy making for women and girls, has not been afraid to voice her opinion since Chakwera and Chilima took office.

'I don't think gender is a priority for our new President,' she says. 'He has told us that women have to wait for 50-50 appointments to public bodies for example, but for how long? Up to five years? But it has only been a few months, so we need to give them time.

'Re-running the election was a big step forward. The challenge now is for the new generation of politicians to change the culture, rid our politics of corruption, and that can take a long, long time.'

Particularly now that the country has to deal with a pandemic. When the coronavirus hit Malawi – the first cases were identified in early April 2020 –

there were fears that it would ravage the 18 million population, already coping with HIV/AIDS, malaria and other communicable diseases.

'There was a lot of fear around,' says Maggie. 'And as the infection rate increased it affected businesses, our schools closed and our health system struggled to cope. We were terrified it would devastate us. Europe and America are struggling to cope, imagine what it could do to Malawi'.

But to date, the expected devastation has not happened. By 31 October 2020, there had been just under 6,000 recorded cases and 184 deaths, and life is beginning to get back to normal.

'It is difficult to say why the pandemic has not been as bad as it has in the UK,' says Maggie. 'People don't travel a lot so our exposure to the world is far less, we have a young population, so that may be a factor. But as yet no one really knows.'

But there is one group that has been severely affected by the virus, prompting one Malawi health writer to describe it as 'the pandemic within a pandemic'.

Writing in a recent issue of *Africa in Fact,* Josephine Chinele describes the unintended consequences of lengthy school closures during the early days of the pandemic, which has seen a surge in teenage pregnancies and child marriages.

Since the schools closed in March to September 2020, Chinele writes that the Ministry of Education registered 18,000 teen pregnancies among primary school learners and 3,931 among secondary school students.

'A whole generation of young girls has been lost to education, it is always women and girls who lose out,' says Maggie Banda.

While the plight of girls forced into early marriages – rightly – dominates global headlines, it is easy to overlook that the country is alive with young people full of ideas and energy, from Wezi Mzumara, founder of Mzuzu Fashion Week, to the students at MUST.

The future of Malawi surely lies with women like Enelesi Nsamila, 22, who graduated from MUST in November 2019 with a distinction in her Earth Science degree. She nearly dropped out of secondary school after her father was paralysed in an accident, but a bursary from CAMFED Malawi (the Campaign for Female Education) meant she could continue her education.

'With science and technology shaping most of current and future development agendas, Malawi and the rest of the world can only attain Sustainable Development Goals if girls are not left behind in sciences. Girls should be competitive and be ready to move out of their comfort zones and go for sciences,' she said at her graduation. 'For instance, Earth Sciences, which

I studied, is important for our national food supply through identifying ideal growing areas and conditions as well as monitoring soil quality. Whether you consider the oil and natural gas that fuel our growing hunger for energy and manufacturing, mining for structural metals for infrastructure or precious metals for use in high-tech devices, it's all about Earth Sciences, and as girls we cannot afford to side-line ourselves from such critical activities.'

Poverty should be no barrier to success, she insisted, 'For me, there is no relationship between poor performance and poverty. If anything, I think poverty should actually drive one to work harder in class so that they can do well and change their fortunes in future.'

But young women like Wezi and Enelesi will not succeed if the governance of their country does not continue to improve, and only the people of Malawi can make that happen, says political scientist Henry Chingaipe.

'There are a lot of us now that are in leadership positions, in the corporate world, in civil society, in government, in universities. We talk, we do analysis, we know the general direction our country needs to take. With the old men gone, we can now start the process and maybe get back on track, but it will take a real shake up of the system. It will take a lot of hard work, but what we need to do in this country is rebuild the state, because the state had been captured and re-purposed, and for many years it was doing things that a normal state should not be doing. I am optimistic that 20 years from now, it should be better.'

And he is confident that Malawi's latest plan, *National Transformation 2063*, to which he is contributing, will make a difference. He smiles ruefully, mindful of the unwieldy ambitions of *Vision 2020*, the first national plan.

'This time, we want a proper document that is practical and that can be implemented. How do we make sure across electoral cycles government is sticking to the national vision? We don't want anyone coming in with their own thing... It is very politically challenging, but we just have to give these people some discipline. There is a lot of ill-discipline in development. You can't have the situation where we are going to have an initiative on maternal health and it is going to be in the office of the President, but when there is a new President, the initiative disappears or loses clout. Development shouldn't belong to the President. It belongs to the government, to the people.'

By 2030, there could be 23 million people in Malawi, with more than two-thirds of them under the age of 30. The lake of stars will be as beautiful as it always has been, and the people as friendly and welcoming. But will they remain as poor, the majority forced to scrape out a living on dusty red soil, degraded by climate change? Will teenage girls continue to drop out of school, to become mothers before they are themselves adults, while young men beg for a day's casual work to alleviate the boredom and despair of unemployment? Will Malawi's middle-class retreat even further behind their compound walls, content with their imported cars, private education and medical insurance, wilfully ignoring the poverty at their gate? Will the rest of the world look on benignly, as it has for the last 160 years, wringing its hands with frustration, muttering 'Malawi, Malawi' as it invests another few million pounds to salve its colonial conscience?

And will the new government, elected with such high hopes, be able to fulfil its promise of steering the country towards middle-income status?

The answer lies in Malawi itself, because, in the final analysis, only Malawians can build their future. Only young men like Alexander Galimoto can transform his country.

At 27 years old, Alexander has already endured a lifetime of hardship. His father died from HIV/AIDS when he was seven years old, forcing his mother to return to her home village and to a life of poverty. He was the first in his family ever to go to university, but dropped out after 18 months, depressed and in debt. He has just survived a short spell in one of Africa's most notorious prisons, for a crime he did not commit, a victim of a corrupt system. He is single, living alone in a rented room hundreds of miles from home, so that he can hold on to his job with an international NGO. But he remains stubbornly positive about his country's future.

'Looking back to 2009 when I was growing up, people were like, "Let's just leave whatever happens, whoever makes decisions for us, let's just do whatever we can." But lately, I've seen people appreciating that they can make change. I've also seen some politicians becoming more serious, like they have been awakened about what has been happening in recent years.

'So, in 20 years' time, even in ten years' time, I think politics will be on a level with South Africa, whereby the citizens can make decisions, they can enforce their politicians to do what they want them to do. Our democracy is getting stronger by the day.'

However, he is quick to point out he doesn't believe in miracles. 'We will be a poor country still,' he shrugs, 'But at least the politicians will make decisions knowing they will be held responsible, not like the old times when nobody cared. Decision-making for us is improving. I don't know if corruption is going to end easily. The politicians have stolen a lot of things and messed up a lot of things while we were sleeping.

'But we have woken up. We are getting wiser and wiser, stronger and stronger by the day. People won't be able just to go to the World Bank and borrow money and mess it up – they will know people will go to their houses one day, they know something will happen.'

He stops for a moment, then with a shy smile, nods and says, 'Yeah, I am hopeful, I'm hopeful for Malawi.'

Timeline

Pre-history – The earliest known relic of the Homo genus – a fossil jawbone dating back 2.4 million years – was discovered in Malawi in 1991.

10,000–8,000 BC – The Akafula people settle on the shores of Lake Malawi.

1st–4th centuries AD – Bantu tribes start to settle in the Malawi region.

1480 – Bantu tribes unite several smaller political states to form the Maravi Confederacy, which at its height includes large parts of present-day Zambia and Mozambique plus the modern state of Malawi.

17th century – Portuguese explorers arrive from the east coast of present-day Mozambique.

1790–1860 – Arab slave trade in East Africa increases dramatically.

1859 – Scottish missionary Dr David Livingstone's exploration of the region paves the way for missionaries, European adventurers and traders.

1878 – Livingstonia Central African Mission Company from Scotland begins work to develop a river route into central Africa to enable trade.

1891 – Britain establishes the Nyasaland and District Protectorate.

1893 – Name is changed to the British Central African Protectorate. White European settlers are offered land for coffee plantations at very low prices. Punitive tax regime forces Malawians to work on these plantations for several months a year, often in very difficult conditions.

1907 – British Central African Protectorate becomes Nyasaland.

1915 – Reverend John Chilembwe leads a revolt against British rule, killing the white managers of a particularly brutal estate. He is shot dead by police within days.

1944 – Nationalists establish the NAC.

1953 – Despite strong opposition from the NAC and white liberal activists, Britain combines Nyasaland with the Federation of Northern and Southern Rhodesia (now Zambia and Zimbabwe respectively).

1958 – Dr Hastings Kamuzu Banda denounces the federation and returns from the UK, where he was a doctor, to lead the NAC.

1959 – Violent clashes between the Congress supporters and the colonial authorities lead to the banning of the organisation. Many leaders, including Banda, are arrested and a state of emergency is declared. MCP is founded as a successor to the NAC.

1960 – Banda is released from Gwelo prison and attends talks in London with the British government on constitutional reform.

1961 – Elections held for a new Legislative Assembly. Banda's MCP wins 94 per cent of the vote.

1963 – Territory is granted self-government as Nyasaland and Banda is appointed Prime Minister.

6 July 1964 – Nyasaland declares independence as Malawi.

6 July 1966 – Banda becomes President of the Republic of Malawi. The constitution establishes a one-party state. Opposition movements are suppressed and their leaders are detained. Foreign governments and organisations raise concerns about human rights.

1971 – Banda is voted President-for-life.

1978 – First elections since independence. All potential candidates must belong to the MCP and be approved by Banda.

1980s – Several ministers and politicians are killed or charged with treason. Banda reshuffles his ministers regularly, preventing the emergence of a political rival.

1992 – Catholic bishops publicly condemn Banda, sparking demonstrations. Many donor countries suspend aid over Malawi's human rights record.

1993 – Voters in a referendum reject the one-party state, paving the way for members of parties other than the MCP to hold office.

1994 – Presidential and municipal elections: Bakili Muluzi, leader of the UDF, is elected president. He immediately frees political prisoners and re-establishes freedom of speech.

1994 – Banda announces his retirement from politics.

1997 – Banda dies in hospital in South Africa where he is being treated for pneumonia.

1999 – President Muluzi is re-elected for a second and final five-year term.

2000 – World Bank says it will cancel 50 per cent of Malawi's foreign debt.

2002 – Drought causes crops to fail across southern Africa. Government is accused of worsening crisis through mismanagement and corruption, including selling off national grain reserves before drought struck.

2004 – Bingu wa Mutharika wins the presidency.

2005 – President Mutharika resigns from the UDF over what he says is its hostility to his anti-corruption campaign. He forms the DPP.

2005 – Five million people need food aid as Malawi bears the brunt of failed crops and a regional drought. Government introduces fertiliser subsidy.

2007 – Malawi begins exporting 400,000 tonnes of maize to Zimbabwe, after producing a surplus in 2006.

2008 – Malawi ends diplomatic relations with Taiwan, switching allegiance to China.

2009 – President Mutharika wins second term in election.

May 2011 – Malawi expels British High Commissioner over a leaked diplomatic cable in which the envoy describes President Mutharika as increasingly autocratic.

July 2011 – Anti-government protests leave 19 people dead. Britain halts all aid to Malawi, accusing the government of mishandling the economy and failing to uphold human rights.

April 2012 – President Mutharika dies, is succeeded by Vice President Joyce Banda. The following month she devalues the kwacha currency by a third to satisfy IMF requirements to restore funding.

October 2013 – President Banda sacks cabinet amid allegations of widespread corruption. Senior Finance Ministry official Paul Mphwiyo was shot and wounded in September.

January 2014 – First of 70 defendants appear in court over the so-called Cashgate affair, the country's biggest corruption scandal.

May 2014 – Peter Mutharika, the brother of late President Bingu wa Mutharika, wins the presidential election.

February 2017 – President Peter Mutharika signs a constitutional amendment raising the marrying age to 18, following a campaign against Malawi's rate of child marriage, one of the world's highest.

March 2019 – Cyclone Idai causes extensive flooding and loss of life in the eastern districts.

June 2020 – Lazarus Chakwera, head of the Tonse Alliance, beats Peter Mutharika in a re-run of the 2019 presidential election, which the courts decided had seen widespread irregularities.

Source: BBC

Notes and sources

This book isn't a policy document or an academic article. But getting the facts right is very important to me.

In the rich world, we take it for granted that the government – or at least its statisticians – know how many babies are born each year, how many children go to school or how many die and from what cause. Elections have been decided on the basis of official statistics on unemployment or health service waiting lists. The systems needed to collect all this information, that have taken decades to develop in the UK and other developed countries, simply do not exist to the same extent – or at all – in Malawi. For example, while the Malawi government conducts a population census every ten years, as we do in the UK, the last official survey of the country's job market was in 2013. The law to compel people to register births and deaths was enacted only in 2015 and is not yet fully in operation across the country.

But there is, nevertheless, a lot of good information out there. In addition to the Census, the Malawi National Statistical Office conducts a regular Household Survey, as well as a Demographic and Health Survey. There is an annual *Statistical Yearbook* covering everything from education and health to exports and agricultural production, while the Ministry of Finance also publishes a comprehensive Annual Economic Report.

External donors often support this work, and they also provide some of the most up-to-date information on areas in which they provide substantial sums of aid – some of the information about HIV/AIDS comes from PEPFAR.

Then there are the major international bodies that have teams of experts to estimate national figures and trends across the world where the data might not be easily available – WHO, the United Nations Children's Fund (UNICEF), the IMF or the African Development Bank (AfDB), among others.

And this book would have been much harder to research without the World Bank's database of over 1,400 indicators that provides information as far back as 1960 for Malawi and other countries, known as the World Development Indicators.

A group of academics based in the University of Oxford have put together much of this information in an easy-to-digest visual form on their website, Our World in Data. In some cases, important information comes from other sources, such as reports in the national press or from academic research.

Sometimes, the existence of several sources of information means that they provide different estimates of the same thing.

Should we believe the Malawi government's own estimate that there are 390,000 young people in the country's secondary schools, or the World Bank's calculation that the total is almost one million? The WHO's estimate of 5,700 road traffic deaths in 2013, or the figure of less than 1,000 provided by the Malawi Traffic Police Service? Where these differences crop up, I have used my best judgement to pick the statistics that appear most plausible, based on Nigel Guy's 35 years' experience as an economic researcher and our collective experience of visiting Malawi since 2005. The main sources I have used are listed below.

Afrobarometer (an organisation that studies social attitudes across Africa) www.afrobarometer.org/countries/malawi-0

Eidhammer, A, *Malawi: A Place Apart*, Lilongwe, 2017.

Goodman, J, *Tobacco in History: The Cultures of Dependence*, London and New York, 1993.

Limuwa, M, Singini, W, and Storebakken, T, *Is Fish Farming an Illusion for Lake Malawi Riparian Communities under Environmental Changes?* Basel, 2018.

Lwanda, J, 'The History of Popular Music in Malawi, 1891 to 2007: A preliminary communication' in *The Society of Malawi Journal, Vol. 61, No. 1*, Blantyre, 2008.

Maddow, R, *Blowout*, New York, 2019.

Malawi Human Rights Commission, *Cultural Practices and their Impact on the Enjoyment of Human Rights, Particularly the Rights of Women and Children in Malawi*, Lilongwe, 2011.

Malawi National Statistical Office www.nsomalawi.mw/

McCracken, J, 'Voices from the Chilembwe Rising: Witness Testimonies made to the Nyasaland Rising Commission of Inquiry, 1915' in the British Academy's *Fontes Historiae Africanae*, Oxford, 2015.

McCracken, J, *A History of Malawi, 1859–1966*, Suffolk, 2012.

Msiska, A, 'The Spread of Islam in Malawi and its Impact on Yao Rites of Passage, 1870–1960', in *The Society of Malawi Journal, Vol. 48, No. 1*, Blantyre, 1995.

Munthali, K, *Malawi: Culture Smart*, London, 2018.

Nervi, L, *Malawi: Flames in the African Sky*, Gorle, 1994.

Our World in Data ourworldindata.org/country/malawi

Pachai, B, 'Samuel Josiah Ntara: Writer and Historian' in *The Society of Malawi Journal, Vol. 21, No. 2,* Blantyre, 1968.

Prowse, M, *A Century of Growth? A History of Tobacco Production and Marketing in Malawi 1890–2005,* Antwerp, 2011.

Ross, K, *Friendship with a Purpose: Malawi and Scotland for Sustainable Development,* Edinburgh, 2018.

Shoffeleers, M, 'Father Mariana's 1624 Description of Lake Malawi and the Identity of the Maravi Emperor Muzura' in *The Society of Malawi Journal, Vol. 45, No. 1,* Blantyre, 1992.

TEVETA Secretariat, *The Tevet Times newsletter, January – March,* Lilongwe, 2019.

The Daily Times times.mw/

The Government of Malawi, *The Constitution of the Republic of Malawi,* Lilongwe, 1994.

The Japanese International Co-operation Agency (JICA) in Malawi www.jica.go.jp/malawi/english/index.html

The Ministry of Lands, Housing and Urban Development, *National Urban Policy,* Lilongwe, 2019.

The Nation mwnation.com/

The Nyasa Times www.nyasatimes.com

The Society of Malawi's Journals are an excellent source of contemporary and historic material societyofmalawi.org/library-and-archives/

The World Bank in Malawi www.worldbank.org/en/country/malawi

Timeline : https://www.bbc.co.uk/news/world-africa-13881367 [accessed 9/2/2021]

UNESCO whc.unesco.org

UNICEF in Malawi www.unicef.org/malawi/

World Development Indicators databank.worldbank.org/source/world-development-indicators#

Luath Press Limited

committed to publishing well written books worth reading

LUATH PRESS takes its name from Robert Burns, whose little collie Luath (*Gael.*, swift or nimble) tripped up Jean Armour at a wedding and gave him the chance to speak to the woman who was to be his wife and the abiding love of his life. Burns called one of the 'Twa Dogs' Luath after Cuchullin's hunting dog in Ossian's *Fingal*. Luath Press was established in 1981 in the heart of Burns country, and is now based a few steps up the road from Burns' first lodgings on Edinburgh's Royal Mile. Luath offers you distinctive writing with a hint of unexpected pleasures.

Most bookshops in the UK, the US, Canada, Australia, New Zealand and parts of Europe, either carry our books in stock or can order them for you. To order direct from us, please send a £sterling cheque, postal order, international money order or your credit card details (number, address of cardholder and expiry date) to us at the address below. Please add post and packing as follows: UK – £1.00 per delivery address; overseas surface mail – £2.50 per delivery address; overseas airmail – £3.50 for the first book to each delivery address, plus £1.00 for each additional book by airmail to the same address. If your order is a gift, we will happily enclose your card or message at no extra charge.

Luath Press Limited
543/2 Castlehill
The Royal Mile
Edinburgh EH1 2ND
Scotland
Telephone: +44 (0)131 225 4326 (24 hours)
Email: sales@luath.co.uk
Website: www.luath.co.uk